# ALWAYS A SOLDIER

# ALWAYS A SOLDIER

Service, Sacrifice, and Coming Out as
*America's Favorite Black, Gay Republican*

# ROB SMITH

POST HILL
PRESS

A POST HILL PRESS BOOK
ISBN: 978-1-64293-575-2
ISBN (eBook): 978-1-64293-576-9

Always a Soldier:
Service, Sacrifice, and Coming Out as America's Favorite
Black, Gay Republican
© 2020 by Rob Smith
All Rights Reserved

Cover photo by Omar Columbus
Cover design by Misha Safronov

Post Hill Press
New York · Nashville
posthillpress.com

Published in the United States of America

# TABLE OF CONTENTS

# FOREWORD

*by Richard Grenell, US Ambassador to Germany*

Rob Smith calls himself "America's Favorite Black, Gay Veteran Republican" as a kind of half-joke to call attention to the idiocy of certain types of identity politics. But Rob is no joke. I first noticed Rob when he decided to come out as a conservative, and was struck by his maturity, and seriousness. I am grateful for Rob's courage to help shine a light on issues that are important.

This book is the story of a young man destined to overcome his extraordinary circumstances. Someone focused on turning his life around. And while I know he was nervous about revealing the mistakes of the past, I also know his intention is to be authentic. His story will challenge others to change their circumstances—rather than be bound by them.

We can all learn valuable lessons from Rob's story.

# PREFACE

This is a work of creative nonfiction. Everything that is described in this memoir actually happened. Though the dialogue may not be exact, it's characterized based on conversations and situations that happened with real people, most of whom are still alive and serving today. For that reason, I decided to use pseudonyms for the names of everyone but myself. I want to protect the anonymity and dignity of the soldiers that I served with. If they read it, they will know who they are, but the world doesn't have to. None of us were perfect, but I aimed to do the best job I possibly could at humanizing these very real people.

There are no heroes or villains in this story, just flawed and imperfect human beings. Real soldiers are not the flawless heroes of military movies, nor are they the bloodthirsty monsters America's anti-military elements would like to make them out to be. If I set out to do anything in this book, it's to portray the humanity of our active-duty soldiers. With humanity comes flaws, and as you will see, we were *all* at times brave and frightened, selfish and selfless, strong and weak. We were all soldiers with our own reasons for signing up for military service, but still meant to give our best in service of this beloved country we call the United States of America.

In case you haven't noticed, I'm black and gay. These two immutable characteristics have defined my life in many ways that you will read about in the coming pages. The racism I faced in the military was omnipresent but not devastating. The homophobia I faced was, at the time, enshrined in military law. Being open and honest about my early days as a gay man is not meant to shock, nor is the candid language used throughout the book.

The memoir portion of this book was originally published in my Obama-era lefty days, but everything about my updated political philosophy that comes afterwards is brand new. After nearly a decade spent trying to get this book off the ground in different ways, I've finally succeeded in releasing a complete work in *exactly* the way I wanted to release it.

I realize that for a great deal of people who will read this book I may be the *only* black gay guy who'd write a book they'd feel comfortable enough picking up and reading. That's a pretty heavy burden to carry, so when I decided to share this work, I wanted to release myself of trying to be "respectable" and just try to tell the truth. So here it is. I hope you enjoy it.

—Rob Smith

**PART ONE**

# BASIC TRAINING

# CHAPTER 1

# WELCOME TO THE JUNGLE

The first time I felt another man's breath on my skin, our noses nearly touching and our lips close enough to kiss, he was screaming in my face. His breath smelled like an unholy combination of chewing tobacco and curdled milk. We were in an outdoor staging area crowded with 125 other recruits for the US Army's infantry basic training program in Fort Benning, Georgia. This was decidedly not how I imagined the first real physical closeness I'd share with another man would be.

"You eyeballin' me, motherfucker?" he said.

His eyes were boring directly into mine as I tried desperately not to react to their steely darkness. I thought, *I must've missed this part in the brochure.*

The ease with which I went from being a merit roll student in my high school to standing in line for infantry basic training not even four months after graduating with one of the top GPAs in the class was almost shocking. Great things were expected from me, the 4.0 honor roll student who would most certainly be going on to some big-time university to become a broadcaster after anchoring the high school newscasts for years. Alas, in a 98 percent black school, where athletics were placed at a higher priority than academics, the guidance counselors didn't quite know what to do with the fat kid who hadn't played a sport in his life. My parents didn't have the money for college, and I just kind of slipped through the cracks. All of the above is how I found myself dialing the number to the Army recruiting office in hopes of doing something and perhaps getting to go to college on the Army's dime.

At that point in my life, I was spending most of my days doing absolutely nothing besides eating, living at home with my grand-mother, and working part-time waiting tables at Denny's. I dreaded the particular hell that was Tuesday Family Free Nights. An assort-ment of baby mamas would come in large groups and shovel free kids' meals down their demon spawn's throats, running me ragged and leaving me a one- or two-dollar tip for the privilege. Surely there had to be more to life than this, but if there was, I certainly didn't know. Maybe it was time to find out.

Over the phone, the Army people said that it was okay that I didn't have a car. They eagerly sent a recruiter over to drive me to the station and talk a little about the Army. I closed the phone book and sat at the kitchen table. I was alone, as usual, in the kitchen of the modest two-story house I'd spent the majority of my teen years in. I was nervous about what I was about to do but strangely excited. I didn't know what I was getting into, but I knew I needed a change. I knew I needed to leave home and go to college, but I didn't know how to get there. Perhaps this was my time to shine, to be all I could be.

There was a knock on the door, and I opened it to see an Adonis. At that point something very powerful came over me. The feeling was new, different, exhilarating, and thrilling. This gorgeous man towered over me, offered a sweet smile, and stuck out his hand.

"You're Mr. Smith?" he asked.

"Uh...yeah," I said, almost forgetting to breathe.

"I'm Corporal Kevin Garvin. I'm gonna take you to the recruiting station so we can have a little conversation."

I had never seen someone so beautiful before, and I was smitten. Tall and lean, he was like a real-life Ken doll. He had blonde hair, piercing blue eyes, and perfectly tanned skin. I couldn't remember having ever met someone so good-looking in real life.

Though I was only vaguely aware of some hidden sexual tendencies just beneath the surface of my outward teenage awkwardness, I knew that I just wanted to be with him. His hair was golden, and his skin glowed. His camouflage uniform fit just right on his lean, muscular frame. I nodded and followed him into his car, a bright blue Camaro. We didn't say much during the ride to the recruiting station, but I couldn't have talked if I'd wanted to. I was nervous, excited, and happy. I felt like I could melt just by being in close proximity to this man. I was vaguely aware of sounds coming out of his mouth as he drove, but I couldn't place them. I was lost in him.

The arch of his eyebrow, the curve of his lips, and the way his smile seemed to start in his eyes and spread across his entire face were all things that I noticed and wanted to have forever.

He was just so different from anyone I'd interacted with before. The west side of Akron, Ohio, was my entire world, and that world was nearly exclusively filled with faces that were black like mine. Corporal Garvin was something fresh and new. He represented the fact that just maybe there was a different world out there beyond what I'd already seen. That thought filled me with equal parts fear and excitement.

For the next few weeks, Corporal Garvin was mine, giving me more attention than anyone had in ages. We went for lunches and talked about the different military jobs I was qualified for. He seemed very excited about one job in particular.

"The infantry," he said over burgers at a local fast food joint one sunny afternoon, "is where the real men go. That's where they do the real shooting, and camping, and all that shit you see on the commercials."

I leaned forward, enthralled by Corporal Garvin, or the prospect of this infantry thing, or some combination of the two. His blue eyes brightened, and his eyebrows rose slightly, as if he knew he was pulling me in, as if he knew exactly how I felt about him. I caught his eye for one brief electric second and looked away, feeling as if I may explode from the direct contact. *Infantry*, I thought to myself, *that's what I'll do.*

At this point in time I would've done anything he wanted me to do. My mother eyed the paperwork that was necessary for her to sign so that her seventeen-year-old son could give the next four years of his life to the US Army. She studied the paperwork intently. A Newport cigarette, burning its way into oblivion, perched between her fingers. Her smooth, deep brown skin was that of a woman much younger than her forty-three years, but her eyes were those of a woman who'd seen it all and learned painful lessons from it. She absently flicked away the ash from her cigarette and stubbed it out in the silver ashtray that sat on the kitchen table. She would have to go back down to North Carolina with her new husband shortly, but I needed her to sign the paperwork for me. I didn't need any convincing or advice. My mind was already made up. I wasn't just gonna be a soldier; I was gonna be infantry.

My mother was a determined woman. She had been largely absent from my life since she'd gotten the courage to leave her abusive husband, my stepfather, five years ago. My biological father reentered my life at this point. Our interactions were strained and awkward, as if his absence from my life between the ages of three and thirteen robbed us of any opportunity of a real relationship. My teenage years were spent largely alone. My mother's participation in my life extended little beyond the moments in the morning when she prepared for work, and I prepared for school. In the evening when I'd return from school, she'd rush across town to spend the evenings with her new boyfriend.

Corporal Garvin said that the infantry was the best of the best. They only took the strongest and smartest men, and they did all kinds of fun stuff like camping, marches, and running. It sounded great, just like summer camp. I had never been to camp. It was exciting. I would go to Colorado for my station assignment after the six months of basic training. Colorado had taken up a mythical place in my mind years back while researching an assignment in the high school library. I randomly flipped through a travel book to a six-page photography spread detailing the state's mountains and vistas. It seemed so green, so exotic, and very different from the dreary surroundings of Ohio. I knew I was going to see this place eventually, but little did I know what I'd be willing to go through in order to get there. My mother looked at me, exasperated.

"Robert, I don't know why you don't just go into the Air Force. You remember Sharon? Her son went into the Air Force, and he says it's real nice, better than the Army."

At this, she cut her eyes brutally at Corporal Garvin. I rolled my eyes. I didn't want to hear this. Her input wasn't needed, only her signature. I'd made this decision, and it was final.

Corporal Garvin had been spending a lot of time with me during the past two weeks. It was the most time that anyone had spent with me in a long time, least of all my mother. She'd rekindled an old flame down in North Carolina and left to move there and marry him right before the start of my senior year of high school. I lived with paternal grandparents, who'd had enough of me by graduation. Not long after, I moved back in with my maternal grandmother to the small house in which we now sat. Her scowls and gruff nature toward me were all the indication I needed of her disapproval of the lack of direction of my barely seventeen-year-old self.

My mother's words irritated me. Who did she think she was to try to give me guidance now? I knew I wanted to do this because Corporal Garvin knew I could. I didn't want to let him down.

"Mom, this is my decision. I'm seventeen. I'm not in school. I can't just live here and work at Denny's forever. I need to do something. I gotta get out of here. You did…. Why can't I?"

I looked over at Corporal Garvin, where my glance was met with warm approval. I silently melted.

"If I do this for a few years, they'll pay for my college. I want to go to college. It's not like you went."

My mother jerked back almost as if she'd been slapped, and looked over at Corporal Garvin.

"I want to do this, so can you just sign?" I asked and smiled at her. "Please, Mom?"

She looked to me and back to him and sighed long and deeply as she took the pen and signed the dramatic swoops of her signature on the seemingly endless paperwork. Just like that, I was in the Army, and two weeks later I would leave for basic training in Fort Benning, Georgia.

The first two minutes of my military experience were a blur. No sooner had I gotten off the bus, retrieved my luggage as directed, and stood in front of it, than I made the mistake of glancing at the drill sergeants out of the side of my eye. They entered the area with their chest-jutting, tough-guy swagger. They seemed somehow larger than life: tall, angry, and terrifying. These big, angry-looking white men were the opposite of the warm and caring

Corporal Garvin. They meant business, and first up on the agenda was to scare the living hell out of all of us.

"Don't fucking look at me, privates!" the first screamed.

"Look straight the fuck ahead!"

My frightened gaze inadvertently met the first drill sergeant's hardened and steely one. I'd never seen an overweight yet muscular middle-aged man move as lithely as he did. He leaped over the other recruits' bags and between their shoulders to move between the four rows of recruits and somehow place his face millimeters in front of mine in the blink of an eye.

I felt every eyeball in the room on me, the lone pepper spot in a sea of bald heads and clean-shaven white faces. I felt weak and exposed. The other recruits were doing their best to focus their attention directly forward and pretend not to notice the scene that was being performed by our new superior for their benefit.

*Why couldn't it have been somebody else?* I thought to myself. *Why can't I ever just blend in?*

In my head I could hear my mother's voice berating me in the loving yet no-bullshit way that had guided me to a near-relentless pursuit of academic success in high school.

*Just couldn't look straight forward, huh? Why can't you ever fucking listen? God, how I wish I had listened when the company commander at the recruiting station back in Ohio taught us how to stand "at ease" with our hands interlaced along the smalls of our backs and told us to look forward no matter what.*

The drill sergeant looked at me, studying me. Although I was trying to maintain my forward gaze, I realized it was bordering on the impossible and decided on a split-second act of defiance. I looked him directly in the eyes, trying desperately to swallow the fear that enveloped me. Maybe this old bastard would respect me for it. Maybe he would think I'm not someone to be fucked with. Maybe I could get his old white ass to think I was some thug from the projects of Detroit instead of a solidly lower middle-class geek from Ohio with a two-parent family background that was like *The Cosby Show*. Well, maybe *The Cosby Show* if neither of the kids were Cliff's, and he was a control freak who beat the shit out of Clair.

I studied the drill sergeant while trying to maintain my gaze. His face was wide and heavy, as age had obviously crept in and started the inevitable decline in his looks. His face was heavily lined, his chin was weak, and his cheeks sagged. The ridiculous drill sergeant cap, which most closely resembled an upside-down bowl on top of a plate, placed an ominous shadow over his hollow eyes. As I looked into them, using every bit of my resolve to keep his gaze, I sensed a white-hot hatred that simmered below the surface. I engaged him there for what seemed like hours, giving him my brand-new don't-fuck-with-me look. In my mind I thought of every rap video, every "hood" movie I'd ever seen with a young black guy killing someone, selling drugs, or robbing someone, men I was told by my thuggish cousins I could never be like because I liked books instead of rap music, writing instead of sports.

The drill sergeant's eyes twinkled, and a smile spread widely across his lips. Suddenly, I was afraid, and I felt a wave of fear unleash within me. I knew what was coming, which was possibly the worst thing that could come out right now. This had followed me since the sixth grade in Ohio, and it appears that it just hopped the flight down to the South. He looked directly at me with that "you're fucked" grin for a few moments more, then stepped back to make his pronouncement to the roomful of recruits that I would be spending the next six months with.

"What are you, a fucking faggot?" he said.

It was less of a question and more of a pronouncement, made loudly enough so that everyone in the staging area could hear it. "This motherfucker was eyeballin' me because he's a fucking faggot! Yeah, that's what you are, right?"

I flinched, taking two steps back and nearly falling backwards over the luggage that was stacked neatly behind me. I quickly regained my footing. That would not be a good way to start this process. I had to think quickly, do something that would end this now.

"No, Drill Sergeant!"

The words came out of my mouth as unexpectedly as the vomit a few hours after I'd had my first shots of whiskey on my seventeenth birthday the previous summer. His head whipped back around toward me. The other recruits and the officers staged in front of us were barely pretending not to pay attention. This was quickly becoming quite the scene.

"What the fuck did you say?"

"No, Drill Sergeant, I'm not a faggot, Drill Sergeant!" I yelled.

"Then stop eyeballing me like you want to fuck me!" he said, pausing for a moment to look at the name tag stitched to my fatigues mid-sentence. I looked up and noticed that he had moved back into position close to my face. This time, he didn't yell, and his words sliced through my fun-and-games attitude like a scalpel through flesh. They were quiet, almost a whisper. These words were intended for me and nobody else.

"You ever eyeball me like that again and I will fucking end you, you motherfucking faggot," he said.

I waited for a smile, for some sign of the showy badass performance he had put on for the company for the last five minutes, but there was none there. It was the real him, and he wasn't a fan of my fake bravado or the little stare-down I had given him earlier. I was confused and looked down, but instinctively looked back up and straight ahead. Through my peripheral vision I could've sworn I saw the faintest smile on his face, but there was nothing happy about it. It was grim and fearsome, somehow devious. For the first time since I had come to Fort Benning and the Army on a whim, I was afraid. Whatever he and his cohorts had in store for me and the other 124 recruits over the next six months wasn't going to be fun. Playtime was over.

He stood at the head of the group of recruits with his hands on his hips, an oddly feminine gesture that belied the rest of his rugged, hyper-masculine presentation. His eyes scanned over us like spotlights, and he licked his lips.

"I'm Drill Sergeant August," he said as he paced back and forth.

"Beside me is Drill Sergeant Thomas." He pointed to another man that I hadn't yet noticed. The other man was tall and thin with sinewy muscle and piercing blue eyes that seemed dead. He stood silently with his arms crossed. His face was heavily lined, the seeming result of years of sun damage. He grimaced, and as his upper lip pulled away from his teeth, I noticed the reflection of light from a gold tooth that seemed to have dulled with time along with his eyes. He had the aura of a coiled snake that was ready to strike at any moment.

"And we're here to turn this group of pussies and faggots into infantrymen that will have the highest honor of being the first in line in the United States Army to defend our country when the time comes. Hooah!"

This last bit caught me off guard. It was a low, guttural sound screamed out loud, almost like a shout. August seemed to catch a bit of our confusion.

"When I say 'hooah!' you say 'hooah!' Roger?"

"Yes, Drill Sergeant!" we all screamed in unison.

My knees were shaking, and I was a bundle of nerves. Somehow this seemed so...not me. I was suddenly struck by a strong and immediate urge: I wanted to go home, right then and there. I wanted to go home badly, back to my days of late mornings and aimlessness and my nights of serving low-level diner food to the unwashed masses and their seed. I looked wistfully to the hill leading away from the base just soon enough to catch the last of the buses disappearing over it, then was snapped back into reality by the grunting and screaming.

"Hooah!"

"Hooah!"

"Hooah!"

"Hooah!"

This went on for about two minutes, a call and response between Drill Sergeant August and us. I half expected us to beat on our chests like King Kong, which would've probably been an equally obnoxious display of masculinity.

"All right, I think we may have some soldiers here!" he yelled satisfactorily, his face relaxed into the look of a man who had just had great sex.

"Soldiers, gear up!" he shouted. We scrambled to put our bags on our backs and gather up all of our belongings. We marched up the stairs to the rear of us and up into the barracks that we were to call home for the next six months.

The room was large, cavernous, and oddly shapeless, adorned only by seemingly endless rows of twin-sized beds and lockers. The blankets were a shade of green that resembled a fresh pile of steaming baby shit and were folded on top of a boxy twin bed that looked as comfortable as a mattress filled with bricks. We stood in a single-file line and marched down the rows, each soldier stopping at a bed on the way from back to front. I noticed that I was to be the last bed in that long row, right by the bathroom and across from a few of the guys I was standing near during the little incident from earlier. I dropped my bags by the foot of the bed and went immediately back into parade rest stance, my hands folded directly above my lower back. Straight ahead of me I looked at the soldiers who were to be my neighbors, wondering who they were, where they were from, and why they were here. I wondered if they asked themselves the same questions about me.

They were both Latino, though one was much paler than the other. I'd never really met any Latinos of any hue, so their presence was intriguing to me. The pale one's name tag read Hernandez, and he scowled at me disapprovingly. Although his head was shaved, the remains were shaped in a widow's peak that suggested he was already losing his hair, even though he couldn't have been any more than twenty-three. He pursed his lips, subtly turned his nose up, and fixed his gaze forward, dismissing me. The soldier to his left was named Rogers. He was baby-faced and beautiful, his skin evenly tanned in a color that resembled one of the caramel drop candies I looked forward to as a child. He also studied me for a moment, but his eyes were wide and kind, his expression one of deep curiosity. He rolled his eyes, as if to say "Look at what we've gotten ourselves into," gave a faint half smile, and returned his gaze forward, though not before he gave a subtle and secretive glance over to Hernandez.

In the corner of my eye, I noticed Drill Sergeant August making his way down the row, his eyes like highly trained daggers looking for their next target. Should they find a soldier standing in the wrong position, a soldier looking around, or even a soldier moving, those dagger eyes would fix on them, and they would be subjected to the special brand of humiliation that August had recently test-driven on me. He opened his mouth to speak, and his voice bellowed out, filling the large room with his presence and instilling even more fear into the recruits.

"Welcome home, men," he said. "This is where you're gonna sleep, shit, and write the letters your girlfriends are gonna be reading in between fucking Jody while you're here." "Jody," of course, being well-known military slang for the types of men who would cozy up to soldiers' girlfriends at home while they were off on deployments or training. The room was so quiet you could hear a pin drop, which is how we heard the snicker coming from the second row.

August's head snapped to his right, and he moved toward a row of recruits that seemed to be tittering.

"Does somebody think something is fucking funny?" he bellowed. "Am I telling a fucking joke? Am I?"

"No, Drill Sergeant!" we all yelled in unison.

"Good! 'Cause if you think Jody fuckin' your girl while you're here is a fuckin' joke, you're wrong, and I ain't pickin' up no dead body if one of you motherfuckers tries to off yourself. That's why we've got fireguard. Every night, two of you will be up every hour on the hour to make sure nobody's runnin' out, or tryin' to kill themselves, or doin' some shit they're not supposed to be doin'."

I felt a white-hot burst of shame at this last statement, as if August had been reading my mind and knew, somehow, that I was a faggot.

"So figure it out amongst yourselves, unpack your bags, and change into your PT [physical training] clothes for some running before chow."

August left, with Thomas right behind him, strangely wordless, but saying everything he needed to say with the turn of his head in our direction, one piercing and nearly otherworldly blue eye gazing directly at us with a stern look on his heavily pockmarked face. The doors closed, and the two men exited. The soldiers all relaxed. We were alone now.

I looked down at my bags, then up at the rest of the recruits doing the same. I felt claustrophobic and trapped. A strange sort of disconnect from reality, like what I had gotten myself into, was finally sinking in. This was not about to be the summer camp that I had never gotten a chance to go to. Nor was it about to be some stupid Army commercial or something that passed through like a montage from a *Rocky* movie. It was going to be long and hard, and I knew already that I was about to feel every second of it. I dumped the gear on my bed and then looked timidly at the shapeless gray sweats with the bold black letters on them that spelled "ARMY." Up until this point, the most exercise I had gotten was my ill-fated attempt to get "in shape" for the track team before senior year in an awkward attempt to move up a social circle, or really to move into any social circle. After what seemed like endless vomiting following one pathetic sprint around my block, that idea was pretty much derailed. I soon returned to my steady diet of whatever was bad for me, and the weight just kept piling on.

I heard a voice right behind me. "Hey you, fag."

I turned around to see a short and pudgy guy with a haircut that would be considered awful even in a room full of Army-style buzz cuts standing right behind me. I felt a paralyzing tension rise up in my legs. Of course, he was talking to me, but I couldn't decide whether to respond or blow him off.

"What?" I asked meekly, the tone in my voice giving this new-found adversary all the ammo he needed.

"Why don't you hurry the fuck up and put your shit on? Everyone else is all ready to go, and I'm not about to get in trouble on account of a pussy like you," he said with the thickest accent I had ever heard. It made me think of the movies I had watched that referenced the Mafia. I wondered if he was from New York or New Jersey. I had only seen those places in the movies, and the people from there looked pretty tough. I was instantly intimidated, even though his short, pudgy stature represented very little in the way of an actual physical threat.

"Look, I...I didn't even do anything. Why don't you leave me alone?" I asked meekly, avoiding eye contact at all costs.

I looked up quickly, and his beady eyes narrowed into small slits as he moved toward me. "And why the fuck should I? I can already tell you're gonna be the fucking pussy of the platoon, and—"

"Look, Boston, why don't you leave that kid alone?"

I looked up from the ground and locked eyes with another recruit about four beds down. He shifted his gaze from Boston to me. I watched as his eyes went from stern to paternal in less than three seconds. He was older, maybe about twenty-eight or twenty-nine, broad-shouldered, and firm. He had a quiet dignity that almost seemed regal, and he looked at me calmly through deeply set brown eyes.

I held the glance for a moment, my frightened eyes locked in the dark pools of his, thanking him wordlessly, then returned to my clothes like this little incident had never happened. Boston muttered something incoherent, then walked off. The recruits had gotten into the habit of calling each other by nicknames back in the staging area, so I figured that his terrible accent was from Boston. It was yet another place I was unfamiliar with, and I wondered if there were as many black people in his hometown as there were white people in mine. There seemed to be a bit of history between them, and I figured that maybe they'd interacted at the staging area before coming over to training. Dallas and I exchanged another glance, then put on our clothes and headed down for a little evening PT.

The sky was orange as the sun set on Fort Benning, Georgia. We headed out in a single-file line onto the fitness field and track that was soon to become one of my greatest adversaries over the next six months. The track was made with red clay and surrounded a circle of grass. Forest and woods surrounded the fitness field. August led us out onto the field, his black Army-issued shorts revealing short, stumpy legs with muscular, powerful calves. Looking at him, I was struck by the fact that this man was at some point in time very handsome, before age and the rigors of the Army had taken over. "All right, men, what we're gonna do now is a fitness assessment. That track is a quarter of a mile long, so eight times around is two miles. I wanna see how fast you can do it and make sure you can finish. We're gonna do a lot of physical shit during this training, so you've gotta be ready. We get up at 0500 hours every fuckin' morning to exercise, and if you don't do well then, you'll be out here at 2000 hours every fuckin' night running 'til you get better, so have at it," he said and guided us all into line at the beginning point of the track.

My breath was short and staggered. I felt as if I was going to hyperventilate. Maybe this would be different than my ill-fated attempt at high school track. Maybe I would be able to do this and hang tough with all of these guys who were in so much better shape than I was. As I gasped for breath just five minutes later and just under two times around the track, I found myself thinking about just how stupid I was to believe any of that crap. The shock of my feet on the ground was foreign. The weight on my chubby body shifted impossibly from side to side. I felt beads of sweat begin on my forehead, just under my nose, and in the folds of the extra body weight along my ample midsection.

One by one, all the other recruits lapped me, and I could see their faces as I heaved, the sweat dripping from my pudgy frame. The emotions ranged from pity to anger to disgust. I could see their opinions of me forming in their eyes. It looked like I was to be here what I was in high school—a loser, the fat kid. The one who was... different. The slew of lean, muscular legs became a blur, and they seemed to go faster and faster while I seemed to somehow slow down, continually out of breath. I could hear August in the background, yelling.

"Come on, Smith! What the fuck? You can't run two fucking miles?" he screamed.

By the time I'd wheezed into lap four, most of the recruits had already finished, and they grouped up on the sidelines, watching me struggle to continue. I could hear their various comments.

*That fat faggot can't even run two miles?*

*What a fucking piece of shit!*

It was the pack mentality that it seemed like human beings always gravitated toward, whether they were in a high school in Ohio or on a PT track in Fort Benning, Georgia.

"Run, Forrest, run!" I heard one of them say, then I looked up just as Boston, my pudgy tormentor from earlier, made his way to the front of the group. He had an evil, ratty little smile on his face.

"No way is he Forrest!" he yelled, reveling in what was obviously a delicious moment for him.

"That motherfucker is too dark to be Forrest. He looks more like Bubba Gump!" At this, the group exploded into laughter and started to chant.

"Bub-ba Gump! Bub-ba Gump!"

I felt the familiar sting of hot tears in my eyes, only this time there was no room to hide in until they either flowed through or subsided, and the tears started to stream down my cheeks. Luckily enough, I was at the other end of the field with my back to my new cheerleaders, and I frantically wiped the tears into my face, mixing them with the seeming rivers of sweat that had already accumulated. Through my tears, I could see a blurry view of the forest beyond the track, and I wondered what it would be like to keep running, to escape this humiliation. As I reapproached the starting point, exhausted nearly to the point of fainting, I noticed Drill Sergeant August standing there with his arms folded and a canteen of water by his feet. He had a look on his face of pure disgust and a deep satisfaction. *I knew what a fucking loser you were, and now you proved it,* I could imagine him thinking.

He picked up the water and handed it to me, the expression on his face never changing. I drank the water as if I had run that mile and a half through the deserts of Egypt. I'd never been so thirsty, never wanted—needed—so much the taste and satisfaction that comes from pure water. I gulped the water down as if I hadn't had anything to drink in months, and when my stomach felt full, I gulped down even more. It came back up so fast I didn't quite realize what was happening at first.

Watery ropes of my vomit hit the sand of the track, splashing Drill Sergeant August's tennis shoes and legs in the process. I could see nothing else, and I could do nothing but feel the fluid being expelled from my body, powerless to keep it from making a mess of August's shoes. I was terrified. This man could do whatever he wanted to me. He hovered over me, a towering figure cloaked in the dark shadows of the evening, the lights that were perched around the field giving him a yellowish glow. He smiled again, baring his teeth in a primal, animalistic power move.

He looked from me to the sky above, then stepped back behind the puddle of vomit that lay there between my legs. He smiled again, then kicked sand over it, sending sand and flecks of dirt onto my body and into my face, some of it coming into my mouth and sticking on the corners of it that were still wet with vomit. I just stared at him, eyes widened with fear. He turned around and walked away toward the barracks, and I sat alone on the field cross-legged for a long time, staring at the woods just beyond the barracks and listening to the sounds of nature. I was once again, as I had been at many things in my short seventeen years on the earth, a colossal failure.

I looked over as the rest of the recruits followed August back into the barracks. The white glow of the fluorescent lights that lit the staging area clashed with the yellow glow of those that lit the track area. I noticed one platoon member walking toward me tentatively. I sat in a daze, staring at my own vomit, but the next thing

I knew, a strong white forearm extended toward me. I looked up to see Dallas, and he favored me with a warm half smile that revealed a hint of his crooked front teeth.

"C'mon, Bubba," he said.

"Let's go get some chow and head up. Lights out in an hour."

As he helped me up and we walked away from the pile of vomit on the track, my head swam with questions. *Who is this guy? Why is he being so nice to me? Why would he risk associating with the platoon loser?* There were so many questions I wanted to ask but didn't, so many thoughts about what had just happened. *What would my platoon members think of me? What did the next six months of basic training have in store?*

What just happened was one of the most humiliating experiences of my life. I felt fat, tired, and useless. I had a deep desire not to quit and a strong feeling that I had to move forward into the unknown under the notion that my vague and undefined future was at stake. As for Dallas, I didn't know why this guy was here, didn't know why he was risking his own fledgling reputation to help me, but I was thankful for him. Thankful that for whatever reason he decided maybe the fat faggot who couldn't run a half mile without puking could use something other than an adversary, that maybe he could use a buddy. I tried valiantly to put the day's events behind me as I walked back up to the barracks with my new friend in silence. However, I found myself unable to escape the sneaking suspicion that a fresh round of humiliation was just another sunrise away. Hooah.

# CHAPTER 2

# BUBBA

The first night of basic training, I returned to the barracks with the stench of failure flowing from me as strongly as the odor from my sweat-drenched PT uniform. My entire body hurt, and it seemed like every newly found muscle in it screamed from shock and agony. I walked into the drab "home" where I was to spend the next six months of my life and let out a long sigh that I hoped wasn't too audible. I looked quickly around me and noticed the other soldiers in the platoon in various stages of undress while getting ready for bed.

The barracks are essentially one big warehouse with rows of beds and footlockers separated only by a pathway in which to get by or be randomly inspected by either one of the drill sergeants. It was lined with small, prison-like windows on the far sides, and I was lucky enough to get placed by one. Each soldier was assigned a bed, footlocker, and full-size locker complete with forest-green covered blankets that had the softness of sandpaper and sheets that seemed to have a negative thread count. The drill sergeants' offices were in the front of the barracks, thankfully completely opposite from my bed, which was closest to the bathrooms. There was an air of clinical precision to the layout and how they obviously wanted things kept.

I walked to my bed and sat down, wincing at the new experience of soreness and tightness in my thighs. My shirt felt heavy with sweat, and I wanted it off of me. I tossed it in the corner by my window and looked at it in disgust. I sat there for a moment in a silent world where I tried to piece together what had just happened. Thus far the voices from the other platoon mates had been noise in the background, but one in particular came into very sharp focus.

"You're fucking fat," it said, dripping with disdain.

I looked to my left to see Hernandez, who had the bunk opposite of mine on the other side of the aisle. He stood up, shirtless. His taut body was cream-colored and lean, and dripped with perspiration from head to toe. His nipples were a dark red and were separated by a bit of definition and the faintest spray of curly chest hair. His lips were pursed in a way that was almost feminine. His beady brown eyes scanned me in judgment. In that instant I could tell that he liked this, liked being the alpha male and disapproving of me. He was in shape and had easily completed the run and was only worthwhile because I was the opposite and had failed miserably.

I had been the fat kid for quite some time, dating back to one long, hot, boring summer between sixth and seventh grade with my grandparents in North Carolina. There, long days of watching television and movies were punctuated only by bouts with massive amounts of fattening food. By the time I'd come back, the damage was done. Over the years I had become quite accustomed to hearing comments about my food intake and my weight from family and the kids at school. Now, in basic training which I was quickly learning was the singularly most intense job in the Army, it was as if years of pizza, hot dogs, soda, and fried chicken had come back with a vengeance, since the weight that they added to my already stocky frame made me slower than all the rest in my platoon.

Hernandez stood up at his bunk with his chest out and chin up. He projected authority and strength, but his willingness to use it to berate me struck me as weak. "You hear me?" he asked, leaning toward me. I leaned over, looking down. I felt weak and pathetic, and he knew it. I knew that people like him could only feel good about themselves when they made others feel like shit, but I felt so physically and emotionally raw that he was succeeding. I wanted to yell and scream at him. I wanted to ask him, why me? I wanted to say so many things that I couldn't because my throat was tight with tears that I was fighting off with everything that I had. I knew if I tried to say anything, the first syllable would be a croaky mess that would open the floodgates of tears and sobs, and I'd decided that I'd had my fill of humiliation for the night.

I looked over at Hernandez. My eyes were glassy, angry, and terrified. Rogers was close to him, as he seemed to be a lot. He watched the exchange with a hint of sadness in his eyes. He looked at me with pity, and at that moment I hated him for it, possibly even more than I hated Hernandez for initiating this incident in the first place. I turned away and looked down, trying to get my breath back to normal and fight back the tears, which seemed to be held back by the mental dam I'd created. Hernandez smacked his teeth, another oddly feminine gesture, then wrapped a towel around his waist and headed to the showers. Rogers followed not too far behind him. After a few more minutes, I did the same, not speaking a word to anyone for the rest of the night.

The next morning I stood in formation with the rest of the platoon on the field in front of the barracks, which had been the site of my bitter defeat just nine hours before. It was around 5:30

a.m., and the sky was a dark blue with a faint orange hint of the sun that would break through in the next hour. The chill of the mid-October early morning wind whipped bitter tendrils around my exposed legs, which had broken out in pimply gooseflesh along with my bare arms. It was unseasonably cold, and I could see my breath. For the first time I wondered what it would've been like to go through this during the summer. Drill Sergeant August walked out with Drill Sergeant Thomas following behind him. I was struck for the first time by the vast difference between the two men in a way that I hadn't been given the chance to during my initial physical training humiliation.

Drill Sergeant Thomas was spindly and almost cartoonishly unattractive. He resembled a living scarecrow, his piercing blue eyes so rich and vivid they almost resembled glass eyes, thus completing the illusion. His legs resembled old bamboo sticks poking out of his PT shorts, and the oversized uniform hung off of him like it would a hanger. On the other hand, Drill Sergeant August had errant rolls of fat that seemed to be eagerly awaiting escape from the constraints of the shirt shoved into his shorts. His legs were thick and muscular. The way the fluorescent light hit the grooves in his deeply set eye sockets gave him an almost otherworldly glow that only increased my fear of him. I was happy to be in the third row, but I remembered that it didn't stop him from getting to me yesterday. I kept my eyes steadfastly focused directly ahead.

August stepped in front of the platoon and began to pace with his chest out and his hands on his hips.

"All right, men, this is called PT. It happens every fucking morning at 0600 sharp, and it consists of whatever the fuck I want to do for however long I wanna fuckin' do it. Now since one of you faggots had such a fucking problem with the run last night, we're gonna try it again."

I could once again feel the eyes and the judgment of the platoon on me, and my heart sank. *Couldn't he just let it go?* I thought. He acts like he *wants* them to hate me.

August took us through the ritual of cadence that we marched to on the long stretch of road that lay just behind our barracks complex. He walked in the front just to the left of us in his now-signature exaggerated chest-out strut, and Thomas took up the rear. I marched in between Rogers and Hernandez. I felt a strong, sudden need to find Dallas in the crowd. We hadn't spoken since the night before, but already his presence comforted me. It looked like I wouldn't be winning any popularity contests here, and he seemed to be the only person willing to be my friend. I finally caught the back of his head and his slightly bow-legged walk, and as if reading my mind, he looked back and gave me a quick little half smile. I felt better but still nervous. My legs screamed with soreness from the night before. I intensely feared I was doomed to repeat my failure in the upcoming run.

Our cadence was slow and steady. I sensed an ongoing dread as it started to speed up along with our steps.

"One! Two! Three! Four! Somebody, anybody start a war!"

We repeated the cadence as we started a light jog. At first, it was almost easy. I felt my body heat up and the soreness going out of my legs while the trees whizzed by on either side of the long road we ran on. I seemed to be keeping up with the bobbing heads that surrounded me while we ran. I tried to breathe as slowly as possible, and everything seemed to be going okay. Then, August decided to turn it up.

The increase in speed was subtle at first and then increased over the next quarter-mile to become just short of a full-on sprint. I could again feel everything in my body fighting against what I was trying to do. The pain seemed like it came from everywhere at once. My lungs felt constricted, my stomach heavy, and sharp bands of pain shot up from my feet through my calves. *It's happening*, I thought. I could feel myself getting weaker and weaker. The next thing I knew I felt the shoulders of my platoon mates bumping against me as I fell further and further behind the crowd.

I hated myself as I slowed down and fell back. I hated that I wasn't as lean and strong as they were, and that I was embarrassing myself once again. The group moved farther and farther ahead. I slowed down even more, though I tried desperately to keep moving. Again I'd had enough, and I stopped on the side of the road, coughing and wheezing. I looked to my left and saw the sun rising above the woodland that lay on both sides of the road.

When I looked up, I saw August jogging back toward me with a look of disgust on his face. This time it was mixed with anger and a dark glee. When I saw him, I picked myself up and moved forward. As weak as I felt physically, there was no way I wanted to repeat last night's teary hysterics. Still jogging, I moved forward at a snail's pace, and August slowed down his running to keep pace with mine. It was just him and me out on this road together. The rest of the platoon had moved so far forward I could only see the small gray dots of their uniforms in the distance.

"You know why you can't make the runs, Smith. Because you're fucking weak. I know it, they know it, and I think you know it, too," he said softly.

I had nothing to say, choosing instead to focus on controlling my breathing and trying to ignore the throbbing pain on the bottom of my feet that hit me like an electric shock every time I put my foot to the pavement.

"What the fuck are you even doing here, son? You think I want to be in the field of battle with a weak little pussy like you?"

His words were brutal, but they were delivered in an even-tempered voice in a calming baritone that I imagined wasn't unlike that of a psychiatrist. He wasn't mocking me or teasing me, just stating facts that I obviously needed to know.

"You know they know it, too, right? Keep fucking up like this and *I'll* be the least of your worries, soldier."

I tried to keep calm and continued to look forward while I ran. The rest of the company had circled back around now, and they passed me on my left as I tried my hardest to continue on. The sun was up now. I could see their faces register the disgust and the pity that I was now starting to get used to. I tried not to make eye contact with them, instead focusing again on looking straight ahead. I didn't look for Dallas because I didn't want to see him. Last night I felt pitiful and sorry for everything that had happened, but this morning was different. I thought back to August's words and how they made me feel. I couldn't muster pity for myself, nor could I muster any hatred for August to match the fear I had of him. As I tried to regain control of my short, jagged breaths, I realized that I couldn't hate August for his words because I knew that they were true.

After that incident and the one before it, my new platoon mates continued to call me "Bubba," after that dark-skinned, simple, big-lipped character in the movie *Forrest Gump*. I never could figure out why, since it wasn't as if they needed an extra signifier for the youngest of only two black people in the entire thirty-person platoon. The name stuck, becoming a not-so-secret shame and the cowbell around my neck for the majority of my basic training experience. On the surface I wanted to believe that the nickname was all in fun, however, something deeper within me told me that there was something else going on with it, something that my mind was far too underdeveloped to understand, like the "grease monkey" chants that were made toward me by my all-white elementary school classmates at the school on the other side of town my mother sent me to. I knew I looked different than everyone else in the platoon but wasn't truly able to understand what that difference meant.

I also noticed that the nicknames were only given to a few of the "losers" in the platoon. The two lean and athletic Latinos who bunked across from me were simply Rogers and Hernandez, but I was Bubba in all his supposedly dark, stupid, and simple glory. Bunking to my left was an older man, who at forty-three looked every bit of his age and then some. His body was thin and frail. There was a blankness to his eyes that, when combined with the fact that he was a forty-three-year-old man in basic training, only added to the sense that he may have been a bit slow. He was very quiet and spoke only in short, curt sentences. As the oldest private in the company, he was of course given the only nickname appropriate: Gramps. Gramps gave me the creeps. There was something unsettling and tragic about someone that old being in such a low position on the totem pole. He seemed shifty and ill at ease in most situations. He was also what could only be described as a nervous drooler.

One bitterly cold evening after an ungodly night run that I'd again failed at, we were called into attention in the barracks for a surprise inspection of our beds, bunks, and boots. We stood in the uniform "attention" position with our hands at our sides in our drab gray PT uniforms. We heard the heavy, foreboding thump of August's combat boots walking slowly and steadily down the two even rows of recruits. The thump of his boots reminded me of the slow, tension-building passing of time on some large, pendulous clock. At that point in time it was the only sound in the world. I struggled to keep my posture and look forward, but I was terrified as I sensed his presence coming toward me. The fear and tension this man could generate in me was palpable. I could almost sense my nerve endings tingling as he approached me. Right in front of me but facing to my left, he did a left face. He was directly in my face, looking me up and down with the faintest of half smiles on his sagging face. I didn't dare look into his eyes, so I continued looking straight through him, only being reminded to breathe as I heard the breath wheezing in and out of his nostrils. Beside me I sensed Gramps's nervousness feeding off of my own. It wasn't long before August sensed it too, like some ancient bloodhound sniffing his prey. He moved on from me and was now directly in front of Gramps. I glanced directly across from me to see Rogers struggling to keep from cracking a smile. Hernandez glared at me.

From my peripheral vision I watched Gramps next to me and noticed a shiny wet substance making its way from the corner of his lips in a painfully slow slog down the side of his chin. He had a look of panic in his eyes as August moved toward him with a puzzled look on his face.

"What the fuck, private?" he asked incredulously. "The fuck? You...drooling?"

Gramps was in full panic mode now. His legs shook as he answered August. His speech was garbled from the drool that had made a home in his mouth.

"Yes, Drill Sergeant."

"Well, wipe your fucking mouth off!" August shouted.

He seemed to be outraged and surprised at this inappropriate display of oral incontinence.

Gramps stood straight up, brought his right forearm to his mouth to wipe off the drool and took a large swallow to cover the remainder. August shook his head and looked at him with a curious mix of disgust, contempt, and surprise.

"The fuck, man?" he growled.

I tried as best I could to betray no movement or reaction on my face. August's back was to Rogers and Hernandez, who were at differing levels of entertainment at this little development. Hernandez had cracked a smile, while Rogers shook subtly but unmistakably, his eyebrows arching up and his eyes watering as he tried desperately to hold in the torrent of laughter that was welling up within him. August exited quickly with only a cursory "Lights out in ten." He was gone as quickly as he had come, leaving everyone within a few feet of the incident to collapse on our beds in hysterics. I laughed partly because it was funny, but mostly because I was relieved that I was, for once, not the butt of the joke. It was the first real laugh I'd had since coming to Fort Benning. It was also the last I'd have for a very long time.

My first few weeks in infantry basic training at Fort Benning, Georgia, were an endless series of failures on various levels. Robert Smith was no more, abandoned during the public humiliation of the very first day of training. I was Bubba, the black fuck-up who stuck out like a sore thumb among the dozens of smart and muscular soldiers in all tasks physical. There wasn't a platoon run I couldn't fall out of, a road march I couldn't fail, or a marksmanship lesson in which I couldn't put my platoon members in danger. One brutally cold fall day, the platoon was to march two and a half miles to the nearest range to practice our marksmanship skills with the M16 assault rifles we'd been assigned after days and days of practicing assembly and disassembly of them.

The drill sergeants paced back and forth as we worked with the weapons, but they didn't institute a strict code of silence as they had in the past. Indeed, the staging area murmured with a sustained but quiet buzz of soldiers chatting, getting to know one another, and helping everyone out.

"Hey watch it, Bubs, you're forgetting the spring," Dallas said to me, taking out a screw that separated the M16 in half and placing it in the aforementioned spring. The spring had rolled over into the section filled with the parts to his weapon. Dallas had become my only true friend in the platoon.

He was a twenty-six-year-old father from Oklahoma with two children. He had enlisted in the Army as a way to take care of them. When he spoke of his two young girls and his wife at home, he got a distant look in his eyes. I knew that he was far away from Fort Benning with its morning PT and road marches.

"I don't know if you've ever been to Oklahoma, man, but there ain't nothing there, and I mean nothing. I know this will help me take care of them. Six months of this bullshit, then it's off to Fort Sill. They'll put me and the family up and everything. Shit, man. Can't beat that," he said.

When he said that, I knew that his wife had a good husband, and his kids had a great dad. I figured his paternal instinct was what caused him to take such a protective role with me, and his actions filled me with a strong sense of awe and hero-worship that remained free of any romantic feelings or sexual urges toward him.

"Bubba, what the fuck are you doing here?" he asked me curiously in his crooked-mouthed, southern-accented way one night after chow before lights out.

"God knows you can't run for shit, but...I dunno. You seem smart and shit. Like you should be in college or something, not here."

I thought about what he said and back to all of my ill-fated attempts to attend my local university, attempts which were never set up or advocated for by the guidance counselors at my high school or my absentee mother. When I thought about it, I felt a sting of resentment towards them all. The resentment was familiar, but this time it was met with a sense of determination that was new and peculiar.

"I do want to go to college. I really do. I mean, it's all I want to do," I said. I felt a need and longing that seemed to reach depths I hadn't yet known existed.

"I think this is how I get there."

Dallas and I ate chow together, marched in formation together, and did pretty much everything together. He was my buddy, my confidant, and the closest thing I'd had to a true best friend in seventeen years. All of this, coupled with my complete and utter failure as a soldier, seemed to annoy Boston to no end. In the days following my two initial humiliations, he had been on a campaign around the platoon to ensure that everyone knew it. Boston was an odd character, short and stout and chunky with harsh, crude features that wouldn't be out of place in *Mad* magazine.

While small in stature, the full force of his personality was enough to make him tower above me and most others in the platoon, but as was typical of guys like him, he went for the easy target in his bullying of me.

"Looks like Bubba the fat faggot fucked up another run," he would say in a faux singsong voice, egging some of the other platoon mates on to join him in the ribbing. Unlike Drill Sergeant August's faggot proclamation of me the very first day, there was nothing indicative of some unbridled joy of gay sex on my part about the way Boston used the word. He wielded the word in my direction like a sword, ready to strike when he felt threatened or wanted to shift the attention away from himself. He used it as an all-purpose slur when he wanted to say weak, lazy, stupid, tired, and all of the other things that I portrayed to the platoon members when I failed at the runs and the road marches or when I fucked up at the marksmanship range. The word stung when he used it, but it made me angry in a way that had only made me sad before.

The only other time I'd heard it in my life before coming to Fort Benning had been on one terrible day in that adolescently political mishmash of status, socializing, and food: the high school cafeteria. Never one to be surrounded by friends, I had nonetheless found a group of fourth-tier kids like myself to have lunch with whenever the library, which worked as my usual lunchtime hideout, wasn't available. Unfortunately, that day another fourth-tier kid and suspected homosexual happened to sit with us. It was then we caught the eye of a popular high school jock that moonlighted in the particular brand of assholedom that popular high school jocks are known to be masters of. I shrank into my seat as I noticed him coming but to no avail.

Soon, he was making his proclamation of me as one of the premier "FAGS" of my high school. He made it known loudly and boisterously to the entire senior student body, which happened to be located in the cafeteria at that point in time. I was trapped, looking down into my food while trying to ignore both the rising chorus of laughter from my classmates and the pitiful looks from the teachers who did nothing to stop it.

Whenever I heard the words "faggot" or "fag," the feelings from that day would come rushing back, and my body would tense up for just a moment as I viscerally re-experienced the hate and ridicule that came from my classmates. When I'd experienced the word from my high school tormentors, I had known that it was used because, for whatever reason, I had been suspected of actually being gay. When the word came from Drill Sergeant August that first day of basic training, I suspected it was rooted both in the weakness implied by Boston's use of it and the suspicion of actual homosexual tendencies that my high school classmates had.

# CHAPTER 3

# THE HARD ROAD

Around the same time I was falling out of runs, making enemies of the drill sergeants, and generally being a complete and utter failure, there was another soldier who was also having a tough time with basic training. His name was Lanter, and he was a young, pudgy recruit who always seemed to be enveloped by an eerie sense of calm, even as he failed at most of the same things. A calm so eerie, in fact, that it was almost creepy. He was eighteen years old, and he wore circular thin-rimmed glasses that always seemed stretched just a little too far on his round, wide face. His build was awkward. He was pudgy but not fat, and his skin was so pale it was almost translucent. The sloppy curves of his body poked out from the unforgiving gray PT uniform we all wore in the mornings.

His features were oddly ill-defined. He always blended in yet remained strangely omnipresent, as if he was studying the rest of us for some as-yet unknown reason. Lanter was free from any sort of physical or verbal abuse from the drill sergeants and other recruits in a way that I never was. Perhaps it was because they sensed a presence from me of an inner-life, a real person that existed beneath the surface. Most of the time Lanter seemed like some pod person from a real-life *Invasion of the Body Snatchers*. He was fully encompassed by some weirdness that existed just beneath the surface that was ready to bubble up and manifest itself if any of us got too close. Lanter never talked, cried, or did much of anything. He simply wasn't there. It wasn't too long before we all realized just how damaged he was.

For me, the tense but tolerable struggles of the first few weeks had given way to a punishing daily ritual of failure and humiliation. Most days would start with the daily ritual of PT, which consisted of falling out of runs over and over again. I would get the usual berating by the drill sergeants followed by the "weak fag" and "pussy" chants of most of the platoon members when we'd return back from the runs. I'd quickly shower and change with my head down, trying to attract as little attention as possible. It was during these days when I really started to notice Lanter and wondered why he was the way he was. He was just as weak and as much of a failure as I was. He never wavered. He possessed a sense of calm that always seemed to lay over him like a protective blanket. When I noticed him at the end of the runs simply giving up and walking when I pushed on through the pain of every screaming and aching muscle in my body, I felt a sense of anger toward him so strong I didn't know what to do with it.

I stood separate from the formation with my sore muscles and sweat dripping down my back. Drill Sergeants Thomas and August screamed at me. I saw Lanter look toward me in his oddly expressionless way while walking slowly back to the barracks. It made me sick. I wanted to yell out to the drill sergeants, the platoon, and the world. Why me? What about Lanter? Of course I did nothing and said nothing. My only movements during those days were grimaces from the horrid breath of the two older men. They got their kicks from berating me. My only movements were subtle twitches of revulsion with my eyebrows when I would see their spittle flecking in my direction and turning to foam at the sides of their mouths.

The words were all the same, some unimaginative version of "weak," "faggot," and "pussy" strung together by "fuck," "shit," and "punk." The usual. The situation was taking its toll on me, and I started to feel like a different person. Before, I never felt the way they described me, but now I couldn't remove the words from my head when I thought of myself or looked at myself in the mirror. Between the verbal abuse of the sergeants and the negative connotations of my "Bubba" nickname that was used even by the recruits who were semi-friendly with me, I was in a valley lower than anything I'd ever experienced.

When I looked in the mirror in the mornings after I'd showered, I saw Bubba. Bubba was weak, dark, stupid, and fat. He couldn't do anything right, and everybody knew it. When I looked into the mirror for a sign of whoever I was before I came here, I couldn't find him. I didn't like who was there. The dried sweat created ugly patches of white salt on my dark skin. Every pore on my body was open as were all my insecurities. They were out in the open and on full display for the world to see, like an oozing open wound. My body started to slow down. I lurched around the barracks like a zombie, and every night I would fall asleep on my side with the wall to my front, staring into the blankness as if looking for an escape from my present situation in the hardened gray concrete in front of me.

During our downtime in the evenings after chow, when everyone else was reading letters from home or writing to their loved ones, I would curl up with my notepad, a pen in my hand and my back to the side of my locker. I would sit intently focused for sixty to ninety minutes, going through pages and pages of paper. On these sheets of paper I would only write one thing, a silent mantra written over and over again with words that I could never verbalize—I hate it here.

I hated it because I'd never felt so weak in my life. I hated it because I'd never felt so *black* in my life. Most of all I hated it because it was the first adult decision I'd made in my life, and it was shaping up more and more to be like the wrong one. I felt like I didn't even know who I was anymore. I was being turned into someone I didn't want to be. I was being turned into the weak pussy, the faggot, the scourge of the platoon, and it was starting to wear at my fragile, seventeen-year-old psyche. The relationship between Dallas and me was also starting to become distant as well, starting with an incident at the marksmanship range.

Through some act of God I hadn't fallen out of the two-and-a-half-mile road march to the marksmanship range on that bitterly cold, early November day, and I was strangely excited about shooting the M16 rifle we'd been assigned. It was a part of our power and our identity as soldiers. The marksmanship range was surrounded by wooded areas all the way around, and the sky was a dark orange turning into light blue as the sun came up. We dropped our rucksacks in formation and then sat down to have some chow before we started. Our meals on the ranges consisted of MREs, which is short for Meals Ready to Eat, small portions of freeze-dried food that were warmed via a small, water-activated heater. I imagined that I'd probably get a better meal by roasting some roadkill over an open fire and grimaced as I prepared that morning's gourmet meal of chicken tetrazzini.

The squad huddled around, trying to keep warm as the wind whipped through the thin GORE-TEX jackets that we wore. I sat with Dallas, Gramps, Rogers, and Hernandez, and Boston wasn't too far away. I looked over at him, and he glowered. I looked away quickly.

"Hey, good job on the road march, Bubs," Dallas said.

I looked up with a smile I hoped wasn't too big.

"Thanks, man," I replied excitedly.

Anxiously looking for a way to get into the conversation, Boston found his chance.

"Yeah, some fuckin' long road march. I can probably hock a loogie and hit the barracks from here," he spat, and then returned to his meal.

His voice was filled with menace, and his antagonizing nature was even more brutal than usual. The stress of basic training was starting to get to all of us, him included. Lately things had become more intense.

The road march to the marksmanship range was sandwiched through all sorts of different training, from bayonet to gas chamber. The trainings were being done in increasingly cold and brutal weather, putting us all on edge. Though my performance was getting better, it wasn't by much, and my failures had oftentimes cost us extra PT on top of what we were already doing. We were tired, hungry, and cold most days, but nobody in the platoon had decided to take any of the extra burdens out on me...yet.

There was an awkward silence as I expected Dallas to come to my aid, but he didn't. He did look over to me as if he wanted me to say something, anything, but he didn't. I looked down, shook my head, and continued eating my meal, silently cursing Boston, as I'd become used to doing. Drill Sergeant August walked over to the platoon like John Wayne himself.

"All right, you're done, men. Whatever you're eating, get rid of it, and let's get to shootin'!"

We begrudgingly threw out the remnants of our meals and headed to the shooting range, looking more and more like the walking dead.

The marksmanship range consisted of six stations that were set up to look like foxholes. Barrels big enough to fit two to three people were dug into the ground. We propped our weapons up on the sandbags that had been provided for us. I huddled in the foxhole with Dallas and tried to remember everything we'd been told about how to hold the weapons. I pressed the butt of the rifle into my shoulder and felt it press against my collarbone. I slid the front end of the weapon into my left palm and my right index finger into the groove of the trigger.

"All clear!" the drill sergeant yelled as we all got ready to shoot. "Fire!"

I focused in on the target, aiming dead center like we were instructed. I'd never been a violent person before, but shooting the weapon felt strangely comfortable. It felt right. I held the weapon tightly into my shoulder to muffle the vibrations of the shooting, but they weren't strong enough to throw me off target.

"Cease fire!"

After we heard the yell, I cleared my weapon and hopped out of the foxhole.

We were instructed to make sure we had our weapons pointed downrange at all times. We walked in a straight line to pick up our targets with the butt of the rifle tucked into our stomachs and the weapons pointed toward the targets and the forest. As the target came closer into focus, I felt a sly smile forming in the corner of my lips. I'd qualified, and qualified well. The bullet holes were all in the desired three-point range, and all but two pierced the black markings that identified the target nearly dead center. I smiled and looked over at Dallas, who broke out into a large grin.

"Holy shit, Bubba!" he said, eagerly clapping me on the back.

"Good fucking job, man!"

"Jesus Christ," I heard from behind me. I had to stop from shrinking away when I saw that Drill Sergeant August was standing right behind me.

"Hmmm. Maybe you're not so worthless after all. Good shooting, Smith," he said and turned to walk back to the beginning of the lane.

I felt happy and vindicated after finally having done something right, so happy that I really didn't want the moment to end. I wanted to ask August something, anything to prolong the moment. When I moved to engage him further, it wasn't until I heard the yells of the platoon that I realized I'd inadvertently swung my weapon and pointed it in his direction. He whipped back at me, and I saw in his eyes what could only be described as pure fury. He bit down on his lower lip hard as he snatched the barrel of the gun out of my hand and forcefully pointed it down while yanking me forward by the chinstrap of my helmet so hard that I bit my tongue as my neck snapped down violently.

"What the fuck are you doing, Smith?" he asked, still grabbing onto my chinstrap and at this point screaming into my face, "YOU FUCKIN' POINTING A LOADED WEAPON AT ME?"

Everything happened so fast I couldn't even comprehend what was happening. I just knew that I'd fucked up. Again.

"N-n-no, Drill Sergeant!" I stammered. "I wanted to ask you a question about shooting."

"Keep that fucking weapon down and don't ask me any fucking questions, private! You fuckin' hear me?"

"Yes, Drill Sergeant!"

"Get the fuck off of my range and make sure you keep that weapon pointed downrange. You fucking hear me?"

"Yes, Drill Sergeant!"

I picked up my qualifying target sheet and walked back uprange, humiliated. I could once again see the eyes of the platoon on me and caught Dallas out of the corner of my eye looking down. I had embarrassed him. As I walked, I felt shame, failure, and disappointment, feelings that were becoming as natural to me as breathing in the chilly air.

For the rest of that long day I watched the platoon members shoot their weapons as I stood behind the range with my weapon at parade-rest position: standing straight up, one hand behind my back, and one hand with the weapon angled so the butt is on the ground pointed out. I'd failed again, but the funny thing was that now there was no room for tears or even a desire for them. Something had changed. I didn't know what it was. I felt tough and hardened, and even though I'd ended the day with another screwup, it had started with an actual victory. That had to count for something.

B ack at the barracks, I peeled off my heavy rucksack, sweat-stained shirt, and BDU jacket. Once again I sat on my hard bed with the aura of failure around me. Gramps, Rogers, and Hernandez said nothing, and it didn't matter because I was in my own world anyway. It was at that moment I started to think about quitting. It would be fine. I could just go back home, but to what? A grandmother whom I didn't get along with? A small town where nothing was ever going to happen and a dead-end job that was going nowhere? I didn't know where this experience was taking me, but thus far it wasn't taking me anywhere good. I didn't feel stronger, smarter, faster, or any of the things that I was told I would feel. Instead I just felt weak, stupid, and pitiful.

As I sat on the bed in a defeated lump, I noticed Dallas making his way over in the corner of my eye. He had a pained look on his face, as if he were about to say something deeply uncomfortable for him.

"How you doin' man?"

I looked at him through eyes that were world-wearier than any seventeen-year-old should have and mustered a slight smile.

"How do you think?" I asked with more than a hint of self-pity.

"Look, Bubba, you just gotta stop fuckin' up, man."

"What?"

"You gotta stop fuckin' up. People are pissed, man. You make all of us look bad. You know how many guys want to give you a blanket party?" he asked, referring to an age-old Army tradition of restraining a weak recruit and beating him with socks filled with soap.

"No," I said despondently.

"A lot," he said.

"Look, I've got a little sway, and I can hold 'em off because I'm older, but I don't know for how much longer. Look, you've got to get it together, man. Man up. I know you can do this shit. You wouldn't be here if you couldn't."

"I'm just tired," I said. "I'm just tired."

"At ease!" We heard the yell from the doorway to the barracks, announcing the arrival of a drill sergeant.

Normally we would hear a "carry on" and continue what we were doing, but this time the tension-breaking command didn't follow.

Dallas and I stood at the head of my bed as Drill Sergeant August walked down the aisle toward us. My stomach tightened with fear as he made his way down, but instead he stopped at Lanter. He stood at ease about nine beds down from me, with that blank expression on his face as always. Drill Sergeant August leaned into him curiously, as one would lean in for a closer view at an exotic fish in an aquarium.

"You wanna kill yourself, private?" he asked softly.

Dallas and I traded stealthy glances at each other, confused.

"Because I've got soldiers coming up to me telling me that you told them you told them you wanna kill yourself. Is that what you want to do?" August continued.

The room was so silent we could hear Lanter draw in his breath as he replied, "I don't know."

"What?" Drill Sergeant August asked.

"I don't know, Drill Sergeant. I don't know if I want to kill myself."

"How the fuck do you not know if you want to kill yourself or not, private?"

"I don't know, Drill Sergeant. I don't think I can make it here," he said softly.

"Don't think you can make it here? Don't think you can, or don't want to?"

"I don't know, Drill Sergeant. Don't want to, I think."

"Oh is that what you want?" August asked him in a patronizing, singsong tone. "You want to go home to your mommy?"

"Yes, Drill Sergeant."

"Or else what? You gonna kill yourself?"

"Maybe, Drill Sergeant."

The way he said this last line gave me chills, and August was noticeably taken aback. Lanter was serious.

"Drill Sergeant Thomas, please see this private to my office and keep an eye on him. I wouldn't want any accidents," he said before turning to the rest of the platoon.

"Is there anyone else who wants to kill themselves? Anyone else who can't cut it?" he asked, and I noticed with horror that he was walking toward me.

"What about you, Smith? You want to kill yourself? You wanna fuckin' go home, too?"

I couldn't answer, so I stayed silent.

"I mean, you may as well, right? You can't do shit. You fuck up the road marches, can't do a fucking push-up, and you haven't made a single run yet. It's been what, two months? And your living area looks fucked up!" he screamed.

Something caught his eye, and he barreled past me and to my locker, where a few papers stuck out.

"What the fuck is this?" he asked, grabbing the papers.

He yanked them out of the bottom of the locker, one by one. They were the papers I'd written on when I was journaling. The papers had the one phrase repeated on them over and over.

"Oh, I see. You hate it here, huh?"

He was working himself into a frenzy.

"Isn't that what this says, you *fucking piece of shit*? You fucking hate it here?"

He had the whole notebook now, and he was shaking it in my face, ripping out page after page after page with the single phrase on it. I felt their prickly edges bouncing off of my face as he balled them up and threw them at me. I looked down at my days and weeks of writing, "I hate it here" scrawled on the letters in handwriting that got progressively sloppier. August was livid, and his face was red and flustered. He seemed out of control in a way he never had been before. I was so paralyzed with fear I could do nothing but sit back and watch this awful scene play out as if it were happening to someone else.

"You know what? I'm gonna give you your wish. Head to my fucking office now. Move, soldier!" he screamed.

I walked down the long path to the drill sergeant's office, feeling once again the tension that came with every soldier in the platoon staring at me. When I walked into the office, Drill Sergeant August yelled "At ease!" at the soldiers left on the floor and slammed the door so hard behind the both of us that it rattled on its hinges.

It was just the four of us now.

August paced the room as Lanter and I stood in front of him. I was shaking. Thomas stood silently behind him. I looked all around at the various awards and assorted military paraphernalia that adorned the space. August started with Lanter, who for the first time seemed a bit shaken up by what was happening. August had since calmed down a bit, and the fiery red color of anger had dissipated from his face. His voice was soothing and almost calm.

"You want to go home or you want to kill yourself, private?" he asked.

"What?" Lanter asked, confused.

"Either you want to kill yourself, and if you do, you'll kill yourself anywhere, or you're saying you want to kill yourself because you want to go home. Which is it?"

"I'm not right for this," Lanter said. For the first time I noticed the hint of a deeply regional Midwestern accent.

"I can't do this. Not anymore. This isn't for me. I don't want to kill myself. I just want to go home."

August studied him for what seemed like an eternity, pursing his lips as he had an internal debate about how to proceed.

"You wanna go home, you can go home, but let me tell you something, private. You may not realize it today or tomorrow or even three years from now, but one day you're gonna look up and realize you made the biggest mistake of your life. If you can't take this, then you don't want to be a man." He said this with what seemed like a sense of deep loss and sadness.

When I saw that, it struck me that I was seeing August for the first time not as an evil, feared drill sergeant, but as someone accepting a failure. Lanter's impending dismissal was his fault, and he was shouldering the blame. The moment passed almost as quickly as it had come, and August issued an order to Thomas.

"Take him into the other office and have him picked up tonight. Have some of the soldiers pack up his stuff. I want him out of my sight," he said.

Thomas complied and walked Lanter into a smaller office toward the back of the room. I looked over at Lanter, but he never looked back at me. I saw only the slightly humped arch of his shoulder as he dejectedly walked into the office, guided by Thomas. August then turned his attention to me.

"So you fuckin' hate it here, huh?"

I stayed silent.

"Fuckin' answer me, Smith."

I shook my head.

"I can't...I can't do anything right," I said, trying desperately to hold back tears. "I can't do anything right, and I've never not been able to do anything right before."

He sighed and looked at me exasperatedly.

"You suck at life, that's for fuckin' sure. Why are you here, Smith?" he asked.

I looked up at him questioningly. "What?"

"Why. Are. You. Here?" he said.

"I've got everybody's scores in here, and yours are some of the highest. People with your scores don't go into the infantry, so why are you here?"

"Thought it'd be fun, Drill Sergeant."

"Fun?"

"Yes, Drill Sergeant. I never got to go to camp or do any of this shit. I thought it would be fun. Different."

"And?"

"And I want to go to college. I can't afford it. My parents can't, either. That's why they never went. I wanted to do this for a few years and go to college, Drill Sergeant."

"But you hate it here."

I thought very hard about his words. Did I really, truly hate it here, or did I just hate the fact that this was all so hard, different, and foreign? Nothing in my seventeen years on earth had prepared me for the types of people I was now forced to interact with every day, or for how physically demanding this was turning out to be. I'd also never failed at anything quite so spectacularly as I was now failing at infantry basic training.

"I hate that I can't do anything right. I can't make the runs. I can't make the marches. I can't do anything."

My voice cracked, and I felt my lower lip quivering, betraying the strength I was trying desperately to project.

"I can't do anything here," I said.

"You can do anything you fuckin' wanna do, private. Do you want to do this? Do you want to be here?"

I thought back to my house in Akron, to the job at Denny's, to everything else in my life that now seemed somehow so very small. In that moment I knew there was more out there I wanted to see. I wanted to complete this and see Colorado and possibly the world. I wanted to go to college and do all the things I'd dreamed of doing. I looked into his eyes and could feel mine becoming glassy. I felt curious and confused as the next words passed from my lips, words I'd never expected to say.

"I don't have anywhere else to go."

I wanted to tell him why I knew this was true, why I knew I could never go back to Akron. Why there hadn't been a real home for me since my mother had moved away. Instead, I said none of these things as the words hung in the air over the two of us. I felt something happening. I think it was an understanding. And I knew that whatever this was, this unspoken connection of understanding between the two of us, it would not extend beyond this room and beyond this moment. I wanted to tell him that something had changed in me, that I wanted to work harder, and I wanted to be stronger—I didn't want to be a failure, and I wanted to make him proud of me if he let me stay, but instead I said nothing. He stepped back, and I saw a shadow of recognition pass through his face. He studied me for what seemed like an eternity, and I met his gaze, eager to let him know that I meant to make this work.

"Go to bed, Smith," he said and walked into the smaller office to join Thomas and Lanter.

Later on that night I was awakened by the shuffling of bags a few beds down from me. I sat up to see Lanter being escorted by military police, making his final exit from the barracks. He seemed broken and despondent. When they'd exited, I walked toward the window by my bed and looked out to the driveway that led down into the barracks. A few minutes later I saw the MP Humvee roar up the driveway and over the hill, out of sight. From the small window I could see the taillights glow in the distance, the flecks of bright red light becoming smaller and smaller until they disappeared.

Lanter was gone, but I was still here. August had given me a choice today, and I'd chosen to stay. I knew it would be hard work, even harder than it had been so far. For the first time I realized what I was running away from and what I had to look forward to. Everyone was running away from something in this place. I was running away from failure, familiarity, and the crushing loneliness of my life in Ohio. I never wanted to go back to that place and how it made me feel. Somewhere deep within me I knew that I was staring a gift horse in the mouth. This experience and everything that it would give me were in some way a path to the better life that waited for me somewhere in the far distance. I wanted to take it.

After that night, something in me changed, and so did my physical performance at basic training. It started the next morning, and as we stepped out into that field to do our regular PT in the bitter early-December cold, I felt a grim determination to be there, to stay, set in upon me. The morning was cold and dark. My usual crushing fear regarding PT was replaced by a burning desire to do better. I didn't know what that meant, but I just wanted to do better. As we stood in formation in our gray Army sweat suits, I scanned August's face out of the corner of my eye for any recognition of the new bond we shared or any indication that he was rooting for me. He had sent Lanter home and could've sent me as well, but he didn't. It instilled a sense of purpose in me, and it meant something.

I had to prove something not only to him but also to myself. I had to prove that he made the right choice and that I belonged there. I covertly scanned his face, but I saw nothing on it that betrayed anything other than the usual gruff drill-sergeant exterior. His black wool skullcap sat on his head, purposeless because it didn't cover his ears. His eyes were as furious as ever. He was breathing heavily, and the visible breath coming out of his mouth and nose reminded me of a bull's heavy breath right before the bullfight. Just before we took off, we locked eyes, and I got what I was looking for, a flash of recognition so brief that it could have been my imagination. It said only one thing: don't fuck this up, Smith. I hoped that I wouldn't.

The morning run started like countless others had for me during the three and a half months I'd spent in basic training so far, but it would end differently. I'd never wanted to complete the runs before. When I thought back to my mental state when starting them before, I realize that I'd allowed the idea of failure to infiltrate my mind before I'd even started. I was determined not to let that happen this time. Some of the soldiers decided to take off their sweatpants and strip down to the black shorts underneath, exposing their legs to the shrill winds of the early morning in Georgia but also cutting down wind resistance. I decided to join them.

The change in the temperature around my fragile legs was so sudden and brutal that I gasped, but I knew that it was what I needed to do. Once again, the cadence started, and I felt my legs carry me forward.

"One! Two! Three! Four!" the drill sergeant said, and we answered, "Somebody, anybody, start a war!"

We sang along eagerly with the chant. The idea of some imaginary war that we were in essence training for was a small kernel of an abstract idea in our minds. This basic training is where we learned how to fight, shoot, stab, and run. This was our war for now. I felt my legs keeping up with the pace and could see my breath coming out in front of me in deep, steady spurts. I looked around the base as we ran and marveled as I had so many times before at the orange glow of the fluorescent lights that lit it overnight and in the early morning. We passed different battalions, different PT fields, and various ranges. For the first time I wondered if there were any other soldiers similar to me out there, soldiers who didn't have any other choice in life except to join the Army and who didn't have anywhere else to go. It struck me then that it was likely that most of them were in the same position.

Returning from my glazed-over stream of consciousness, I found that I was still hanging in with the run. It was longer than I ever had before. As we turned the corner, which indicated the three-quarter mark of the circular route we'd run many times before, I felt a familiar pang in my stomach and my shins. I wanted desperately for it to go away, desperate to avoid a repeat of the failure I'd exhibited so many times before, but here it was now staring me in the face. The failure taunted me with the deep pain that crackled north in my shins with every step I took and with sharp, jabbing pains that felt like someone punching me in my sides. My lungs felt as if they couldn't take in enough air for me to control my breathing. I pushed through and kept running.

I tried to keep up with the platoon but could feel myself slowing down and falling back.

I fell back but not out. I was near the back of the platoon as I fought with everything I had in me to continue and to complete the run. It would be my first completed run, and never in my life had I wanted something as badly as I wanted to complete the run with the platoon that day. I looked up, and the familiar glow of the lights of our battalion PT field beckoned to me up ahead. It was like some white light I was running toward for my redemption. I saw it, wanted it, could taste it, but instead I felt the familiar slowing of my legs until the platoon was much further ahead of me. I'd failed again. Though I knew I'd failed in staying with the platoon this day, I was determined not to quit and not to give up. August had believed in me, and I wanted to believe in myself for once. It was a new and strange feeling, but it was intoxicating. Even though the platoon was a bit in front of me, I told myself that I would not stop.

When we finally made the right into our PT field that day, I came up only a few hundred feet and a couple of minutes behind them. I still failed to complete the run with the platoon, but in my mind it was still a minor achievement. As I made my place in the platoon, I scanned the eyes of my platoon mates for the usual signs of hate and derision, but I saw none there. As Drill Sergeant August led us through our usual stretches, I looked at his face. When we locked eyes again for a split second, I could've sworn I saw a sort of contentment in his face. He'd taken off the wool cap now, and it didn't hide the deep recesses of his eyes. They were narrowed into slits, but the gaze wasn't angry or domineering; it was strangely settled. Maybe I didn't see the subtle curve of his right cheek form into a satisfied smirk. Maybe I was reading too much into it and looking for something I wanted to see. Maybe that slight tilt of his head forward wasn't directed at me but rather was trying to get one of the last kinks from the physical training we'd just endured out of his neck. Perhaps all those small, subtle signs I saw in him that morning, the signs that indicated he was somewhat pleased with my performance, were created in my head. Maybe it was just wishful thinking, but I didn't think so.

The not-quite failure of the run was the start of a different time for me at basic training. Little by little, I got faster and stronger, until I was not only completing the runs, I was leading them, as well as the road marches and other physical events that we were made to endure during basic training. During that period, I felt like I was finally becoming what I'd set out to be. It was what basic training was supposed to be and what they were there to make me become. A soldier. As the weeks turned into months, I was finally in the homestretch of US Army basic training. Old rivalries were about to rear their ugly heads, and I was soon going to be dealing with an unexpected arrival…and departure.

# CHAPTER 4

# GOING ALL THE WAY

Drill Sergeant Lucas entered our lives two months before our projected graduation date into the hallowed ranks of US Army infantry soldiers. He arrived late due to completion of some other intense training that I imagined he had glided through like Denzel Washington facing some seemingly insurmountable task in an action movie. His presence was strong, and he seemed so much larger than life. He towered above me. When I looked at him, he appeared to be gazing down at me with a knowing, almost comforting gaze. His skin was an even darker and richer shade of brown than mine. It served to enhance the regal aura around him. He was attractive, but I wasn't attracted to him. I had this strange sense that I wanted to *be* him. I wanted to walk the way he walked, and carry within myself the same unshakable confidence that he seemed to possess. Drill Sergeant Lucas was calm, with a confident authority that made you afraid of what was just beneath the surface. He didn't yell, scream, or intimidate like the other drill sergeants. It made you think twice before crossing him or doing anything other than exactly what you were supposed to do. Even the drill sergeant hat, so awkward and bulky on the others, seemed to fit him just right and enhance the presence that he brought to the table. He was tough and determined, knowing that he could face whatever was thrown at him. I wished that I could be like that, and I was actually well on my way.

After the incident with Lanter, I'd managed to do a complete one-eighty in terms of my success in the various tasks we were given. The change came not a moment too soon. One of the most common sayings in the US Army is that pain is only weakness leaving the body. I found the pain leaving right along with the weakness in my body and, more importantly, my mind. I was not only completing the runs but was even calling cadence once or twice. One chilly afternoon as we finished a grueling twelve-mile road march, I felt a certain smug cockiness in the fact that I was able to pass some of my former adversaries who were falling behind in the road march.

There were physical reminders of the months of training. My feet were in awful shape, covered with dead skin that I would hesitantly pick away after the marches and runs. I had lost quite a bit of weight over the past four months along with the weakness that once plagued my mind and body.

Unfortunately, the attention wasn't always positive. I found myself becoming increasingly adversarial with Boston. I'd caught him giving me pointed stares after some of my more recent successes, narrowing his already beady eyes into evil little slits when I glanced in his direction after a run or road march. The situation came to a head the chilly afternoon after the twelve-mile road march, when we both found ourselves in the barracks changing out of our stained, sweaty BDUs.

"So what, you're hot shit now, right?" he asked me as he walked up to my bed, his thick accent turning "you're" into "yah."

I rolled my eyes and looked over at him.

"No," I said.

"So why the fuck were you passing people? Why the fuck are you being a show-off?" he asked, encroaching further into my space.

Boston had never had any trouble completing the tasks, but he was still fat. His brown t-shirt clung to his body, exposing his round stomach and the fatty deposits that jutted out from his chest like the apple-shaped developing breasts of an adolescent girl. He was still breathing heavily from the road march, and his cheeks were dark red from the bitter February chill outside. It wasn't until I realized that I had to look down at him that I noticed how short he really was.

"I wasn't showing off," I said, staring directly into his eyes. "They were falling behind, and I needed to catch up."

"That's fuckin' bullshit, Bubba. Oh what, you think because there's a black drill sergeant you gotta be hot shit now?"

"What the fuck does that have to do with anything?" I asked, wild-eyed.

His words were a bitter reminder of a hard truth that I'd tried to ignore for the most part.

Some of the taunting I'd faced earlier had as much to do with being a black boy in a sea of white faces as it did with my failure at the various tasks. For the first time, Boston was starting to piss me off. Not only was he a fat little shit with an awful accent, he was probably a racist too. He started to move closer to me, and I wondered what would happen if we were to get into a fight. I'd never been in a fight before. Ever. The closest I'd come was a few weeks back when the drill sergeants thought it would be fun to do boxing training. They set up a makeshift boxing ring on the PT field, and paired us up by size and weight. I had no idea what to expect. I was paired with Springer, a lightweight guy from Indiana who nevertheless had a mean left hook that sent me down for the count very easily.

"No, I think you think you gotta show off because you're not the only black boy around here anymore."

"Fuck you. Get outta my face, Boston."

"What the fuck you gonna do if I'm in your face?" he asked, this time sticking a pointed finger in my chest.

Just then, I looked up and saw Dallas heading over to my bunk with a worried look in his eye.

"Hey, Bubba, what's up?" he asked, surveying the situation. Boston turned around and looked up at Dallas angrily.

"Why don't you get the fuck outta here, Dallas? This ain't got shit to do with you."

At that point, something changed in Dallas, and I saw a shadow go over his face that seemed powerful enough to darken the entire room from the midday glow of the windows.

"What the fuck did you just say?" Dallas asked him.

My back was against the wall, and my eyes darted around looking for an exit to the situation. I didn't want them to fight. I didn't want anyone to fight. I just wanted to get the fuck outta there. My anger for Boston was being overtaken by a strong desire to defuse the situation that was getting more volatile by the second.

"Okay, whatever. Let's just go downstairs and check the laundry or something," I said to Dallas, grabbing his arm, but he was unmovable, a stone-faced statue staring intensely at Boston.

Dallas continued, his eyes boring a hole into Boston.

"What the fuck did you just say to me you fat fuck?" He advanced toward Boston.

Boston stood his ground, but I could see his eyes wavering with fear.

"Get the fuck outta here, Bubba," Dallas said to me, using his left hand to push me away as his right drove a hard fist into Boston's chin.

Boston's eyes widened in shock as the blood started to flow from the corner of his bottom lip.

He started to throw wild punches. His height made them only body blows. Dallas solidly landed two more punches to Boston's jaw. The men were grappling now on the floor. An excited "Oh shit!" came from the entrance to the barracks.

"Get the drill sergeants!"

I panicked and exited down the stairs at the rear entrance to the barracks. I arrived downstairs just in time to see the drill sergeants heading upstairs. I shook my head and found myself near tears, wondering how on earth this had all happened. I cursed myself because deep down I knew it was my fault because I wasn't strong enough to fight my own battles. I ran back upstairs and entered the barracks from the front just in time to see Dallas, having pinned Boston to the ground, wailing on him with a fury that belied his gentle demeanor.

The drill sergeants pulled Dallas off as he screamed a litany of curse words. I caught a glimpse of Boston's face, which was now bloody and frightened. Tears streamed down his cheeks, making a clean line through the blood and grime which now lined them. We locked eyes for a split second before he rushed to the bathroom to clean up. I felt an odd sense of power wash over me. There was no doubt in my mind that he'd gotten exactly what he deserved. Unfortunately, the situation wasn't consequence-free for Dallas.

Dallas, my only real friend in basic training and the only person who ever stuck up for me when I needed it, was written up. He was given a bad conduct discharge from basic training and sent home the very next day. As much as I enjoyed what had happened to Boston, I wished it hadn't, because my feelings were overwhelmed with the crushing loss of a good friend. I felt guilty knowing I was the reason behind his untimely exit.

Soon after he left, I found a note that he'd somehow placed in my locker before he'd left the base. I found it one night after dinner. I opened it and read:

*Hey, Bubba,*

*Man, you did it. I couldn't be more proud of ya. You stuck it out and finished, and you've changed a lot from that kid I met the first day here. Now you are becoming a man. Just keep on the way you are and you'll be a leader to many. An inspiration to all new recruits. I can't tell you how happy I am for you. And I wipe the tears back when I say that, one from joy but one because I hate to see the good friend that I have found in you gone. I hate to say goodbye. That's the only hard part. I don't like very many people, and when there are ones I like, they always seem to have to go their own ways, but if they are bettering their lives like you are, I can't complain. I just hope you keep your focus on your goals—meet them, then surpass them. Just give me a call or send a letter once in a while, okay?*

Private Dallas was the first real friend I ever had and someone who sacrificed his military career sticking up for me. In the days that followed his exit, I thought about what a chickenshit I'd been and how weak I really was. For all of my newfound strength and success, I'd still managed to get bullied by a guy I had at least three inches and twenty pounds on. I'd let a true friend take the fall for me. I never saw Dallas again. The circumstances surrounding his exit started to generate some discussion among the other recruits, specifically Hernandez, who seemingly never missed an opportunity to tell me how much of a failure I was.

"He went home because of you," Hernandez said to me the next evening as we were changing out of our gear from nighttime PT.

"That man had a wife and kids, and he went home fighting for you. You're such a fucking pussy, man."

I looked over at him and shook my head, narrowing my eyes. I simply couldn't understand why this person was so intensely concerned with kicking me while I was down. It was yet one more part of basic training I'd had my fill of. I thought a great deal about

Dallas and my role in getting him kicked out. It factored into one of the deepest fears that I had about myself, which was that I was toxic. At seventeen years old, Dallas was the first friend I'd ever made in my life. The only thing he had to show for being a friend to me was a one-way ticket back home and one last paycheck from the US Army. It was something I felt deeply ashamed of. I'd spent so many of the years prior to enlisting in the Army in a constant state of loneliness and isolation. If my own damn parents didn't want anything to do with me, why would anyone else? In the time after Dallas left, I retreated further into myself. I kept up my routine of success in the tasks at hand, but I was moving through a fog— not because of Dallas's absence but because of my role behind it. Hernandez's smug superiority was coming through at a time when I really didn't need it, and it was time to say something.

"What the fuck is your problem, man?" I asked, sitting on my corner and leaning in as if I were a student waiting for an interesting answer from a professor. "I mean, really," I continued. "What do you want from me? You give me shit about not making the runs, and I'm making the runs. Man, people like you just want something to talk about. Why don't you worry about your shit, and I'll worry about mine?"

I couldn't believe the words as they were coming out of my mouth, though my small feeling of victory was overshadowed by a moment of panic as Hernandez seemed to narrow his eyes even more and stood up from his bed. As always, Roberts was watching from the next bunk. He stood up to place his hand on Hernandez's chest to stop him. Hernandez looked over, and I noticed that thing again, that small spark between the two of them that would always come up at the oddest moments. They locked eyes for a brief moment and walked toward the other end of the barracks. I seemed to have stopped breathing. The air came rushing out of me so forcefully it felt like I had taken a punch to the gut.

I thought more about Dallas being sent home, but I knew I couldn't let it bother me for too long. I thought back to what I could've done, and back to the blankness and fury that was in Dallas's eyes right before he attacked Boston. What would telling the drill sergeants of my role in the fight actually do besides put me at risk of getting a one-way ticket home right along with him? No, I couldn't do that. As I'd gotten more and more successful at the tasks, the vision of Colorado became more and more clear in my head. It was where I would start the new journey into the next phase in my life. Someday this would all be over, and I'd sit down in that college classroom and look back on all of this and know it was worth it. It wasn't my fault that Dallas couldn't control himself. What was done was done, and I had the final five weeks of basic training to worry about. It was a long road that was nearing its end, and in Drill Sergeant Lucas I'd found an unexpected ally.

One bitterly cold morning the platoon sat huddled on the M16 range. We had gone out for final qualifications. The sky was an endless pool of drab gray, and the barren trees framed the weapons range where we'd just fired. For all of my previous shortcomings, I was a hell of a shot. I had qualified expert along with only three other people in the platoon. This time, my qualification was thankfully free of gun-waving theatrics with Drill Sergeant August. August hadn't attended, leaving us to the devices of Drill Sergeant Lucas. Lucas was decidedly different from August. Where August was all chest-thumping, loudly vocal authority, Lucas ruled with a fist that was quiet though still iron.

When he would walk the line of the soldiers during PT or on the range, I felt my heart swell with something that was new to me: pride. Lucas was a late addition to our class because he was changing his military career. I was now one of only three black soldiers in the entire 124-person company. It felt good to see this man, who was as black as I was, in such complete control and authority over the recruits in the company. I had begun to see him as my secret surrogate father in a way. I had certainly spent more time with him in the past four weeks than I'd spent with my father in the past four years. My own father hadn't been a major part of my life since I was three years old. His absence was the collateral damage in a nasty breakup with my mother over his cheating ways.

I didn't have my father, but I had Drill Sergeant Lucas, who was so powerful, strong, and regal. As we sat in the bitter cold that Sunday morning at the M16 range, wrapped up in our various layers of military-issued hats, gloves, and coats, Drill Sergeant Lucas gave us a little pep talk before we were to march the ten miles back to base. He was always doing things like that meant to motivate and encourage us, though a Sunday-school teacher he was not. He was known for making a recruit drop and give him fifty push-ups for as little as looking at him the wrong way. On this day, however, his words were gentle and motivational.

"So men, we're coming up on the end. Even though we've lost a few people, the shit always happens that way, so don't worry about it," he said with a hint of a southern drawl.

I sat up, cross-legged and alert as if I were in a kindergarten class. I looked at him, and we locked eyes briefly. In the moment I caught his gaze, he gave me a slight smile, and I returned it and looked down.

"And we have Private Smith kicking ass on those road marches and runs, and shooting the shit out of these targets, huh?" At this point something miraculous happened. I heard a "Yeah, Bubba!" come from somewhere behind me, and the guys started clapping for me.

I smiled but tried not to smile to brightly or broadly. I had a new tough-guy image to maintain. Hearing their applause and Lucas's words filled me with a greater sense of accomplishment than I'd ever felt before. School always came easy to me, so getting good grades was never a big deal, but this? This was hard. This was grueling. This was blood, sweat, and tears. I'd given my soul over to this just to know that I could do it. I'd literally worked my ass off. I had the scars, calluses, and now respect of my fellow platoon members to prove it. In that moment I loved Lucas. He'd given me the one thing I'd never really had before in my life: self-respect. At that moment it took everything I had in me not to run up and hug him like an excited five-year-old hugging his father after getting a puppy on Christmas morning.

At this moment, though I looked at Lucas and could see his mouth moving, everything else was a blur. I could hear nothing but his words being repeated over and over in my mind on a glorious loop. When we packed our gear up to make the ten-mile trek back to the barracks, I took the lead in the march because I knew I could. I knew now that whatever I had in me that had been developed over the past few months was enough to succeed and enough to take the lead. Some people fell out of the road march that day. The winds were harsh, and the pavement was hard and cold. The metal of the rucksack dug into my shoulders and rubbed against my bones. I'm sure it did to everyone else in the platoon, but failure was simply not an option. Not after that. As we turned the corner to see the now-familiar brick-red building that had housed our lives for the last five and a half months, I looked past the platoon and back to the soldiers that had fallen behind. They weren't my problem. I'd barely broken a sweat.

The events of recent weeks had completely changed my reputation within the company, and it felt good. No longer did I feel the crushing anxiety that used to come with doing the morning runs or the road marches to the ranges or whatever else they threw at me. I was well on my way toward becoming an infantry soldier. It finally felt like I was achieving something substantial. The taunts and teasing, so merciless in the first few weeks of training, had subsided almost into oblivion. Lucas hadn't been aware of me at my worst, but August had, and one evening after chow he pulled me to the side as the other soldiers cleaned their plates and headed back up to the barracks.

"C'mere, Smith!" he yelled as I attempted to rush past him.

I obliged and stood in front of him in the obligatory parade rest stance, legs spread shoulder-width apart, hands clasped behind my lower back, eyes directed straight forward. It seemed like our adversarial first day was a million years ago, not the five and a half months that had passed in reality.

As I kept my eyes straight forward, I could feel him studying me, seeing if I would meet the eyes that were scanning me. He looked at me as if he'd never seen me before, and I knew immediately what he was looking at. I'd dropped nearly twenty-five pounds in those five months. Though I didn't really notice it, the change seemed to attract a lot of attention from others, especially one day in the barracks when I'd taken my shirt off, and Roberts had looked at my stomach in awe.

"Look at your ABS!" he'd said excitedly, pointing to my flat stomach.

"Those," he said while jabbing his finger at the muscles, "are fucking hard to get!"

I knew what August was looking at as he studied me like one would study a racehorse in a stable, and I welcomed the attention. The new smug and superior voice in my head relished all the attention.

*Look at me,* it said. *You thought I couldn't do this, motherfucker, and look at me now.* "At ease, Smith," he said with that southern twang of his.

"You're doing good, Smith, real good. You ready for the final march?"

"Yes, Drill Sergeant!" I said in full-on soldier mode.

When he spoke of the final march, I felt the slight pang of fear and anxiety return from whatever dark recesses my recent success had banished it to. Among the recruits, the final march and nothing more had dominated conversations as of late. By all accounts, it was to be a grueling forty-mile road march completed within a twenty-four-hour time span with no rest in between. The mile markers would be punctuated by challenges that brought together elements of all the training we'd been given thus far. It would consist of grenade throwing, bayonet knife training, urban territory training, and everything in between. We would be required to satisfactorily complete them all, or we wouldn't be allowed to graduate basic training and gain ownership of the elusive blue cord.

The blue cord was something that was given only to infantry soldiers in the US Army. It signifies the status as the most elite, toughest, and grueling job in the Army. It was something to aspire to, and provided we all graduated basic training, we would be presented with it during the ceremony. To me, the cord meant the final phase of acceptance and knowing that I'd completed the training that had beaten me down to my very essence and was now in the process of building me back up again. My success in this, the toughest thing I'd ever done in my seventeen years on earth, meant that there was very little I couldn't accomplish, least of all obtaining a college degree when these four years were over.

"I know you got all these runs and marches licked, and that's fine and dandy, but you don't make the final march, you don't get that blue cord," he said with a slight smile.

When I looked at him, I knew that his smile wasn't adversarial or devious, and in that moment I understood him more than I ever had before. August wasn't here to babysit or to handhold; he was here to create men. Infantrymen. He was challenging me one last time, not because he thought I couldn't do it, but because he knew I could.

"Carry on, Smith," he said, still smiling.

I looked at him and returned his smile.

"Roger that, Drill Sergeant," I said, all the while thinking, *You wanna try me? OK, motherfucker, game on.*

The morning of the grueling twenty-four-hour final march was a bitterly cold one. The late March wind was crisp, and I could hear the slight crunch of the frozen dew on the grass under my feet as I marched into formation with the rest of the platoon. We carried a rucksack that had been packed and inspected to weigh sixty pounds. I could already feel the heaviness of its weight on me, both physically and mentally, as I looked toward the road we would start on. It was the same road we'd started runs and road marches on so many times before, but now it felt different. This was the final stretch. Before me was a goal that I surprisingly now desperately wanted to reach. I thought back to the first times I'd done runs and road marches on that road, and to all the times I'd failed on it. I found myself strangely disconnected from who I was then, as if that person was an old friend who had outgrown his place in my life. I was now stronger, faster, and leaner, and while the next twenty-four hours would be painful, I knew I would be able to finish this.

"At ease!"

I was broken out of my thoughts by the booming voices of the various platoon members as Drill Sergeants August, Lucas, and Thompson took their places at the head of the platoon. Drill Sergeant August stepped up to speak, a certain sense of fearsome pride etched all over his face along with the lines of age that covered it.

"Privates, God willing, in thirty-six hours you will be able to call yourselves infantrymen, but the next twenty-four hours are going to separate the men from the boys. If, during the next twenty-four hours, you fall out of a run, a road march, or fail to complete a task, you will be removed from the training and sent home. Let me direct your attention to the trucks behind us. They will be on the road behind us the entire time, and will serve to take any of you back to base should you fail to complete a task. All right, gentlemen, let's get a move on." He launches into a steady jog, and we're off.

As the run begins, I feel an all-too-familiar sense of panic as my legs start to move as well, keeping up with the pace of the rest of the platoon. I wonder how long this run will last. Five miles? Ten? Fifteen? A few miles and an hour down the road, it dawns on me that I haven't tightened the straps on my rucksack nearly as tightly as I should have. It's now bouncing up and down as I jog, pressing down hard on my shoulders and exposing the skin on my hips to the metal bars of the rucksack's frame. What starts as a slight pinch begins to become more and more like an intense scratching feeling, and it's with a mix of fear, pride, and pain that I realize the skin on my hips is being rubbed raw as it bounces up and down. I hear the voices of the other platoon members calling cadence, but in my mind I'm far, far away. My voice is likely among theirs, but I don't know for sure.

The pain of the frame is becoming intense. I want to stop so badly to readjust, but I know I can't. I lean over and shift the weight of the rucksack to my upper back, experiencing a split second of absolute terror when I feel as if I'm about to topple over, but I don't. I move my M16 strap around my neck. When I reach back to my hips to feel the damage I feel the excruciating sting of the dirt from my hands mixing with the open cuts and the warm, sticky blood. I pull my t-shirt down as far as I can and tuck it into my pants, and then shift the rucksack back down. I tighten the pack enough so that this time it's more secure. Now I feel better. I unstrap the M16 from my neck and carry it at the ready in front of me, joining in with the cadence being sung. The crisis is averted. There is no real physical tiredness, nor is there any more pain in my legs or feet. I'm here and present, just a few hours from completion of this goal that has in the past few weeks and months become the most important goal in my life. My voice becomes more and more prominent as I see the sun peeking over the silhouette of the trees in the woods that surround us.

We break from the run and slow down into a march. I can see the looks of relief on the soldiers' faces. They are as sweaty and tired as I am. As if choreographed, we all simultaneously dig into our utility belts and pull out canteens of water, which were once room temperature but are now naturally chilled by the weather. The water is cool and crisp as it rushes down my throat, though I'm careful not to overdrink and risk throwing it all up. I drink slow and steady, and relish the break that we're getting before the next phase of the march.

Soon enough, it's time to break for lunch, and the company sets up in an area that is just off of the main road to have our MREs for lunch. By any other standards, the meals are absolutely terrible, but I relish the flavor of my chicken tetrazzini as if it were a five-star meal at the best restaurant in the world. I chew hungrily and furiously, and as I look around, I notice that my other platoon mates are doing the same. We are deathly silent, as the drill sergeants are standing over us after having already warned us that there will be no talking and that we will only have fifteen minutes to eat. When we finish, we throw the garbage into a larger bag that is tossed into the bed of the larger truck that has been trailing us since the beginning, serving as a grim reminder of the price of failure.

After marching for a few more hours, we make a right into the woods and walk for what feels like a few hours as we go deeper and deeper into the woods. I have no watch, so I have no concept of time. I look directly above to try to gauge where the sun is. It appears to be about midday. *Good*, I think. *Six hours down, eighteen to go.* When I look behind me, the relative comfort of the road moves further away, and when I look forward, I'm shocked to see a steep hill that we are being motioned toward to climb. The top seems to be about a half mile up. I look frantically from side to side for another way, but Drill Sergeant August looks at me sternly and points straight up. There are a few soldiers ahead of me, and I can hear them struggling and panting to make their way up. They periodically lose their grips on the tree roots that they're using for balance and slip while trying to get a firm hold of the muddy earth with their boots.

I take a deep breath and hit the wall of earth, grabbing ahold of the first deeply set tree root I see and pulling myself up. It takes everything I have to pull myself up high enough so that I can gain footing on a small rock, but I do it. I can feel the weight of the rucksack pulling me back as if it were a person grabbing onto my neck. At this point I'm holding onto the root of the tree so tightly I can feel it digging into my palm and drawing blood. I hold on with all my might because I don't want to lose even the four feet I've gained thus far. I look to the right of me and see another root, then another, then another, and after a few minutes I'm like a professional climber, though the pain in my arm, shoulder, thigh, and calf muscles is damn near unbearable.

I look back and can see the top of August's head as he is guiding the other soldiers to follow me. He's crowning, and the missing hair creates a large bald spot on his head. At that second I'm overcome with awe at his dedication to what is happening here. This truly is his life. I can see that now in a way I never had before. I look back up and keep on climbing, finally reaching the top. My bruised and bloodied hand searches the unseen ground just past the top of the hill for another conduit to lift me up. I don't feel another tree root or rock, but a rough, calloused hand takes mine and lifts me up with a firm yank and a bit of help from my foot. I'm not surprised to see that it's Drill Sergeant Lucas. He projects a look of pride as we lock eyes for a split second, then I head to join the rest of my platoon mates in formation.

We exit the woods and jog onto a dirt road, farther into the base than we've ever gone before. I feel as if I'm venturing deeper into the belly of the beast. We're directed to line up in two rows, and as we're doing so I hear the all-too-familiar sounds of dry heaving followed by the heavy splash of vomit hitting the dirt. I look over and see Boston puking, and my expression is neutral and unfazed, as if it's the most natural thing in the world. Everything in me wants him to fail, but he takes his place in formation almost immediately after he's done. I send him a look of smug superiority that he doesn't notice.

On each side of the two rows are metal containers, which are filled with rounds for the .50-caliber machine gun. Their heavy weight is made known by the firmly etched impressions of the containers into the ground where they sit. Lucas points to a marker about a half mile down the road. He tells us that we are to run the length and back while carrying our rucksacks and one ammo container in each hand. I barely have any time to process this direction before I realize that I'm one of the first in line.

Hernandez is directly in front of me, and he is off like a bullet, grabbing the ammo boxes and running as fast as he can. He looks gangly and uncoordinated. The rucksack shifts sloppily from side to side, and the ammo boxes are weighing him down on both sides. When he turns around to come back, his face is dripping with sweat. His eyes look pained, a prominent vein that runs down the center of his forehead throbbing intensely. He gets closer and closer, and suddenly he is right in front of me, dropping the ammo boxes down and making his way toward the end of the line. The drill sergeants are yelling for me to continue. I tighten up my straps, grab the ammo boxes, and begin to run. I'm taken aback by how heavy they truly are.

When I first grab them, they weigh my arms down so much I feel excruciating pain in my shoulders. My arms feel as if they're about to come right out of their sockets. As I am running, I trip and topple to the ground. Dirt flies into my face as I hit knees first. I feel a jolt of pain in my right knee that's as strong as an electric shock. For a split second, I'm completely immobilized. The rucksack has inched its way over my head and I'm still holding onto the boxes. I immediately rock myself back and use my thighs to lift me back up. I hit the halfway point and turn around, feeling the pain that consumes my body but at the same time emboldens me.

As I'm finishing up, I see the faces of the platoon, and I realize that the silence ban has been lifted. They're cheering. Not only are they cheering for me, but they're cheering for the rest of the soldiers who are doing the same thing. I feel a low, guttural sound form in my stomach, and a roar comes out of my mouth. I'm now screaming and cheering along with everyone. As I look at the faces of the platoon members who were once my adversaries, I realize that they want me to succeed as much as I want myself to. I hit the finish line, drop my ammo boxes, and proceed to the end of the line to cheer for the other soldiers in the platoon.

Day is turning into night, and the relative calm of the woods is taken over by the sounds of various crickets and bugs while we continue the march to our next point. Twelve hours down, twelve more to go. The thought is comforting. As night falls, we march until it is pitch-black, and I again lose concept of time. The drill sergeants become mere shadows that guide us with their flashlights. We approach a large space that breaks from the woods, and I can make out shadows of a mock city.

The buildings are largely empty on the inside but are designed to resemble establishments that can be found in any city. I can make out a post office, a church, and a few houses. Drill Sergeant August tells us that the space is used for guerrilla warfare training. I vaguely remember practicing the lineup on some cold morning a few months back in between lessons with the bayonet. He guides us over to a large hill just outside of the complex where we are to set up guard over the "city" to simulate an early morning attack. We are set up in a half-moon, pulling guard on the outside of the city with our weapons pointed in. We're given blank ammunition, and the bright red adaptor that is muzzled into the barrel of our weapon serves as a constant reminder that this is only training, not the real thing. Whatever the real thing is, it's an abstract thought in my mind. I don't think of war but of training. This is the logical next step in my life, and all of our wartime simulations have been from wars like WWII and Vietnam, long ago fought in different eras and different worlds than the one that is before me on this cold night at the end of my training.

I lie on the ground with my weapon at the ready and with soldiers on either side of me, all of us awaiting an unseen, imaginary threat. Time marches on, and we are deeper into the night. My body temperature starts to drop. The sweat that has drenched my clothing all day is now working against me, joining the crisp wind and creating a cold shield that is almost like an igloo around my body. I start to shiver and notice that I can see my breath. I look up and see the shadows of the drill sergeants pacing back and forth. My eyes are starting to get heavy, but I know that I cannot sleep. *Perhaps I'll just rest my eyes for a moment though, just a moment.*

When I open my eyes, it takes me a moment to remember where I am and I immediately go into panic mode. My eyes dart back and forth, fully expecting the drill sergeants and the rest of the soldiers to be standing over me, having failed once again, but they are not. I look to my left and right, and see some soldiers vigilantly holding guard. I lock eyes with a few of the others and find that my terrified state is reflected in theirs. I haven't been found out. Good. I don't know how many hours I was out, but I notice the first hints of light blue forming in the sky. It tells me that it's almost morning and that this final test of infantry manhood is almost over.

Out of nowhere, we hear a loud bang, and it's with a sense of excitement and bemusement that I realize it's a grenade simulator. We're off, and the next hour is a haze of running in and out of buildings and participating in mock guerrilla warfare. Of course we have no idea what we're doing, and I have a strong sense that the drill sergeants don't either, but it's fun. We take it seriously but not too seriously. In some way we all know that we've survived this process and that we're now officially on the road to becoming infantrymen.

We walk with our chests jutted out proudly as we finish the last hours of the road march back to base. I look around me and am again struck by that feeling of being different. This time though, my difference isn't in my sexuality, which has become clearer to me by the moment; it's a difference that I share with the other soldiers in the platoon. It's a difference that separates us from them—infantrymen from non-infantrymen. I'm proud, and when we break into a run for the last few miles of the march, I'm not in the least bit tired. It feels as if I'm running on a cloud.

Soon after dropping our rucksacks and our gear in the staging area, we're headed to the cafeteria for chow. We're tired, bruised, and bloodied, but not broken. We're all here. Nobody failed the march. As I make my way through the cafeteria line, I notice Drill Sergeant August posted in his usual spot, ensuring that the soldiers are completely silent as they move through. I take great pains to look straight forward, but I feel his eyes on me and am not surprised when he calls me over. What does surprise me is when he smirks and extends his hand. Neither of us says anything. The gratitude is written all over my face just as the pride is written all over his.

Two weeks later, basic training graduation had come and gone, and I found myself sitting in the airport. I was headed back to Ohio for a quick break before heading onward and upward to Colorado. The graduation itself was relatively uneventful. Drill Sergeants August and Lucas plied my mother with the requisite bullshit about how I'd ended up an outstanding soldier. She beamed and took credit for everything that I'd done in that way that had increasingly gotten under my skin over the past few years. I'd gotten into the habit of freezing my face into a false smile that would make a pageant queen proud whenever I got the sense that one of her self-congratulatory screeds was coming. That smile was front and center during the excruciating meet-and-greet period after the actual ceremony in which we were finally awarded our coveted blue cords.

"Well, you know I always told him to work hard, because he knew I'd pop him good," she said to Drill Sergeant August, grinning like a loon as the three of us stood in the hot May weather.

"I always told him to study and work hard, hard, hard."

She repeated that as if we'd somehow missed the message about what an incredible mother she'd been. It was at these times that I always wanted to scream at her. I wanted to tell her how angry I was at her for abandoning me and for ignoring me after her breakup with my stepfather. I wanted to tell her that maybe if she'd been around and paid even an iota of attention to me during the last few years of high school, I wouldn't have been subjected to what I'd just been through and God knows what lay ahead just so that I'd have a shot at college. I wanted to tell her how furious she made me when she took even a bit of credit for what I'd just achieved when she barely wrote me during basic training. Instead, I said nothing. I kept smiling, awaiting the chance to make my exit. If I didn't know any better, I'd swear August was as relieved as I was when we finally left.

After saying my goodbyes to my mother and grandmother, I found myself looking ahead to Colorado and my next adventure. As I sat in the airport waiting to go back to Ohio to pick up some things, I wondered what it would look like, what the unit would be like, and what my fellow soldiers would look like. My mind was moving so fast I couldn't tame it, so I decided to pick up a magazine, and what I read in the magazine shocked me into a state of near panic.

Right there in *Rolling Stone* was a four-page story detailing the murder of Private First Class Barry Winchell, a soldier who had been beaten to death by a unit member who found out he was seeing a transgender person. Although I couldn't process in my head what exactly a transgender person was, I knew it had something to do with being gay, and that this something-to-do-with-being-gay had a lot to do with why this guy was beaten to death. The article had tons of pictures and information, and I devoured it all. It went into the military's "Don't Ask, Don't Tell" policy, which according to the article meant that you could be kicked out if you were gay. Now the question that the recruiter had asked me right before I entered made sense.

Of course I answered that I wasn't gay, but what did I know? I knew I liked guys, that I was sexually attracted to them. I was also aware that this was some kind of deal breaker in the military. If I were found out to be gay, I would be dishonorably discharged and booted right out of the Army. Not only did I run the risk of being beaten to death, I could also be fired and be denied my college education and all of the benefits that the rest of the soldiers got after their time was finished. I looked back to the article and a picture of PFC Barry Winchell, this person whom I'd never seen or heard of before, but whom I was now linked to by virtue of our shared situation. His pale, expressionless face was so much like the soldiers' I'd just finished basic training with. I wondered what was going through his head as his roommate beat him to death with that baseball bat. I started to think of all the ways that things could go wrong at my unit, and all of the ways that my career and life could now be in danger. That's the moment I decided that I had to keep the secret at all costs. I wished I could have ended the day as excited as I was when it had begun, but I could not. I ended the day very afraid.

**PART TWO**

# WHAT
# WE DO IS
# SECRET

# CHAPTER 5

# A CHILLY RECEPTION

Small pictures in the beat-up old book in my high school library so many years ago had left me unprepared for the visual beauty that met me upon my arrival in Colorado. The mountains were stunningly picturesque, with the recently ended winter's snow still resting on their peaks. They were surrounded on all sides by a gorgeous expanse of blue sky that made me wince with its brightness. The colors on everything seemed to pop, as if they were all turned up just a bit brighter at this level of elevation. While the plane swooped to make the runway, I looked at the different suburbs and different houses with their pools and cars. It was so different from my small town in Ohio that it was a lot to take in.

Even on the brightest days of summer, Akron, Ohio, seemed to be a dirty, dingy place. It was as if all the failed hopes and ambitions of its citizens were somehow released into the air and absorbed into everything around it, draining the sky of its color and the sun of its brightness. Potholes littered the streets, and houses were stacked up next to each other like soldiers shoehorned into shoulder-to-shoulder formation. Packs of random people running the streets aimlessly were not an uncommon sight in my neighborhood.

Colorado was so different. It was a place where people had the actual lives that I'd only seen on television. It was a place where two-parent families lived. They had picket fences and children who loved them. I felt this place seducing me with its bright colors and promise of a new beginning. Oddly enough, it felt like home.

I was directed by the people at the unit that I would be met by a Sergeant Brandon at the gate, and after picking up my bags and looking toward the airport exit, I was certain that I'd found the guy. Sergeant Brandon was a short, stocky man, and his camouflage BDUs didn't hide the fact that he had a bit of a stomach underneath his jacket. He stood with his back so straight that he was nearly leaning backwards, an obvious attempt to appear taller. He had a slight double chin that was clearly freshly shaven. He wore an awkward, pained expression on his face. It appeared as if he was attempting to look imposing or important, but to me he just looked rather constipated.

A leggy, high-heeled blonde walked self-importantly in front of him, inadvertently dwarfing his short frame. I caught a glimpse of uneasiness in his eyes as they darted back and forth, scanning the room to see if anyone took notice of this. I approached him uneasily, not knowing exactly how I would be expected to perform my military bearing, but he immediately relaxed as we locked eyes.

"Private Smith?" he asked, firmly.

It was more of a statement than a question.

"Yes, Sergeant."

"Very well. Follow me, Smith," he said and guided me out into the parking lot.

He drove an old GMC SUV riddled by the slightly sour smell that comes from years of lost cigarette butts, stealth French fries lurking underneath floor mats, and stale air fresheners. I sat in the seat and immediately rolled down the window as Sergeant Brandon fired up the engine, the sound of which resembled a growling dog as he revved it up. He cocked his eye in my direction as if looking for a macho affirmation of the truck's power. *Is this what guys do?* I thought to myself as I gave him an awkward nod and turned toward the window to take in the fresh Colorado air. Most of the trip was driven in silence, and I began to think about how the hell I was going to be a "man" here.

Basic training was too intense and condensed a time period for any real questions about me to be dredged up, but I knew that this would be different. In one of the final weeks of basic training, I'd had a conversation with one of the other black soldiers, a specialist who had come from a different military occupational specialty (MOS) just to do the final infantry training and get his cord. He'd told me that unit life is different. He told me that the guys not only trained together during the day but that they hung out most nights and weekends as well. Most squads became real close friends. That was exactly what I was afraid of. If anyone suspected anything, I could be fired, or, even worse, beaten to death like Barry Winchell. What if there was nothing to suspect, though? I'd only messed around with two guys at that point. Most of what was going on in my mind was more of a desire to do more than any actual action, so in that car ride I decided to do the straight thing. Who knew? Maybe it was just a phase. Maybe I could be normal. Whatever that was.

"So where you from?" Sergeant Brandon asked, jolting me from my thoughts.

I looked over at him and felt a wave of disgust when I saw his lower lip stuffed with chewing tobacco. He reached between us to grab an empty water bottle that was swimming with slimy saliva and tobacco refuse, and spat out another gob of it expertly into the opening of the water bottle. The sour, acrid smell of the tobacco and its refuse hit my nose, and I felt my stomach turn.

"Uh, Ohio, Sergeant," I said.

"Yeah?" he said, getting an obvious kick out of my answer. "They got black folks in Ohio?" The question caught me off guard. Everyone in my life so far in Ohio had been black. If there was some covert large white population there, they certainly didn't live on my side of town. My concept of "black" and "white" was an abstract thing, made more abstract by the fact that, save for a few teachers in my high school, I didn't have much contact with white people. They were people on the shows that I watched, people reporting the news, but not people I had any interaction with whatsoever in my daily life.

"Well, they've got one," I said, trying to match his machismo and bravado.

"Guess so," he said, turning his attention back to the road.

I watched him carefully from the corner of my eye, trying to gauge whether he'd sensed anything. If this was going to work, I'd have to try on a different persona here than I'd had at basic training. The last thing I wanted to do was be the platoon loser, or, worse yet, the platoon faggot. Again.

My midday arrival at the unit came at a time when many of the soldiers were nowhere to be found. I assumed they were out doing other tasks, training, taking late lunches, or sleeping in their own rooms in the barracks that surrounded the unit headquarters. The headquarters themselves were abuzz with all of the many jobs that went into a day's work in the Army. Some soldiers were doing desk work, others were filing, and still others could be found randomly scattered cleaning equipment or just shooting the shit in various platoon offices. I noticed that the soldiers in the unit were fairly racially mixed, with black, white, and Latino soldiers working side by side. This fact made me feel good, as my token black boy status in my basic training unit had been an underlying source of discomfort for me. After being processed in, I was told where I'd be staying and that I was lucky to have a single. I headed through the landscaped lawn that separated the buildings to see my new digs.

The room was small and barren, save for a twin-sized mattress and a generic wooden dresser that sat awkwardly placed in the corner. The room was on the third floor of the building. I walked through to the window that offered a clear view of the parking lot below, the expanse of the base, and of course the mountains that seemed to surround everything in Colorado like silent protectors. I sat on the bed, gathering my thoughts about what exactly the next few years of my life were going to be here. Sergeant Brandon told me that most days were generally the same:

> Formation at 6:20 a.m.
> PT at 6:30
> Breakfast/Shower from 7:30 to 8:30 a.m.
> Formation at 9 a.m.
> Daily Activities until noon
> Lunch until 1:30
> End of Day Formation at 5 p.m.
> Lather, rinse, repeat.

It seemed simple enough, if a little mechanical, but then again I gathered that mechanical is definitely what worked in the military.

Brandon said that there were generally different types of training set up during the week, and every once in a while, they'd go to the field for a few weeks. For the most part it was routine. They weren't aware of any impending deployments, and the last major war had been the Gulf War. No one was expecting any wars anytime soon. That was good enough for me. The countless repeats of *Full*

*Metal Jacket* we'd watched in the days before basic training graduation had exposed me to a version of the Vietnam War that was the closest I ever wanted to get to any kind of battle.

A few hours later I put on my BDUs and headed out to the final formation of the day, which was held in the parking lot behind the unit headquarters. The air was springtime-warm but not too hot. I felt confident in my uniform, even though I was wearing the E-2 (Private) rank, signifying to anyone who cared to look that I was newly out of basic training. Fresh meat. The skeleton crew of earlier was replaced with about thirty soldiers of various heights, races, and sizes. They all surveyed me as curiously as a toddler would survey a younger sibling as I moved my now gangly frame toward the formation. I locked eyes with Sergeant Brandon, who waved me over. "Welcome to the squad," he whispered quickly as he moved to rush me into place before the platoon sergeant came out to take charge of the formation.

I stood straight up in formation while I tried stealthily to size up the guys in my squad whom I'd be spending the most time with at this unit.

We stood in four rows of seven, with each squad making up a row of the formation. Sergeant Brandon was the lead, and next to him was a tall, lean white man who looked to be about thirty. The white guy at one point may have been good-looking, but whatever good looks he had were marred by scaly, leathery skin that was scarred by acne. He had deeply set, piercing blue eyes with pupils that were pointed at their target with laser-like precision. Next up was a heavyset black guy who was probably the darkest person I'd ever seen besides my grandfather or myself. His skin tone was darker than the varied chocolate tones I was used to seeing when I looked at the rest of my family members. It seemed to be just a few shades lighter than coal. I noticed thin beads of sweat breaking out on his acne-covered forehead and dripping down the sides of his face, which was surprising to me because it didn't seem all that warm out. His facial features were surprisingly delicate considering how severe the rest of him appeared. His small, round face was in bad need of a shave. Small, ragged hairs broke out all in his beard region, sharing space on his chin and cheeks with small pimples and razor bumps. His ample stomach sagged over his belt, and his beady eyes peered out from behind small, circular-rimmed glasses. I wondered what his name was and what he was like. We were the only blacks in the squad, so we definitely had that in common.

*Is there anything else we have in common?* I wondered. *Would we be friends?*

Beside him was a short, thin white guy, and right next to me was a small, fair-skinned Latino who also had acne and glasses.

When formation broke up for the evening, Sergeant Brandon took us all to the side and introduced me to the soldiers I'd spent the past fifteen minutes in formation sizing up. The heavyset black guy was Specialist Howard; the tall white guy with the leathery skin, Sergeant Norman; the white guy, PFC Wharton; and the Latino, PFC Lantos.

"Now listen up!" Sergeant Brandon said as he made his way to the head of the half circle he'd placed us in.

"This is Private Smith. He's new here, fresh off the boat from Benning. Hooah!" He moved almost comically, as if this were some great joke that he was sharing with everybody. He had an air of manic, intense energy about him, as if he were a child afflicted with ADD. He always seemed to be moving. Even in formation earlier, I could notice him slightly swaying from side to side.

"So he got a single room, but all you privates live together anyways, so I expect for you all to hang out and shoot the shit from time to time," he continued.

"How the fuck did he get a single?" Howard asked in a dry, sarcastic way.

I tensed up. He cut his eyes toward me, and I looked back at him to see a playful expression on his face. I relaxed a bit.

"Hey, you watch your fucking mouth, Specialist," Brandon said, grinning at Howard.

"Yo, Brandon, I'm going to my girl's house," Norman said, making his way off to his car while giving me a half-hearted "Welcome to the squad, man" and a pat on the shoulder.

"Thanks, Sergeant," I said.

"Don't worry about him, man," Wharton whispered to me. "He's kind of a prick."

"Anyway, welcome to the squad and all that shit," Brandon said, making his own exit.

"Formation's at 0620 tomorrow morning, private. I gotta get home. The wife's making meatloaf!" With that, he was gone, and I noticed the rest of the platoon had dispersed, leaving Howard, Wharton, Lantos, and me.

"I gotta go too. See ya, Smith," Lantos said and trailed off.

Howard said something about a computer game he needed to get to, and Wharton made a half-hearted comment about us getting together sometime, and within a few minutes they were both gone as well.

I stood by myself in the lot behind the unit headquarters for a while and walked around, still somewhat in awe of my surroundings. I walked to the sidewalks that surrounded the barracks and out to the main road by my building. I gazed out at the looming mountains as the sky went from a light blue to a reddish-orange and finally to dark. I thought to myself that I'd never seen anything more beautiful in my life, and was so thankful to be there and away from the dreaded and dreary small-town life of Ohio.

The next few months were spent becoming acclimated to the military life at Fort Carson, Colorado. I was up at dawn, in formation by 6:20 a.m., and sweating my ass off during PT by 6:45. The elevation in Colorado was high, but thankfully there were no repeats of falling out of any runs. After a small adjustment period, everything was fine, and I found myself completing the various runs, road marches, and PT tests with ease. I spent most nights and weekends alone, reading books and watching various television shows, save for the times when I would hang out with some of the members of the platoon and some of my squad members.

Howard and I had sparked a tentative friendship that was based on the shared love of all things dorky. We spent many nights in his barracks room watching the latest episodes of *Buffy the Vampire Slayer* and *Angel*, debating the plausibility of the latest plot twists of those absurd—but to us deathly serious—vampire soap operas through mouths stuffed full of pizza, hot wings, and breadsticks. Howard was also a constant buddy through the various field training exercises that we would go through. Our squad was a true combat infantry squad, which meant we were trained in the various weaponry and trench/urban warfare skills that would be needed of us in case the country ever went to war. The various instructors on the ranges we spent our days training talked a lot about WWII, and most of the tactics we studied were straight out of that era. During these exercises Sergeant Brandon would grumble under his breath about how out-of-date the training was, but we slogged through it all.

On the many nights sleeping in the field under the stars or by the tanks that provided background support, Howard and I would talk about our goals in life. Neither of us seemed to include more than a few more years of military service in our plans.

"You know," he said to me, during an early-summer night in one of the expansive field training areas of the base, after a long day of training, "I just want to have a good job back in Texas with a wife who loves me."

As I looked over at him in the dark, he was almost invisible, lit only by the full moon that cast a bright fleck of light on his spectacles. I wondered if he'd ever have that, and found my thoughts wandering toward dating and relationships of my own when I quickly directed them elsewhere. I shared with him my dreams of going to college when this was all said and done. I told him about doing a great job as a news anchorman at my high school and that I wanted to go to college for journalism. I shared lots of things with Howard that I shared with nobody else in the platoon, though I kept my deepest secret guarded closely. He was quickly becoming my best friend. I knew that he could never know that I was gay, or at least that I thought I was.

I'd thus far managed to avoid any mention of a girlfriend and was able to sidestep situations I felt were potentially dangerous. I avoided any trips to bars or clubs, which wasn't hard because, at seventeen, I was still far too young to get into most places. In fact, in those early days I was more or less asexual. I had no sexual urges for anyone. I had no real way to contact anyone outside of the base, nor was there any outlet besides masturbation for me to work out any sexual energy. The limited options worked out well enough for me to keep any idea of my sexuality at bay, and for a while everything was perfect. For those first few months, the tension between the desires I had and who I thought I was becoming were kept at bay due in large part to the limitations of the options to explore any of it. My impending eighteenth birthday would soon bring the issues into the forefront of my life in a very public and unexpected way.

Turning eighteen isn't much of a milestone in the lives of most people. You're not technically "legal," you certainly can't get into any bars, and you're still light-years away from even being able to rent a car. At Fort Carson, eighteen was the magic number because it was the age at which entry was gained into the finest non-alcoholic strip club that Colorado Springs had to offer. Déjà Vu Showgirls was a nondescript building that sat in a lonely lot at the end of a block of various pawnshops, payday loan places, and questionable banks that seemed to sprout up in the military town like vultures waiting to descend upon the earnings of the young soldiers who populated the base. A simple sign with the club's name in bawdy pink letters was the only thing that gave any indication of what was to be found inside. The location on the main strip that led back into the gates of Fort Carson was the only reason I'd seen the outside as many times as I had.

The club had a mythical quality and reputation for me based upon the way it was spoken of by the various soldiers. Many times after final formation on Fridays, I would hear conversations with different variations.

"Yeah, hitting up Déjà Vu tonight. Don't tell the old lady," followed by a knowing grin, laugh, or fist pound to seal the deal of what was obviously the worst kept secret among the platoon members.

I began to find myself curious about Déjà Vu, but not because I was interested in any of the naked female flesh that was sure to be on display. I wondered what the hell straight guys got from popping boners in a room full of other men. It all seemed very homo-erotic to me.

One Wednesday afternoon, I found myself hanging out in the unit headquarters with Sergeants Brandon and Norman shooting the shit, when a boisterous black sergeant entered the area. His name was Sergeant Kane, and he had a huge reputation among the soldiers for being a bit of a player and a party guy. It was shocking to me because he had a body that resembled a Buddha statue and a personality that was right out of a B-level '90s movie about life in the "hood." He was a lot of fun and good for a few laughs. I figured it was why he maintained his reputation. I could tell from seeing some of the soldiers' girlfriends who hung around that the steady paychecks the soldiers brought in were certainly a bigger selling point than any of their physical attributes.

Sergeant Kane walked toward us, and like Sergeant Brandon, he used impeccable posture to camouflage a portly frame. He looked from Brandon to Norman to me with his chin up, sizing me up and exerting his authority over the situation.

"Fuck ya'll talkin' 'bout?" he asked.

"Nothin' much, Kane," Brandon said. "Just tryin' to get the fuck outta here."

Kane looked at me.

"Sup lil nigga, what yo name is?" he asked, in a faux ghetto voice.

He must've read the shock on my face as I tried to figure out how to respond, so with a twinkle in his eye he straightened up and asked again.

"What's your name, private?" This I responded to.

"Private Smith, Sergeant!"

"Right," he said, and turned to Norman and Brandon.

"Hey, man, how old is this dude? This motherfucker looks like he just stopped breastfeeding like last week or some shit!"

At this, Kane, Brandon, and Norman laughed. I wasn't offended and took it as a joke. I was, at this point, a few days shy of my eighteenth birthday.

"Yeah...like this motherfucker don't need water in his canteen; he needs Similac!" At this he burst into near hysterics.

When he'd settled down, Kane turned back to me.

"How old are you, private?" he asked.

"Seventeen, Sergeant!" I responded, adding, "I'll be eighteen in a few days!"

Inwardly I cringed at how young I must've sounded to these men who were all in their late twenties and early thirties, at least.

"Eighteen, huh?" Kane said, looking me up and down and studying me.

"You tasted any pussy out here yet, man?"

The question caught me off guard, and I looked at Kane as he studied me, awaiting my answer. He reminded me not of my high school tormentors, but of every older cousin who had ever asked me the same thing throughout my years of high school. Those questions started at thirteen and never really stopped, probably because of my hoodlum older cousins who had started smoking, drinking, and presumably fucking sometime after their fourteenth birthday. I tried to figure out how to respond and could hear myself stammering as if I were listening to someone else.

"Yeah, I mean, uh, no, I mean, I haven't tasted.... I don't like to eat.... Well I could but I don't have a car, so...."

Sergeant Kane smiled and put a hand on my shoulder, still with one eye on Norman and Brandon. "Relax, man. That's why you've got us! You said you turn eighteen in a few days? Why don't we all go out to Déjà Vu to celebrate? Only strip club in town where you can get in at eighteen."

Norman and Brandon smiled at this, and as I looked around I noticed that more and more people from the platoon were joining in on the conversation.

"Yeah, time to take ol' Smitty to the strip club!" Brandon said, who had become accustomed to his new nickname for me.

He spent a great deal of time making sure it stuck in the platoon. This was starting to become a thing. I looked around in abstract horror as I noticed more and more side conversations happening around me, all centered around the big trip to Déjà Vu that was going to be happening on Friday night to celebrate Smitty's eighteenth birthday. I found myself in the middle of Brandon, Norman, and Kane, powerless to stop what was happening. I had the distinct feeling of being a small fish who was on his way to being devoured by piranhas.

The two days leading up to the strip club trip felt like a march to death row. I was paralyzed by fear and worry about what could possibly go wrong. I'd never seen a naked woman before in my life, save for some adolescent fooling around with my junior high girl-friend when we were both fourteen, and that certainly went nowhere fast. I was so afraid of the trip to the strip club. I inwardly cursed myself for mentioning my birthday in front of everyone and wished I'd stopped the trip from becoming such a big thing around the platoon. Just a few hours prior I'd been stopped by the fear-some company first sergeant, who told me to have fun at my birthday party, gave me a slap on the back, and chuckled to himself as he headed back into his office and closed the door.

*What the fuck have I gotten myself into?* I thought.

There was a part of me that wanted to go through with it only because I wanted to be sure that I was gay. I wondered if I could go into the strip club and see a girl I liked and suddenly be cured, as if being gay was something that could be turned on and off. Besides, who said that it wasn't? I remembered back to a conversation I'd had with classmates in junior high school. As thirteen-year-olds, we had what we were sure was a very adult conversation about sex and sexuality. In it, someone mentioned that everyone goes through a "gay phase." I eagerly—and stupidly—offered up the fact that I'd already gone through mine, which was in hindsight maybe not the best way to go about the private negotiation of one's sexuality during adolescence.

There was a part of me that deeply wanted to desire women. I hoped that perhaps I could go to the strip club and feel some tin-gle for them that wasn't there before. A tingle that had been thus far reserved for some of the sexy men I'd sneaked covert peeks at on the covers of *Playgirl* at the few porn stores I'd ever had the guts to venture into. Maybe the whole gay thing was just a phase. Perhaps I could walk through the doors of Déjà Vu like they were the gates to the inner sanctum of heterosexuality. I could be automatically cured of my gayness by the nubile, nude female flesh that was sure to be on display in abundance. Maybe that's what I wanted most of all.

Friday night came, and I found myself standing in the parking lot outside of Déjà Vu flanked by Norman, Kane, and PFC Wilton from my squad. Wilton was a fun-loving, partying type. He'd jumped at the chance to attend my birthday party at what I was soon figuring out was one of his favorite places. In the days before, he'd talked excitedly about how hot the strippers were, the classiness of the club, and the free lunch buffet they sometimes had on the weekends. The visual of nude female flesh jiggling over old hot dogs in a tin server repulsed me. I couldn't really pinpoint whether it was the nude female flesh or the hot dogs that did it. Trying to figure it out only underlined the image in my head, so I figured it was best to just forget the entire thing.

The evening was warm and still. The 9:30 p.m. arrival gave us the cover of darkness from the prying, judgmental eyes that were cast toward the establishment by the many cars whizzing back and forth on the main road adjacent to it. I'd officially turned eighteen that day, but I felt younger, as if I were reverting back in age due to the fact that I was once again venturing into uncharted territory. Various stragglers followed us from the platoon, but nowhere near the crowd that buzzed on the unit floor. There were maybe fifteen of us in all, and I only knew those who'd come from my platoon.

The other faces were unfamiliar, from other platoons that I didn't interact with most days. I certainly didn't engage with them in the kind of training that bonds you to your fellow soldiers. We walked up to the front door. I caught a glimpse of darkness with flashes of bright pink lights inside. The thin walls shook with the bass of the speakers that played whatever club song the strippers inside were gyrating to at this very moment. I handed my military ID nervously to the bouncer who guarded the entrance into this inner sanctum of displayed womanhood. He was a tall, bald, burly white guy. I had to keep myself from looking too hard for too long. A few moments later, I stepped through the doorway and into a different world.

The club was large, expansive, and dimly lit save for multiple strobe lights that hit the various mirror balls hanging from the ceiling, giving it a permanent pink glow. I looked to my right to see a large stage with three metal poles, each with a different stripper attached to it. On the far right was a caramel-skinned black girl with long, brown hair that was obviously a wig. Her body was lithe, but not toned, and her small breasts jiggled along with her small stomach as she wrapped her body around the pole. She contorted her body into a flip up as she spread her legs into a V-shape pointed directly at the audience.

Old white men with gray hair in various stages of balding hooted and hollered, tossing dollar bills strategically thrown to land right in the center of the V of her legs. All the while, the girl maintained a look that was somewhere between boredom and titillation. She clearly enjoyed the attention, yet maybe wished she could get it from another source.

Center stage was a buxom, blonde stripper who wore a strawberry-colored wig. Her moves were nowhere near the black girl's, but she made up for it by calling attention to her breasts. It struck me that not only were these the first real breasts I was seeing but that they were enormous. On some level I knew I was supposed to like what I was seeing, but I really didn't. I mentally scanned for any trace of activity in my pelvic area, and realized I'd felt nothing since my private fantasy about the bouncer a few minutes prior.

I was broken out of my trance as I felt two thick, heavy hands on my shoulder. I turned around to see Sergeant Kane's smiling face.

"Look at that. Man, you don't even know what do with all this pussy, huh?" he asked.

"Oh, I know exactly what I'd do with it," I said, shocked at how easily the macho line escaped from my lips. He laughed.

"Now that's what the fuck I'm talking about, Smith. Which one you like?"

My confusion must've been fairly obvious, because he smiled and explained the situation to me. The strippers did the pole shows for everyone, but they also did private dances. I followed Kane's finger as it pointed toward a private area broken off by streamers that led down a short hallway.

"That's where you go for the private dances," he said with the confidence and authority of an old pro.

"That's where the shit goes down."

I was nervous at exactly what shit was meant to go down. I played along anyway, nodding up and down in what I hoped was a sincere-seeming interest in the assorted details he was offering up about the ways of the strip clubs.

"Some of them are just strippers, but some of them are hoes too," he said.

"Watch out, because the hoes will try to take your money first and then complain and get you kicked out so they don't have to do shit. So which one you like?" he repeated again, this time with a bit less patience.

He'd maneuvered his arm around me, and I felt trapped. I wished I could've followed Brandon and Norman, who'd casually found a seat not too far away from the stage and were absently flipping through the wad of one dollar bills. I scanned around very quickly, and my eyes fixed in on a young, pretty, caramel-skinned black girl who looked maybe about twenty-two or twenty-three. Her body was firm and supple, and she had no tattoos. Her medium-sized breasts swung from side to side in the thin pink bikini top she wore as she walked around. I was struck by the natural curviness of her body. We locked eyes briefly, and she smiled sweetly, taking her cue to head over toward us. I felt a flash of fear, and I looked downward, looking up only as she approached us.

The pink and white strobe lights sparkled off of her blonde wig, and she placed her hand on my shoulder, giving a light squeeze as she introduced herself.

"Hi, my name is Monica. Would you like to buy me a specialty drink for twenty dollars?"

Sergeant Kane lifted his eyebrows and looked at me, and I nervously fumbled in my wallet and pulled out a twenty to hand her.

"Thank you. I'll be right back." She took the twenty so easily, I hardly recognized it slipping out of my hand. She disappeared into the crowd of people and into a back room marked "employees only," presumably to drink her specialty drink in private. I looked back at Sergeant Kane with wide eyes, and he burst into laughter.

"Man, you a young motherfucker," he said in between fits of giggles.

"Your young ass just fell for the oldest trick in the book. This place is non-alcoholic. What fucking non-alcoholic drink costs twenty dollars?

I relaxed a bit and started to join in with his laughter. "I don't know, but it had better be a fucking good one," I said.

"So what's up, man? You want a private dance with her?" he asked.

"Uh, yeah," I said. "I mean yeah, I guess. How much is it?"

Sergeant Kane looked at me paternally. "Don't worry about it, kid. We'll work it out."

With that, he disappeared, and I stood in that spot for a few minutes as I watched Kane, Norman, and Brandon have a discussion about getting me the private dance. The next thing I knew, Monica's long arms were outstretched in front of me, and I was being guided into the private room for my dance.

The room was dimly lit, save for pink and blue backlights that were strategically placed along the walls. Monica and I were just another pair of moving shadows in the room. When I looked from side to side, I could see other pairs of shadows as well, lean and thin shadows of women and their rounder male counterparts who sat on their hands while the women danced around them, sometimes touching them, sometimes not. Monica lovingly placed my arms within a few centimeters of her hips, and then playfully shook her head as she placed them on my sides and pushed my hands under my thighs. I felt the skin of her cheek against mine as she brought her lips to my ears and whispered a soft, simple, and firm "No touching."

She began her show, and I was consumed with fear and nervous energy. We locked eyes as she took off her thin bikini top, exposing her pert, medium-sized breasts and small, hard nipples. I could see the gooseflesh on her areolas stick out as she rubbed and massaged them, stopping to pinch her nipples while never losing eye contact with me. I was frozen with fear, which caused me to have the opposite reaction. I was very, very uncomfortable. She straddled me with her strong thighs and started to grind to the soft beat of Sade's "Smooth Operator" as it played in the background. She rode me softly, arching her back and shaking out the wig on her head. She placed her hands above her chest almost as if to pray, then brought them down between her breasts, grinding and throbbing the entire time. I was deeply embarrassed and had no idea what to do about the situation.

Monica opened her eyes to look at me. She brought her hands to my outer thighs and began to massage them slowly, moving in slower and slower, and then finally heading to my dick. Her hand was on my dick now, and I wished with every part of me that I could respond with the erection she was working for. I could feel her squeezing my dick and balls. I thought she might be looking for signs that she was in the process of bringing it to life, but I felt nothing and neither did she.

I closed my eyes desperately trying to think back to things that had aroused me in the past, but I still felt nothing. Monica was visibly frustrated now. She would have to bring her "A" game. She stood up from me and spun around, placing her ample ass in my face, and it reminded me of two warm muffins. She did away with the flimsy bikini bottom material. I now found myself face to crotch with a beautiful woman and everything that came with her, yet I was still not aroused. As she spread her legs in front of my face, I was now exposed to what apparently drove other men crazy, but I felt nothing. She looked back at me as she gyrated. I could sense the boredom on her face as she gyrated back and forth, up and down, around and around. I looked at her, through her, and inside of her, and at that point I felt a deeply instinctual knowledge that there was nothing there for me. I found her neither sexy nor appealing, despite the fact that she was probably the most beautiful woman within one hundred miles of this establishment. That thought scared the shit out of me, because I knew exactly what it meant.

After a few more minutes of this, Monica made another half-hearted grab at my crotch, but I was already mentally checked out. She dejectedly put her thin bikini outfit back on and led me back out onto the main floor, where Brandon, Kane, and Norman waited. I looked awkward and ashamed. She stuck out her hand in front of Sergeant Kane.

"A hundred dollars," she said flatly and then looked at me up and down. "It's a shame you wasted your money. Kid couldn't even get hard," she said and made her exit back onto the dance floor to finish her shift for the night.

# CHAPTER 6

# RABBIT HOLE

After the night at Déjà Vu, my mind was confused and jumbled. I was fraught with complicated thoughts that seemed to be constantly at odds with each other. I thought I could be straight, thought I could like girls and be normal like everyone else, but I was quickly finding out that that wasn't the case. I'd wanted so badly to get an erection as the stripper fondled me. Had it come, I would've been free to be a normal, red-blooded heterosexual male among my fellow soldiers, but my dick was telling me another story. It was now official. I guess I really was a fag.

While trying to figure out what that meant, I'd find my mind drifting back to thoughts of Barry Winchell. His death scared me. Could I be the next PFC Winchell? I didn't know whether these guys in my platoon or squad were just a few beers away from a fag witch hunt, but I certainly didn't want to find out. The aftermath of the stripper incident had created an invisible but very real barrier between most of the other members of the platoon and me. Word had spread rather quickly, and the other soldiers didn't quite know how to take it. Sergeant Norman was sure there was only one possible reason for my lack of response to the stripper. In the weeks and months after the incident, I noticed his behavior become colder and more aloof. He'd work coded gay references into the most rudimentary conversations between me and the other squad members.

When he did so, I'd notice a chill in his demeanor as cold as his icy blue eyes, and I could feel their weight upon me. His behavior freaked me out so much that I made a promise to myself to keep my burgeoning sexuality as quiet as I possibly could. I realized I could trust no one with the secret that could kill more than my career and shot at an education. If I got kicked out, there would be no college for me, and my future and career as a broadcaster would be gone right along with it.

I kept to myself for most of the remaining summer and fall months that followed. I found myself becoming increasingly isolated from my fellow soldiers and retreating into a lonely world of self-doubt and fear. There was no one to turn to or talk to about my sexual orientation. I didn't feel safe enough to talk to any of the other soldiers, so there was only one real place to turn for solace. During a slow afternoon, I found myself sneaking back to the barracks from the motor pool, where the rest of the squad was shooting the shit and pretending to work on their vehicles, to give my mother a call.

I opened the door to the barracks room slowly and discreetly, and picked up the phone to dial my mother. I wasn't sure why I felt the need to provide a teaser to a conversation that we wouldn't be having for two months, but a strong sense of relief had come over me ever since I admitted it to myself. *I am gay. I like guys.* I heard her warm yet gravelly voice on the other end. She'd obviously been smoking.

"Hello?" she asked.

"Hey, Mom, it's me. How you doing?"

"Fine, and you?"

"I'm okay. What are you up to?"

"Just driving, Robert. What's up?"

"Um, nothing." I felt my throat begin to close up. I suddenly became tense and nervous, and I was struggling to find the words to say.

"So why are you calling me, Robert? I'm on the road driving."

Husband number three lived in North Carolina. He worked for a truck driving company that delivered loads of various products all across the country. She'd moved down my senior year of high school and embarked on a career in driving, leaving me to live with paternal grandparents for the remainder of my time.

"Um, okay. You know I'm coming back home for Christmas, right?"

"Yes, Robert, I know."

"Well there's something I wanted to talk to you about."

There was a long, uncomfortable stream of absolute silence. I could hear the wind whipping in the background from the cracked window of her eighteen-wheeler. I wondered what city she was driving to this time, what the scenery was like wherever she was, anything to fill the silence. After what seemed like forever, she continued.

"What is it? You're not gay are you?"

The words hit me like a well-timed punch to the gut. My knees buckled a little bit, and I stumbled onto the corner of my bed, shocked.

"Well, what if I was?" I asked in a quiet, little boy voice.

"Robert, you know that's not allowed in the Army," she said. "You also know that's not God's plan."

Her voice was cold and harsh. Unforgiving. Whatever the words to respond to this were, I couldn't find them.

"Do you hear me?" she asked.

I felt as if I was adrift, as if I was floating above myself watching this happen. It wasn't supposed to happen like this. I was supposed to call and give her a primer that I wanted to talk to her about something, so that maybe it wouldn't be such a big shock when I told her during the holiday. When I did tell her after Christmas dinner, she would hug me and tell me that she still loved me, and that I was her son no matter what. I would hug her back as tears of joy streamed down my cheeks while flurries of perfectly soft white snow fell outside. That was how it was supposed to happen, but that wasn't what was happening. It was happening now, and I wasn't feeling the love.

"Yes, I hear you," I said in a low, defeated croak.

"And you'd better not tell anybody else, either. You hear me, boy? Those people there are not to be trusted, and you can't be getting kicked out. How you gonna pay for college if you get kicked out? Where are you gonna live?"

"I don't know, Mom."

"I know you don't. Is that what you called me about? I've got to get back to driving. Call me next week."

She hung up, and I sat on the edge of the bed, motionless. Soon after, I realized I was crying. Out in the distance, I could hear the faint chant of soldiers calling cadence while they ran. Their voices comforted me. When I heard them, it was almost as if I wasn't so alone, and it was only when they stopped that I knew I was.

The night I decided to end my life, I sat alone in my barracks room just a few weeks after I came out to my mother. In the weeks after my admission to her and her subsequent rejection of it, I'd sunken into a deep depression. I was lost, lonely, and consumed with self-hatred about my sexual orientation. I knew the fact that I would never be like other people was what bothered her the most.

Though I wanted deeply to talk to someone about my feelings, I knew I couldn't. I wanted escape. I figured that the nothingness that death would bring would certainly be better than anything I was experiencing at the time.

If I had told anyone about why I wanted to kill myself, even a chaplain or a mental health person at the VA hospital on base, I would have been discharged under the "Don't Ask, Don't Tell" policy. I stood to lose everything, even if they helped me beforehand. I knew very little about how people went about suicide but knew that I didn't have the stomach to slit my wrists. I remembered vaguely reading about how any pill taken in a large dose could result in death, so I'd bought an economy-sized bottle of Tylenol from the gas station that was walking distance from the barracks, meaning to partner it with a bottle of cheap vodka I'd swiped from an impromptu party that some soldiers in the building had thrown a few weeks back. I walked into the bathroom in my barracks room and closed the door, stealing one last glimpse at the night sky just beyond the window.

The fluorescent lights bounced against the cold steel of the counters, toilet, and tub. It served to create a harsh whiteness that was almost clinical, as if I were in a hospital bathroom. I sat on the tile floor and curled against the tub, feeling the hard steel pressing into my spine. I looked down at the bottle of pills in my left hand, the bottle of vodka between my knees, and then at the telephone in my right. I couldn't remember picking up the phone to bring it into the bathroom, and found myself dialing my sister's number as if in a daze. My sister and I had never been extremely close, but that night I didn't know who else to call. I closed my eyes and exhaled in relief as I heard her voice on the other end of the line. Her tone went from annoyance to concern to frantic damage control as I found myself telling her about what I had planned for the evening.

For hours and hours that night, she listened to my problems and concerns as nobody else had before. She told me that she would always love me no matter who or what I was. I sobbed as I listened to her words, and I could hear her own tears and choked-up voice through the other end of the phone. After many hours, when she was absolutely convinced that I'd abandoned my plans of suicide, she hung up the phone and went to bed. I sat in the bathroom that night thinking and crying for a very long time, and eventually cried myself to sleep. When I woke up the next morning, the first thing I saw was the bottle of pills that had rolled out of my hand and into a dark corner behind the toilet, abandoned. I picked them up, placed them calmly in the medicine cabinet, and left the bathroom.

Though I was starting to personally come to terms with being gay, the loneliness was starting to become more intense. My sister regularly called to check up on me, but my mother's words were seared into my impressionable mind. They embedded a fear that kept me from really engaging with my other platoon mates. After the stripper debacle I'd been afraid to go to any more off-base events with the guys after hours. I figured perhaps it was best to stay away. One night, some of the guys on the squad were drinking and hanging out in the barracks. I could hear the muffled sounds of the thumping music and faint yelling going on in the rooms around me, but I didn't hang out, partly out of fear, but mostly because I had other plans.

I sat in my barracks room alone, curled up with my new discovery, a computer I had bought at a pawnshop near the base. It looked as if it had been through hell and back with its previous owner. The monitor was sticky and stained with what I hoped were only various juices and coffees. Ancient particles of food rested in between the keys. I looked in wonder at this new tool that was going to help connect me to others like me outside of the base. My distorted reflection in the monitor screen was replaced by the ubiquitous windows symbol as I booted it up for the first time.

Back in high school, I'd heard about this site called gay.com. It was one of those chat rooms where you could talk to gay people in your area and possibly even meet up to hang out or something. I had never been brave enough to go, but now seemed like the perfect time. Lately it had seemed as if I was the only gay person in the world. *It would be nice to meet a few more people like me*, I thought. I connected to the internet and opened up the browser. The blinking "I" of the cursor continued to go on and off, as if it were mocking me for being too afraid to move forward. I took a deep breath and typed "gay.com" into the address bar. I instinctively looked behind me, though it was impossible for anyone else to be there.

Safely freed of my irrational fear that someone was spying on me, I hit the "enter" key and watched as the screen immediately filled with images of hunky young men and web banner ads for gay cruises and vacations. All of the men were young and athletic, with muscular bodies that seemed to be free of even a hint of fat, and all of them were white. My exposure to any and everything gay was limited to this site and a new show, *Queer as Folk,* that I watched religiously every Sunday night, and without fail all the men were white, with perfect bodies and lots of money and amazing lives. Among the gays on television, white skin seemed to be the prerequisite to the lavish life of luxury all these men seemed to lead. If there were any gay guys that looked like me with these lives, I sure as hell didn't see them anywhere. I looked down at the dark brown hands that rested on my keyboard and frowned, silently cursing my grandfather for the coloring that he passed on to me. I knew it was what had drawn the drill sergeant to me that first day of basic training. It was an uncomfortable reminder of the "Bubba" nickname that I'd been branded with during basic training and the evil cries of "grease monkey" that I'd received from my white classmates during grammar school.

Afraid to use my real name, I settled on Griffin99, the name of my high school mascot and my graduation year, as an alias and dutifully filled out the online profile. When the photo selection tool came up, I paused. *Would any of the soldiers in my platoon be able to see this?* I thought nervously. My mind furiously scanned through all scenarios, and I decided to use a photo that I'd taken at a beach the previous summer. The sun reflected off of the camera, making me seem a bit lighter than I really was, and my teeth were bared in a jovial, fun grin. I looked like, well, the boy next door.

My heart was racing in fear, but I was determined to find a way to cut through the isolation I was feeling, to find a connection. *Besides,* I thought, *anyone from the military who sees the photo here obviously has as much to lose as I do.* Although I'd convinced myself to move forward, I felt a strong sense of relief that I could make my profile picture private and only accessible to those I'd be chatting with personally. With the double-click of the mouse, I entered the "Colorado Springs" room of gay.com and found myself adrift in a sea of screen names that ranged from innocuous to suggestive to downright vulgar. NiceGuy27 and RedHead86 could be found alongside JockAss4U and Looknfordik, and for the first time it crossed my mind that people could be using this site strictly to find sex, which was kind of scary.

It had been three years since my first sexual encounter in high school, the nice twenty-five-year-old guy who seemed to appear out of nowhere in his jeep. I was walking my route to school when he started talking to me. The chats and visits escalated from riding alongside me as I walked to picking me up from my job once or twice a week. It had been three long years since the night he'd moved his hand further and further up my thigh in his car until we had sex in a dark parking lot in the back seat of his car, lit only by the vague and harsh yellow light of the Swenson's Hot Dogs sign that was erected just a few hundred feet away.

I'd spent the rest of that school year feeling like a stranger in my own body, convinced that I was dirty. I felt a sense of shame about what I'd done that was so deep and all-consuming, I'd instinctively duck down when I saw a jeep that looked like his and started walking a new route to school to avoid him. I'd been successful up until a day when I found myself waiting at the bus stop on a chilly fall day, running late for my new job at a movie theater across town.

He pulled up to me as he had that first day, but now there was nowhere to hide. I was exposed. He rolled down the window and leaned out. I noticed everything about him in a different light. His dark-brown skin, the way his stomach hung over his jeans, the way how, when you actually looked up close, he looked more like thirty-five than twenty-five, and of course the lazy eye that seemed to be looking away while the other looked so deeply at me I felt as if he could see my developing soul.

"Hey," he said.

I could feel everything within me instinctively retreat. I looked down, fixated intently on the cracks in the sidewalk that needed to be fixed seemingly along with everything else in that crummy city.

"It's been a while," he said and smiled.

I looked up at him and then quickly looked away. The smile was lecherous and seedy, and it made me feel uneasy.

"Yeah, I guess it has," I said in a hushed tone. He looked behind him, as if to check for any oncoming traffic, but there was nothing. It was as if the two of us were the only ones in the world.

"Need a ride?" he asked.

"No," I said, and he shifted in his car uneasily.

"So, when are we gonna link up again?" He smiled that seedy smile again. I could see the gold tooth near the back of his mouth, and it made me want to vomit.

"I don't think that would be a good idea," I said, still avoiding eye contact with him.

"Okay," I heard, and by the time I looked back up, I saw nothing but the back of his jeep. He drove away and out of my life, never to be seen again, but to be felt for quite some time. Back at my computer, I shook off the memory, happy to leave it behind.

The main room of the gay.com site was broken up into two rooms. It had a public chat room and a private one in which you could talk to different members personally. I scanned the names and looked at some of the profiles. I wanted to see if there was anyone I'd like to connect with. The men in the room were almost exclusively white and older. For the first time, I got a terrifying glimpse of what gay life could be like in my thirties and forties. I feared that this was all that was in store for me. My thoughts were interrupted by the deceptively juvenile sound cue letting me know that I had gotten a private message.

"What's up?" the message read.

It was from a guy with the screen name CoSprings78.

I clicked over to his profile and saw a nice-looking, clean-cut white guy who had to be around twenty-three or twenty-four years old. The "78" in his screen name obviously referred to his age. He had dirty-blonde hair and blue eyes. His photo was one of those photos in which some unsuspecting party had been cropped out of the picture, so as not to steal any of the attention away from the main event. The guy was cute, if maybe a little doughier than the borderline porn stars whose photographs lined the borders of the gay.com website. I decided to engage him, ignoring the other message boxes that were rapidly popping up on my computer screen from other members. I'd found someone cute and interesting to talk to. He'd be enough for now. I was a one-guy man.

"What's up?" I answered tentatively, still occasionally glancing behind my shoulder, looking for the nonexistent threat.

"Nothing much, man. Just chilling out alone," he said. "Yeah?"

"Yeah."

"So what's your name? I'm Rob."

"Chris here. Nice to meet you, Rob."

"Same here, man. So what do you do?"

"As far as what?"

I chuckled at his naiveté. Obviously when you ask someone what he does, it's for work. Were all the guys on here this dense?

"For work," I typed, rolling my eyes with a half smile on my face.

"Oh, lol. I thought you meant something else.... I'm a student at CU."

"Oh, cool. That's really great. I want to go to school someday."

"Yeah? What do you do now?"

"I'm in the Army."

"Whoa! No shit?"

"No shit, lol. I want to get out and go to school for broadcasting."

"That's really great. I'm sure you'll do it."

"Yeah, I think so too."

"So what brings you here, Rob?"

"Just kind of bored, I guess. Wanted to maybe meet some gay people. It's like I'm the only one around here."

"I know the feeling. I'm from Iowa. It was kinda like that there too. Well, you've got me, lol."

"Do I?" I typed and noticed myself getting flustered.

"If you want. You're pretty hot. I like black guys."

"Yeah? Why is that?"

"I don't know. I just do."

"Well, I guess that's lucky for me."

"I guess it is. Look, it's getting late, but I'm free all day tomorrow if you want to link up and chill or something. Soldier boys are off on Saturdays, right?"

"That we are."

"Well, there we go."

Chris and I exchanged numbers and agreed to call the next afternoon to set something up. I was thrilled and nervous. I instinctively logged out of the chat room immediately after our conversation, not wanting to taint anything with any more conversations with the other men on the site. I'd found my connection, Chris. I turned off the computer and the lights, and laid down to go to sleep. I instinctively rolled over to the side like I usually do, my mind utterly consumed with the idea that perhaps tomorrow night I'd be sleeping with someone on the other side of me. No sex, just a little kissing and some cuddling. Yes, that would be nice.

I woke up the next day oddly refreshed and relaxed, feeling as though I could take on the world. It was one of those fall days in which everything was in perfect alignment for the season, and the colors of the trees and the sky shone brilliantly. I was always impressed with the weather in Colorado. The seasons came right on time, and weren't too harsh or too mild. Sometimes it was so beautiful I would feel as if I was in a postcard, walking down a block with no worries in the world. Due to living on base, I was constantly surrounded by the militaristic aspects of my life. It was on days like this when I would walk around the base alone that I often wondered what life was like on the outside. The military was beginning to feel a bit like prison, a place where I had to do my time, where I was being held back, where I couldn't be myself. The computer and Chris and gay.com were the first steps toward claiming something I didn't even know I was missing until now. These were the first steps toward having a life outside of the one I was regimented into every day.

It was early, and I didn't plan on calling Chris until afternoon, so I decided to take one of my walks around the base. I left my barracks room and walked out, as always with a bit of stealth to my movements. I didn't want to run into any of the other soldiers. I had been acting like this more and more on base lately. I figured that if I wasn't going to be like everyone else and wanted to avoid any more disastrous attempts to fit in, it would be safer for me to just stay away.

I walked down the main street that housed my company's section of the barracks, looking distantly at the off-duty soldiers doing their comings and goings in and out of the buildings that looked like little apartments. I looked up at the sky and marveled at the large, imposing mountains that seemed to surround this little corner of the universe that was Fort Carson. They were just like the mountains I had seen in that travel book in the high school in Ohio, and though it was only a few years back, it felt like a lifetime ago. So much had happened; I felt like I was living in dog years. I wondered what I was missing out on, what was passing me by as I was stuck on this treadmill of Army life, moving forward but never really ahead. Maybe with Chris and exploring this new gay thing I would be able to find some sort of balance, to find an outlet to have the fun and experiences I felt were lacking. Overwhelmed with a fresh feeling of excitement, I decided to walk back to the barracks and give Chris a call. Besides, it was only forty minutes until noon.

Chris agreed to pick me up at one of the public fast food places that littered the military base. Since I didn't have a car, it was easier that way. I was surprised that he was willing to drive on base, but I was happy either way, happy to finally be getting off base with someone other than the squadmates for once. I was excited to be meeting someone new, perhaps my first real gay friend. I supposed I looked like some kind of teenage hustler loitering at the Burger King on a busy corner of the base, but I didn't care. Chris described his car as a blue Ford Focus, and I felt a rush of excitement when I saw it pull up. I looked down into the car and was excited to see that he was even more handsome in person. He had sandy blonde hair and a crooked smile that I returned as I sat in the passenger seat.

"Hello, Mr. Rob," he said and smiled.

His teeth were damn near perfect, and his jeans and V-neck T-shirt hugged his semi-doughy frame just right. He was built like a football player who had let his body go just a bit. I wasn't sure what my type was, but this was certainly a contender.

"Hello yourself," I said.

I rolled down the window, happy to feel the breeze in my face as we escaped the base if only for a few hours. I looked over at Chris, who seemed calm and self-assured. He squinted his eyes into a narrow gaze as he navigated the light traffic to lead us off base. He looked back over at me and smiled. I smiled back.

"So what's on the docket today?" I asked.

"I don't know, you tell me." He placed his right hand on my thigh as his left navigated the steering wheel.

I felt a wave of attraction come over me and became instantly hard, struggling to camouflage it, a sight that he noticed and chuckled at.

"I don't know, man. What do people do for fun around here?" I asked.

He glanced over at me and looked me up and down. "Oh, we can do lots of things for fun," he said and smiled.

I looked down bashfully and glanced back out of the window.

"I mean, we could go grab some food and see a movie or something if you want to," he said, and my eyes brightened at the suggestion.

"Yeah, that would be great!" I said with what I hoped wasn't too much enthusiasm.

"Yeah, that works, but let's stop by my place first. I want to grab something."

"Sure, man. You're driving." I leaned back toward the window, enjoying the air of freedom as it whipped my face.

Chris's apartment was cavernous and unwieldy. It was located on the third floor of a house on a picturesque tree-lined block just near the end of the Colorado University campus buildings. The furniture was typical college-kid style with mismatched couches, chairs, and futons undoubtedly scrounged from a variety of garage sales and street corners. Books and paperwork were thrown around as far as the eye could see. The absence of sun exposure coupled with the dreary blue paint served to create a lifeless, stale atmosphere. It was as if all the vibrant colors that had once existed in the apartment long ago had been sucked out of the room and replaced with different shades of the same drab, muted blue/gray mixture. In the kitchen, ancient dishes piled in the sink, and the kitchen table seemed plucked from the same humble beginnings as the rest of the furniture. I stood in the middle of the living room, silently taking in Chris's apartment as he closed the door behind me.

I felt his presence behind me, coming ever so closer until our bodies were nearly touching. He was taller than I was, and I felt the faint brush of his stubble against my ears while his hands wrapped around my hips and down the front of my thighs. As I felt his thin lips kissing the back of my neck, I felt apprehensive yet exhilarated. Something in me felt as if this was wrong, that this was not how I wanted the day to go, but the attraction overwhelmed me so much that I began to question it. What exactly did I expect was going to happen when we came to his apartment?

My vision went in and out, fading to black and back into life again as my eyes rolled back, closing and opening in between bouts of ecstasy. I tried to summon from some deep and powerful place the strength to break away from him. I had a desire to have an experience that was somehow more romantic than the one I was having, but I couldn't stop myself. My body was overwhelmed with a toxic mixture of neediness and desire, and it proved to be stronger than the prudish and hopeless romantic that had simply wanted to hold hands and go see a movie. I turned to Chris and looked into his eyes, and though I sensed not even a hint of romanticism from him, I closed my eyes and kissed him. We devoured each other hungrily, with him willingly meeting and at times surpassing my own excitement at only my second real sexual experience with a man.

If I was going to do this, I wanted to pretend that I was in love, pretend that Chris was going to be my boyfriend. I wanted this encounter to be more romantic at its core than the casual mid-afternoon online meeting of lips, tongues, and bodies that it was becoming. Neither of us made a motion for the bedroom, as there seemed to be some sense that whatever this was should be confined to this public space in his apartment. When it was over, I felt a pang of shame and regret, as if I had done something I shouldn't have.

I didn't know if what had just transpired was his intention all along. The encounter filled me with mixed emotions that clashed in my mind, as if someone had taken a handful of opposing puzzle pieces and thrown them at each other in midair, colliding and then falling completely out of place. I had wanted it, liked it, needed it, but wasn't sure if I was ready for it. I would probably have felt differently if we'd gone on a date first, or if he'd at least attempted to do something with me other than take me straight to his apartment for sex. I had uncomfortable flashbacks to my high school experience. This thought made me think I wasn't ready for this, that I was being used again, and that what happened wasn't good. But I liked the experience, liked the closeness, liked his lips on my skin and reveled in the memory of his mouth on my dick. He looked over to me with an expression that I couldn't decipher between contentedness and boredom.

"So, do you need a ride home?" he asked absently.

I did.

For a while, gay.com was the gay friend I never had, linking me up with various men throughout Colorado Springs and the surrounding areas. I never felt that there was anything wrong with what I was doing. In fact, it was almost expected from most of the people I met. The days became hazy, one leading into the other as the sexual experiences notched up on my bedpost. I would do my basic military functions during the day, then at night, if I wasn't alone in my room, I was out meeting different men in the city. It felt intoxicating and powerful. There was something about my photo and me that attracted all these men to me via the power of the internet. That power was enough to get them to make the trek all the way on base to pick me up so that we could spend time together. Sex was all that happened with most of them, and I rarely saw them twice.

In the six weeks since I had discovered gay.com, I'd been with at least five men of various ages and body types—more men than I had been with in the entire eighteen years prior to that first login. The encounters were like fast food. They were filling in the short term but ultimately unsatisfying. I continued the behavior in the weeks and months ahead. The men varied in age and were from all walks of life. The only thing they all had in common was me and the fact that none of them were seen more than once. As the time passed, I became so adept at hiding the behavior that I didn't notice the burgeoning relationships with my fellow soldiers slipping away.

Promotions and field training exercises came and went. They were secondary only to my sexual exploration, which became the primary focus of my life outside of the base. It wasn't until many months after that first encounter, when a national tragedy met with a personal one, that I would be lifted out of my sexual haze.

# CHAPTER 7

# FALLING DOWN

The day two hijacked planes hit the twin towers, I was at home visiting my mother after doctors found a cancerous tumor in her colon. She'd broken the news over the phone on a rare night in for me in her trademark no-nonsense tone. I was devastated. My mother's mortality wasn't something that crossed my mind very often. I'd always felt that even after an apocalypse she'd still be around, probably smoking one of the Newport cigarettes that had now put her life in danger. Since I came out to her, our relationship had taken on a "Don't Ask, Don't Tell" feeling of its own. Our conversations had become increasingly shorter and less frequent, and over time calling her had become a chore.

On the night she called me with the news, I was in my barracks room alone. I'd declined so many invitations to hang out with the other platoon members at this point that they didn't even come around anymore. I preferred to hang out with Howard on my own time, and, of course, my online friends, who were a constant presence in my life.

When my room phone rang, I picked it up and was surprised to hear a worn-down, gravelly version of my mother's voice on the other end.

"Robert?"

"Yes?" I replied hesitantly.

"I just called to let you know I'm sick, boy," she said with the same gravelly tone to her voice. It sounded like she'd just been gargling with small rocks. I was struck with an immediate and sharp pang of fear at her admission.

"What's wrong with you?" I asked softly.

"Cancer," she said.

With her news, every image of a cancer patient I'd ever seen started flowing into my brain. I remembered seeing kids with leukemia on the news, women who were breast cancer survivors, and people who'd had all different kind of cancers but had the same look. They have hollow eyes, shrunken cheeks, and a deadening in the eyes indicating how the disease had trampled their spirit. This is the look my mother was soon to share. I felt my eyes well up with unwelcome and surprising tears, and my voice wavered as I continued the conversation.

"What kind of cancer, Mom?" I asked, already figuring that I knew the answer.

Her cigarette smoking had been a source of contention between us for years. On previous visits to see her, I would make an admittedly annoying spectacle out of coughing when she lit up or rolling the window down in the car as she smoked. I would tell her that it was dangerous poison, and she would tell me to mind my own business. Now, the smoking had finally caught up with her. As disturbed as I was by her admission, I felt a small, shameful sense of vindication as we spoke, and I hated myself for it.

"It's not cancer per se, Robert, but it's a tumor. In my colon."

The words "cancer" and "tumor" proved too much for me to handle, and I collapsed on my bed as I felt the strength leave my legs.

"So what does it mean?" I asked softly.

"It means I have to have surgery for it, Robert. And chemo," she said matter-of-factly.

I sat with my head between my legs on the corner of the bed as the tears streamed down my cheeks.

"Okay, okay," I said. "Do you want me to come home, Mom?"

I wanted her to say yes, that I was her only son, and that she needed me there to help her through the surgery and chemo. Just once I wanted to hear from her that I was loved and needed, but I got no such thing.

Instead, she flatly replied, "You can come home if you want to, Robert."

I paced around the room while the drops of tears from my eyes became a steady stream. When I hung up the phone, I was over-come with waves of emotion that induced strong, powerful sobs that quaked from unknown depths within me. It seemed like I was crying for so many things that night that they were all fighting to be expelled from my body first. I cried for my mother and for the relationship with her I wanted, but knew I'd never have. I cried for the pain and hurt that I knew she was going through, and I cried because of the fact that I knew it was a mirror of my very own pain.

The isolation I felt from the other soldiers was all-consuming, and a part of me knew that my dalliances with the men from gay.com were meant to be a Band-Aid for a problem that required sur-gical attention. I wanted attention and companionship, but all I was getting was sex. In a sense, my life now was a *Twilight Zone* alter-nate-universe repeat of my teenage years, except this time I was in control. I was doing the abandoning.

While it may have made more sense for me to go the opposite route and cling on to the various men I slept with, I did no such thing. I took great pains not to give my telephone number out after a few incidences when, to my surprise, a few wanted to see me again. I knew that could never happen. I could never be seen out in public in the relatively small military town of Colorado Springs with another man. I would take their numbers and promise to call when I had no intention of doing so, and when faced with their online profile names, I blocked them and effectively cut off all communication.

As I sat on the bed and cried for most of that night, I realized I was repeating behavior that was done to me. The more I thought about it, the more destructive it seemed. I began to wonder if this was what being gay was like, if I was destined for nothing more than empty encounters like the ones I'd been having for the rest of my life. I felt ashamed when I realized how many men I'd been with in such a short period of time. When I looked around, the barracks room seemed smaller than it ever had before, and I looked disdainfully at the computer that sat on the desk adjacent to me. I felt happy that I was getting an escape from it.

Sergeant Brandon approved two weeks of emergency leave. I was back in Ohio to visit my mother shortly after her surgery. Stepping foot back in Ohio after having lived in Colorado for well over a year now was like stepping from a Technicolor dream to a gray, dull nightmare. My father picked me up from the airport, and I grinned in amusement as he pulled up in his beat-up 1989 Honda Accord. I found it funny because he could've easily afforded so much more.

My father was a gregarious and handsome man, and for as long as I'd known him, he'd been an aficionado of working out and healthy eating. My military lifestyle made fitness a nonnegotiable part of my daily routine. I never quite understood his dedication to the gym, though I knew it was one of the things that defined him. He was thick and muscular, and made a habit out of wearing tight shirts meant to show off his barrel chest and strong arms. Our relationship was more big/little brother than father/son, because I'd only known him for six years.

My parents divorced when I was three years old, and shortly afterwards my mother found the man whom she would devote the next nine years of our lives to. That man would spend the next nine years terrifying my sister and me and physically and mentally abusing my mother. Outwardly, we were the prototypical, middle-class, respectable black family with a two-parent household and two bright children. Behind closed doors, things were a different story. Her husband, Ray, was a perfectionist who would wield his tall, lean frame like a weapon of intimidation against us all, but he particularly terrified me.

If I brought home anything less than a B from my schoolwork, I would feel the weight of his beady eyes on me through his thick bifocal glasses and promise through tears that I would do better next time. If there ever was a disciplinary problem at school, I would be made to strip naked, and he would beat me with his thick leather belt for ten minutes at a time. I would cower nude in the corner of my room when it was over, my chin resting on my knees and tears streaming down my cheeks. As he exited the room, the whip of the belt made an audible snap against the old wooden door as he dragged it behind him. I was also sexually abused by Ray between the ages of five and eight. It would take many years before, with the help of therapy, I connected the hypersexuality of my teens and early twenties to the abuse I endured at the hands of that violent and confused man.

The violence from him toward my mother would come at the most random times. A bloodied nose here, a hard, open-palmed slap to the cheek there. My eight-year-old self would sit cross-legged in the basement watching the over-the-top '80s videos on BET's *Video Soul* with my older sister when we'd hear the commotion coming from upstairs. The thumping and banging would thunder through the thin ceiling like the drumbeat to the same sad song. We would look sadly at one another, and, without missing a beat, she would grab the remote control and turn the volume all the way up so the noises were shielded by the heavy percussion of Shelia E.'s "The Glamorous Life" or the funky beats of Cameo's "Candy."

I was twelve and my sister seventeen when we finally escaped that nightmare. We left the home we'd shared with Ray in a late-night blur of screaming, physical violence, and the blue and red flashes of police car lights. Afterwards, we moved in with my grandmother into a small house just a few blocks around the corner. My mother took her newfound freedom as a sign that she was simply done raising children.

She was an attractive, lively, and boisterous woman who was always popular with men and had lots of friends. After the move, she quickly became used to leaving me to my own devices at home. My grandmother worked long hours, and my sister had since become pregnant with her first child and moved out to be with the father. During those years, my mother was a ghostly presence in my life. She was someone who was seen only in the morning before work then briefly in the evenings before leaving to live her new life, one that didn't seem to include me. It was in those years that she decided to make my father a part of my life again. He and I would begin the awkward dance of getting to know one another as an adolescent and adult.

During my high school years, we became more or less friends. We would spend time catching up via inexpensive buffet meals at

the restaurants across town or going to see the trashy horror movies that I'd grown particularly fond of. Although we spent time
together, my father was still a stranger to me in many ways, and
while I knew that I liked him, I didn't know if I loved him as a son
should love a father. There was a silent but impenetrable distance
between us, and his freewheeling nature would sometimes give
way to a hint of darkness and resentment toward my mother's role
in our lack of a relationship.

"You know she kept me from you," he said inexplicably one afternoon as he drove me back home after the two of us had spent
an afternoon together. "She had you thinking that man was your
father, and that hurt my heart. That hurt me deep inside."

We'd maintained a relationship throughout my time in high
school and when I entered the Army. He was the first person I called
when I knew I'd be back in Ohio for that week in early September
2001. As I sat in his car coming back from the airport, I saw only the
grim, dreary signifiers of a dying city surrounded not by visually
stunning mountain vistas but by never-ending flatlands of gray as
far as the eye could see. The buffet restaurants, pawn shops, and
used car dealerships that used to signify home now felt alien to me.
My father and I made casual conversation during the ride, but he
soon ceased to engage, perhaps feeling the distance that was coming from the fear of what lay ahead for my mother.

My mother stayed in the house with my grandmother while she
recovered from her surgery and started an intense period of chemotherapy. The husband she'd left town for during my senior year
of high school stayed at their home in North Carolina, working.
I'd only met the man she'd abandoned me for a few times. He was
the catalyst for her mid-career change from administrative office
worker to truck driver. From what I saw, he certainly didn't seem to
be worth uprooting one's life for and moving back to the sticks, but
in a way the behavior was a trademark of my mother's. Men defined

her. She always seemed to be searching for something more than what she could find in herself when she chose a man, and thus far in her life she hadn't been very successful. Although her behavior sometimes repulsed me, nothing could prepare me for how she looked when I walked into the bedroom of my old house.

Her usually vibrant brown skin was pale and blotchy, and she had dark bags under her eyes. She lay on the bed in the center of the room in what looked like a hospital gown, and when she looked at me, she quickly threw a blanket over her colostomy bag and averted her eyes in shame. She seemed as uncomfortable being seen like this as I was looking at her. I walked over to the bed and kissed her softly on her forehead, trying to be strong and keep the tears that were welling up in my eyes at bay. She pursed her lips and looked away in embarrassment. Seeing her like this seemed to melt all of my negative feelings toward her. I just wanted her to be better. All of my memories of her had been memories of strength. I saw that the chemotherapy and the cancer were robbing her of that strength. I wanted to help her get it back.

During the next few days at home, we spent more time together than we had in years. We watched television and ate, and I shared with her some of the stories about my military training. I showed her pictures of how beautiful Colorado was. We were mother and son, and though I cursed her cancer, I relished the chance to spend quality time with her. The topic of my sexuality didn't come up explicitly in conversation, but she did give me a tantalizing glimmer of hope that her views had changed in the year since we'd last spoken on the topic.

One afternoon I sat on a chair beside her bed as we watched *Judge Mathis* and waited for my father to pick me up to go to lunch. I noticed her staring at me intently and turned to face her. I shook my head and smiled. "What?"

"You know I'll always love you, right? No matter what," she said gravely.

The words caught me off guard, but they strangely didn't come as a surprise.

"Yeah, Mom, I know. Love you too," I said and pecked her on the cheek before rushing to meet my father in his car in front of the house.

Though I was fully resigned to come out to my father, I had great reservations. I took solace in his laid-back temperament, but I was still frightened by the possibility that he could take it very badly. The year prior, I'd had my first real experience with homophobia, outside of my high school, and it shook me to my core.

While visiting for Christmas, I thought it would be a great idea to attend church with my grandmother on the other side of town. It was a church that was different from the one I'd attended from childhood through most of high school. The small African Methodist Episcopal Church (AME) I'd attended was warm and inviting. I had nothing but good memories of participating in church plays, summer camps, and bible studies. I'd never once heard anyone mention "gay" or "homosexuality" at all, let alone in a way that was disparaging or unkind. While the sermons could undoubtedly get a bit boisterous and preachy, the overwhelming message seemed to be of love, repentance, and worship. On that Christmas morning, I would discover that my grandmother's church was a different story.

As I sat in the church, I watched the heavyset black preacher become more and more consumed by hatred as his sermon continued. He ranted and raved, and spittle flew from his lips as he wiped sweat from his brow.

"And then..." he bellowed after going on and on about sin for what seemed like an eternity, "You've got these punks and faggots and sissies running out in the streets doing God knows what!"

I recoiled in my seat as if I'd been punched in the face. I was deeply disturbed and uncomfortable by the laughs and cheers of all the supposedly good Christians that surrounded me. I felt a small but very real jab of fear, as if I were sitting in the middle of a rabid pack of dogs that could turn on me at any moment. The preacher kept on raving, but I mentally checked out and slumped in my seat. In my mind, I imagined myself making a big, bold statement about what he'd just said by standing up and stomping out of the church, but instead I said nothing and continued to bide my time until the sermon was over.

I'd never seen someone who seemed so utterly consumed with hatred for gay people before, and it was frightening. He was the only adult man I'd ever heard say anything referring to gay people. It shocked me that he did it from the pulpit in a place that was supposed to be welcoming to all people. I felt ashamed of him, and it took every bit of resolve that I had to keep his words from making me ashamed of myself. Though I knew my father was unlikely to react with that vehemence, it still occurred to me that he could be harboring similar thoughts that were as latently venomous as the preacher's.

When my father and I arrived at the buffet-style restaurant, I felt stiff and uncomfortable. My appetite was generally voracious, but I picked absently at the plate of chicken, fish, and salad that sat in front of me. My father ate his food as if he were being timed. He looked at me quizzically between forkfuls of food, though he said nothing. Our conversations were never particularly deep or meaningful, but I knew this one would be. I felt that the conversation we were about to have would either destroy our relationship or take it to another level. I tried unsuccessfully to eat my food, then pushed it away.

"Dad, I have something to tell you."

He raised his eyebrows at me in between massive spoonfuls of mashed potatoes. "Yeah, what's up?"

"I'm gay," I said, wincing as I prepared myself for the worst.

"Oh, yeah, I know," he said nonchalantly.

I was floored. *Did I just miss something here?* "You know? How?"

"You know, when you stayed with your grandparents your senior year of high school after your mother went to North Carolina, I saw something pop up on the computer when I used it. Gay.com I think it was. I put two and two together. Your dad ain't dumb."

"Oh," I replied quietly.

He pushed his plate forward and looked at me intently, then broke into the calm, engaging demeanor that was his trademark. He pushed his chest out and pulled his hands back, the classic "live and let live" gesture.

"Hey, man, look. If that's who you are, that's who you are. I mean, am I supposed to get huffy and puffy about it? What, am I supposed to stop loving you?"

"You love me?"

"You're my son, right?"

"Right," I said and broke into a huge smile.

For the next two hours and three plates, I shared with him all my fears and frustrations about being gay and what I was going through in Colorado. He listened intently. I told him about my dreams of college. He said that since I was nearly halfway through my term of service already, I shouldn't give up. In those moments, I felt completely free to be myself with my father. Even though there were years of our relationship that were taken from us, we seemed to be on the path to getting them back.

I was scheduled to return to Colorado on September 13. Just two days before, I sat in my old bedroom watching television as the smells of the bacon and eggs that my grandmother was preparing wafted into the room. A nondescript network news show played in the background, and I noticed with a bit of alarm that there was a breaking news alert. The news was coming out of New York City that two airplanes had just crashed into the Twin Towers, and there was no word about whether or not it was an accident. I rushed into the kitchen to join my mother and grandmother. We sat transfixed as the news played the footage of the planes crashing into the towers. I was horrified. I slowly felt their eyes upon me as we all came to the slow realization about what this meant.

Throughout the day, word trickled out about the attack and the motives behind it. We sat glued to the television as if there was nothing else going on in the world. In a way, there wasn't. In an instant, my mind became flooded with the images of all the war movies I'd ever seen. The future was uncertain, and it scared me. When I'd enlisted in the Army two years prior, going to war wasn't even on my mind. I never thought that I'd see war in my lifetime. Wars were things from the past, relegated to history books. They taught us about how the Americans pulled together during World War II or were torn apart in the aftermath of the Vietnam War.

I was struck with a clarity that my life was about to change. It was because all the abstract things that I'd been preparing for over the past few years had become reality within the span of a few short moments. The words were on the tips of all of our tongues. We dared not speak them, because to do so would make the situation even more real. America was certain to soon be at war, and, being stationed in an infantry unit, my skills were soon to be called upon.

After days of flight cancellations, I finally managed to reschedule my flight back to Colorado. When I arrived on the base, I was surprised to see my platoon and company gearing up for some kind of move. I was told to pack up all my equipment and report to the rear of the unit headquarters, where we staged and awaited direction. I stayed close to Howard, as his presence remained calming. We withdrew our weapons from the armory and were told that we were to stage in a field house near the north side of the base to await further instruction. The entire area was cordoned off by razor wire. It was made very clear to us that none of the lower-level soldiers were to go in or out, period. Guards were stationed at the front gates at all time, and roving guards walked the perimeter 24/7.

We were there in case we needed to be deployed at a moment's notice. A few weeks prior, we'd received orders that we were to deploy on a six-month training mission to Kuwait. It struck me as very unlikely that a low-level infantry unit like ours would somehow be called in to launch some sort of offensive in Afghanistan, but like a good soldier, I kept my mouth shut. The weeks in the field house were maddening. Soldiers were aimless and bored. We were constantly teased by the tantalizing smells that came from the Burger King. It was located just across the street from where we were all "staged," which made the whole thing seem even more ridiculous.

Roughly 350 soldiers in the infantry battalion were stationed in the field house that was no larger than a football field. We slept on cots that were practically right atop one another and ate MREs for all three meals. After ten days in the field house, a wave of sickness went through the troops. Several soldiers were afflicted with simultaneous bouts of vomiting and explosive diarrhea. The field house wasn't equipped to deal with that many people. The toilets backed up and overflowed, forcing their closure and the delivery of port-o-johns. The air became stale and heavy with an unbearable smell, as we'd been forced to keep up questionable hygiene habits in the field house. After three long weeks, we were notified that we were free to resume our regular lives and duties on base. We returned to the unit headquarters to turn in our weapons and to be debriefed. For the weeks leading up to our Kuwait deployment, we paid close attention to the developments in the media concerning Afghanistan. The knowledge that there was a real war going on led to increased intensity in our training.

We landed in Kuwait shortly before Christmas, unafraid of any potential for combat because we were assured that it was close to zero. Kuwait was a friendly place for American soldiers. For those six months, we did very little else besides pull guard shifts, work out in the makeshift gym, eat food, and write letters to our friends and family. Every so often we were allowed to go into Kuwait City. I was struck by how beautiful it was, especially by the water. We walked through the malls and near the beaches, and had I not known any better, I would've thought we were in Miami or someplace less exotic. A few of the squad members also experienced downtown Kuwait City and the many different counterfeit goods that one could purchase there. The Kuwaiti vendors relished shoving gold trinkets and watches in our faces while they stated, "I've got the bling-bling," in their best heavily accented English.

Kuwait was more or less like a field trip, but one evening, I got an ominous harbinger of what awaited us in the future.

It was a calm, crisp night. I was alone on a guard shift. I kept eyes forward on the border of the camp. I was joined by the company's first sergeant. He was a tall older white man with the slight hint of a southern accent. When he came up to me, I immediately locked into parade rest position, but he immediately put me "at ease" and lit up a cigarette.

The night was so dark that we were both just barely discernible figures in the darkness. I saw only the faint light of the cigarette tip as he guided it to his lips and smoked.

"He's up there," he said to me, motioning toward the north with the cigarette that dangled between his fingers.

"He's up there, and we're down here."

It was well known that Kuwait bordered Iraq. It was where US forces had succeeded in pushing Saddam Hussein's forces back when they tried to take over Kuwait nearly a decade before. With the Afghanistan war at full mast, there were small rumblings that Iraq may be next.

He looked down at my rank and squinted as he tried to make it out.

"You know why we're here, Specialist?" he asked.

"Keepin' Kuwait safe, First Sergeant," I answered eagerly, laying it on a bit thick.

"Well yeah, but we're here in case that asshole up north decides to start any more shit," he said coolly. "And if he does, then we're here to be the first ones in the fight. You got that, Specialist?"

"Roger that, First Sergeant," I said, and he walked away, the light of the cigarette tip becoming fainter and fainter until it disappeared into the night.

It would be a little over a year before I realized how right he was.

# CHAPTER 8

# AN EDUCATION

I returned from Kuwait with an abundance of money in my checking account due to the extra cash the US Army provides for service overseas. I decided to buy my first car. Sergeant Brandon accompanied me, and as we walked onto the lot on that sunny May afternoon, I could see the salesman looking at me hungrily. I settled on a blue 2001 Hyundai Accent, which seemed small and efficient enough to get me around. I'd just barely passed my driving test with Sergeant Brandon's help a few months before. The car became my best friend. I finally had an entry into the world outside of the base that came free of the strings that were attached to the many men I had met and had sex with in my earlier days on base. After returning from visiting my mother shortly after 9/11, I had found myself meeting the men online less and less. I'd become bored with the process. Now, I was onto bigger and better things.

By this time I'd learned to steer clear of Sergeant Norman, as his harassment was becoming less and less thinly veiled. Although the incident at the strip club had happened going on two years prior, it still colored his opinion of me. When we were put in a situation together, I would look into his steely blue eyes boring into me and feel the hate radiating off of him. It scared me, and as always that mental image of bloodied, bruised, and beaten PFC Barry Winchell still haunted me. His story was my omnipresent passenger, reminding me of the fate that could await me should I become too comfortable with things or ever slip up.

Shortly after returning from Kuwait, the squad members stood in line returning our equipment after a short day of training on the firing range. I carried the M249 saw machine gun on a strap around my shoulders. I was proud of my shooting for the day and inadvertently caressed it as one would caress a cherished toy or a lover's cheek. I'd become the squad's saw gunner almost by accident. One day, Howard was too sick to go to training, so I shot the weapon out of curiosity, and it was love at first sight. I liked how powerful the weapon made me feel and how much damage it could do. Since we'd come back from Kuwait, the feeling of the world seemed a bit different than it was before deployment.

The United States of America was at war. I'd never thought about that possibility when I'd joined the Army, but now it was always present in the back of my mind. I would wonder what it would be like in the mountains of Afghanistan. Would I be able to perform? Would I be able to trust my fellow soldiers enough to get the job done? The thoughts scared me. I would push them out whenever they came, but I couldn't help but think about it every time I shot the machine gun on the range. I instinctively knew that one day this weapon may mean the difference between life and death, so I'd better fucking know how to handle it.

I stood in line returning the equipment with Sergeant Brandon, Sergeant Norman, and PFC Lantos, and the conversation turned to the weekend plans of the squad. Norman turned to Brandon, his six-foot, two-inch frame towering over Brandon's short, stocky one.

"What you doing this weekend, man?" he asked.

"Nothing much, man. Wife wants to go to the fucking park or some shit. You'd think we'd been gone for six months or some shit," he said, and they all laughed.

I stood behind them silently. When Norman was involved in any kind of conversation, I instinctively shrunk back, not wanting to bring any attention to me. I knew that he knew about me. I felt it in the way his looks toward me always seemed judgmental, sneering, and seething with hatred.

He looked over at me, and I quickly looked down. When I looked up at him, I noticed that he was wearing his trademark sneer.

"Where you going this weekend, Smith?" he asked with a taunting, singsong tone in his voice.

"Uh, I don't know, Sergeant. Maybe just hang out around the barracks," I said.

"Yeah, you do that a lot, huh?"

"Yes, Sergeant," I said. He moved toward me and smiled.

"You sure you don't want to go to Hide 'N Seek?" he asked.

"What's that?" I said, slightly intrigued.

"It's a fag bar. You'd be right at home there, huh?" he said, and started to snicker.

I felt locked into the moment and absolutely terrified.

"Um, no, not really," I managed to mumble and quickly moved to return my equipment and walked away. I looked back at the line to see Norman laughing and joking with another soldier, and when I locked eyes for a brief second with Lantos, I could've sworn I saw empathy.

I found myself in my barracks room later that night once again in front of the computer, but this time it wasn't for online sex. Sergeant Norman, as creepy and terrifying as he was to me, had provided an opportunity that I'd never really been aware of until now. I typed "Hide and Seek Colorado Springs" into the Google search bar and anxiously clicked on the website. After I winced at the choppy yellow and black flash animation that opened the site, I looked at the information. Hide 'N Seek, as I was informed via the text on the website, was Colorado Spring's hippest gay and straight inclusive bar. It was open on the weekends until 5 a.m. It was twenty-one plus until 2 a.m. and eighteen plus afterwards. I cringed at having to wait until 2 a.m. to get in, but I knew exactly what I was going to be doing this weekend

I'd only been to one other gay club in my life. It was a small hole-in-the-wall called Club X in Sandusky, Ohio. I'd spent the summer after high school graduation working at an amusement park and truly exploring what "gay" meant for the first time, at least on the dance floor. The first time I entered, it was like sensory overload. It was the darkest place I'd ever been to in my life, lit only by a strobe disco ball and the lights of the bar. I looked to my right and saw boys dancing with boys and girls dancing with girls for the first time in my life. Their bodies dripped with sweat and glitter, sparkling as the glitter bounced in the strobe lights. There were many nights that summer I spent twirling, being free on the dance floor. I thought back to those nights as I made the decision to go to Hide 'N Seek just to check it out.

The night I was to make my initial trip to the gay bar, I paced around the small barracks room in anticipation. It had been a while since my nights at the gay bar in Ohio. I modeled my clothing choices after the men on *Queer as Folk*, which I still watched religiously every week, fully absorbing the show's ideas about gay life. I walked into the bathroom and looked at myself in the mirror. I wore a black A-shirt, chosen to show off the muscles I'd gained from the days spent working out in Kuwait, and a skin-tight pair of leather pants I'd bought from a discount store a few days earlier.

There were a lot of men in the club scenes on *Queer as Folk* who wore leather clothes, so I figured that was the popular look. As I pranced back and forth in front of the mirror while keeping an eagle eye on the clock, I imagined what it would be like to walk into the gay club. Would men want me? Would I be desired? I thought so, and it made me even more excited to make the trip.

I put on a large coat and walked out of the barracks room and to my car. I instinctively looked around to make sure nobody noticed me, got in the car, and pulled out as silently as possible. In my hand I held directions that I'd printed out, and I was surprised to see that the club was only a fifteen-minute drive from the base. When I pulled up to it, I was struck by how ordinary it looked.

It was a small building offset by two outside patios on both sides. An ancient awning hung over the entrance decks. Several men hung out lazily on the old patio furniture that decorated the decks. I summoned my energy and exited the car, the brisk wind stimulating gooseflesh on my bare arms. I put my chin up, my shoulders back, and walked to the end of the line where other patrons waited to get in. Frightened but aware, I continued to look around and behind me for any sign that someone had recognized me as a soldier. I thought back to the decal on my car that was used for entry into Fort Carson. Did anyone see me get out of the car? Would anyone here be able to recognize the decal and turn me in? I tried not to let the thoughts get the better of me. I did my best to hide any anxiety while I waited in line. I decided that I wouldn't look back to the car, so even if anyone recognized the decal, they wouldn't be able to see that I was the one who owned the car.

I studied the guys in the line in front of me. They were young, thin, and white. My presence commanded attention from some of them. I looked at my watch and noticed that it was 2 a.m. on the dot. After waiting in the line for what seemed like an eternity, I noticed it begin to move. The line behind me had grown. I was far too nervous to look anyone in the eye, so I glanced back, taking in only shoulders, tight jeans, and scuffed up shoes. After moving through the line, I entered the club and into a different world.

The club was dark with pockets of light. To my right was a small dance floor that was populated by a few guys who seemed to be in their forties or fifties. One was a heavyset shirtless man who wore a nose ring and what looked like a leather strap on his bicep. Tiny beads of sweat formed on his bald head. His chest was full of furry black hair that was separated by two large, protruding nipples that were both pierced. A thin bead of sweat ran down his nose and was caught in his thick brown mustache as he moved to the thumping techno music. Beside him was a lanky white guy who was also shirtless. Beads of sweat also resided upon his slim, hairless chest. My face became a grimace of horror when I realized that my leather pants looked like theirs. I was absolutely mortified that I was dressed in a way similar to them. The heavier one locked eyes with me. I headed straight forward and to the basement like a cockroach scurrying at the bright flash of lights in the kitchen.

Making my way through the hallway, I noticed more guys who were around my age. The place was filled with the stench of old beer. My shoes stuck to the floor as I walked down the narrow staircase. I could see ancient messages written on the wall. "Johnny G sucks cock, 719-233-9584." "Allan P takes it raw." There was something exciting, sleazy, and dangerous not only about the messages but about where I was. I was scared as hell but secretly thrilled to be breaking the rules just by being here. As I walked deeper into the labyrinth of the dark club, I found myself further away from all the stresses that dominated my life at the base. Sergeant Norman's harassment, the constant fear and worry that someone would figure out my sexual orientation, and the new promise and threat of war were all relegated to a place far away as I explored this dark and mysterious new world of Hide 'N Seek.

When I made it into the basement of the club, I found myself overwhelmed by the thumping sounds of hip-hop bass. The men upstairs were primarily older and white, but now it seemed like I'd found where the younger black men were hanging out. Missy Elliott's "Work It" played in the background as the men on this dance floor contorted their bodies with the rhythm. Their sweat wasn't a source of disgust or fear for me. I wanted to join them. I moved closer to the dance floor as if being pulled by some unknown force. The dance floor was packed and lit by a single blue light that met with the red strobe lights from the bar area, giving everything an eerie green glow. The almost coal-dark skin of some of the black men on the floor along with the light created an intoxicating visual that I desperately wanted to join. I looked over my bare arms, realizing that my skin matched their skin. I felt like I needed to be there, and soon enough I was, dancing the night away to countless songs over the next few hours.

I felt confident, alive, and sexy as I danced flirtatiously and sexually with all comers, embracing the moment and my newfound freedom. The next time I looked at the time, it was 3:30 a.m., but I had no intention of stopping after my first introduction to Hide 'N Seek. I was having too much fun.

"I know you," I heard a voice to my right say.

I looked over to see a strange man standing right next to me.

He was a tall, lean black guy, just slightly darker-skinned than myself. His hair was cut into the standard military high and tight, but it was grown out on top in a small curl that had more than a few specs of gray. I gathered that he was about thirty-five years old. He had delicate features and looked at me with a sly smile. I shook my head and looked down at my water as if it were the only thing in the room. The music continued to pump hip-hop so loudly that we were both nearly screaming at each other just to hear. "No, I don't think so," I said dismissively.

"Oh no, I do," he said. "I think we may work in the same area."

I looked over at him with a frightened expression on my face. He smiled.

"Fort Carson, right?" he asked, and his grin got wider.

"Your superiors know you like to make out with boys, soldier?"

He must have seen the freaked-out look on my face because his expression softened, and he burst into laughter.

"Relax, man. I suck dick too. Yeah, it's a bunch of us fags in the Army," he said. I looked at him distrustfully, unsure of how to continue. "What, you think this is a fucking sting operation? Do I need to let one of these studs fuck me right in front of you to get you to believe me? How about that fine one you were slobbing down on the dance floor? Looked like he couldn't leave quick enough when he found out you weren't givin' up any of those cookies," he said and gave me a swat on my ass.

I remained silent.

"Come on, kid. I need a cigarette. I'll fill you in on exactly where I know you from."

I followed him through the darkness of the club and out onto the patio near the front. We both sat on the old furniture, and I stared out into the parking lot as a steady stream of people stumbled in and out. I was nervous and scared. I didn't know how on earth this person knew who I was, but I knew he had the ability to kill my career. I sat across from him, and he looked at me knowingly with a world-weary expression on his face. His eyes never left mine as he pulled a cigarette smoothly out of a pack then lit it and blew the smoke to the right of him. I sat as nervous as a kid in the principal's office.

"So where do you know me from?" I asked hesitantly.

He smiled.

"My name is Sergeant Scott Bond. I manage inventory for the battalion. You're an infantry boy, right? I'm always in your unit headquarters. I don't know how you didn't recognize me." I started to relax a bit.

"Yeah, I'm infantry," I said.

Scott smiled.

"You're a fag, too, ain't that right?" I looked down, answering only by nodding my head. "That's fine," he said.

"So am I. I told you I was, boy. What, you think you're the only fag in the Army? Child, please."

"So what are you gonna do?" I asked.

"What you mean what am I gonna do? What the fuck is there for me to do?" he asked. "What, you think I'm gonna turn you in? What the fuck would that look like? Relax, boy. Nobody's gonna turn you in."

I looked into his eyes as he said it, and I was struck by an honesty that lay just beneath the surface. At that moment, I trusted him. Still, I was unsure of why he'd even bothered to come up to me.

"A few other boys in your unit are too, you know," he said.

Now I was intrigued. I let the last of my defenses down and moved forward.

"Really? Who?"

Scott smiled again and chuckled a bit.

"Wouldn't you want to know? Okay, I'll bite. Small guy, Latino but looks white. He's fucking a captain over at the Air Force Academy."

My eyes widened with the revelation.

"Holy shit. Lantos?"

"Yeah, that's his name," Scott said as if he was trying to remember the name of the mailman. In that moment I thought back to Lantos, and suddenly it all made sense. He was extremely quiet, almost as quiet as I was. I never heard about him hanging out with the other people in the platoon either. In fact, I never heard anything about him. All the while he was a fag just like me.

"Holy shit!" I repeated and burst into hysterical laughter.

"I'm telling you, these children think they're the first gay ones on the planet," Scott said almost to himself as he leaned back in his chair and took another drag from his cigarette.

Over the next few weeks and months, Scott and I became fast friends. I relished the time we spent together. I wasn't alone anymore. I finally had a gay friend to do things with on our off-time. Scott prided himself on being my guide for the gay world that was so new to me. Between biweekly trips back to Hide 'N Seek, we sometimes went on excursions out into the city. We ventured up to Denver, where he took me to my first gay pride event. I marveled at the floats and the parades. There was such brightness and joy from all the people marching with pride just for being gay. As I stood there with him, my surrogate big brother, I wondered if I would ever be comfortable enough with being gay to be as free and open as the people in the parade.

During that time I still took great pains to keep my life hidden. I studiously avoided being photographed or caught on any local news cameras at any of the events. As the parade marchers passed, I looked over at Scott, who absently flicked away the ash of his Newport cigarette. Though he was kind and a bit flirtatious, his face seemed harsh and world-weary. His was the face of someone who had seen and done it all many times over, and he seemed a bit tired.

"How long have you been doing this for?" I asked, curious.

His eyes rolled up, and he smiled. It was a bitter smile, filled with disappointment and regret. When he smiled like that, he seemed to be thinking of opportunities passed, not to mention the passing time of a life lived in the shadows.

"For too damn long, brother," he said and blew out his cigarette smoke. "For too damn long."

As I looked at him I wondered what kind of toll living in secret had taken on his life. Were there ever any opportunities for him to live openly and freely? Were there ever any opportunities for him to be happy? As we stood on the street in the hot summer sun, my mind was filled with millions of questions, not only for myself but for the other soldiers who were forced to live like this. How could they do it? In my mind I knew that my time in the Army was only temporary, but what about those soldiers whose time was more permanent? What about the ones who loved the military so much that they wanted to make careers out of it? What was to become of those forced to live and love in secret just because they were gay?

"Have you ever been in love?" I asked.

I imagined how naïve I must've sounded to him. Young, dumb, and full of fuckin' cum, as he would say. That same sad, wistful smile came over his face.

"Yeah, I was. Once," he said.

"Was he a military guy?"

"No, man, he was a civvy. White boy, too. Could you fuckin' imagine this black queen with a white boy? Name was Greg. Now ain't that about the whitest fuckin' name you've ever heard?" He'd stealthily replaced his old cigarette with a new one and continued to puff away, chuckling to himself.

"What happened?" I asked softly, not wanting to disturb what was obviously a very happy memory for him.

"We were together for five years, but he couldn't take it," he said.

"Couldn't take what?"

He turned to me and looked at me sternly, as if he were a teacher correcting a dumb student who just didn't get it.

"Couldn't take sneaking around. Couldn't take me being too afraid to go out to eat or to hold his hand. Couldn't take it. Couldn't take this," he said and stomped out his cigarette on the ground.

Scott said he had a surprise for me, and when we got back into his car after the parade, we drove around Denver until we entered a beautiful park. It was late afternoon inching into the evening, but the air was still thick with midsummer warmth. Again, I was struck by the greenness of the grass and the colors that abounded. I was also struck by something else—everyone in the park seemed to be gay. Outside of Hide 'N Seek and the parade, I'd never been around so many gay people in my life, but this energy was distinctively different. Men of all colors walked around the large oval of the park, some scantily clad in short shorts, some in jeans and T-shirts. As we walked, I became suddenly self-conscious of the clothes I'd worn, an old T-shirt and some blue-jean shorts. My crisis of self-confidence was cut short by the cries of "damn" and the whistles I heard as I walked by. I grinned and chuckled to myself. Those were not things I was used to hearing.

We walked around the park for about an hour without speaking. When I looked at Scott I realized that my line of questioning earlier had reminded him of his lost love, placing him into a bit of a funk. He wasn't with me that afternoon at the park. He was with Greg. Perhaps he was remembering when they fell in love or when they first kissed. As I romanticized their relationship in my mind, it made me wonder when I would find something similar for myself.

Scott and I rode back to the base in silence that night. As I looked out of the car window, I was mesmerized by how clear the sky seemed and how bright the stars were. I found myself once again awestruck by the mountains. I looked over at Scott, my new friend, and was thankful that he had come into my life. The education I was getting from him was different from any I'd gotten before. I don't know what I would have been doing without him. It would turn out that because of Scott I would meet the man who would shake my life up personally right at the same time the military was about to do the same professionally.

Over the next few months, Scott and I continued with the big brother/little brother relationship that we'd begun to build. I found myself greatly enjoying the time we spent together off base. Back on base, I was known as a solid, if unremarkable, soldier. I wasn't involved in any disciplinary actions. I was known for being someone who got the job done. With the revolving door of new soldiers, officers, and platoon leaders, the memories of my strip club debacle and questionable heterosexuality seemed to drift into the backgrounds of the minds of many of the soldiers.

Recently, I'd struck up a friendship with another soldier named Wale, whose wife ended up providing the perfect cover. We had an easy, natural friendship. I would spend a great deal of time with Wale, his wife, and his son. Wale's wife was gorgeous and definitely the type of woman that I knew I'd be with if I was straight. She had short hair and gorgeous brown skin. She was the spitting image of the pop star Kelly Rowland from Destiny's Child. The friendship between the three of us struck up rumors among some of the newer soldiers that I was sleeping with her.

The rumors continued to follow me around, and I did little to avoid them or put an end to them. At this point, I had the intricacies that went into the careful construction of my dual lives down to a science. A big part of that was allowing others to believe the lie about Wale's wife. It painted me as someone who was morally questionable. That fact was secondary in importance to the fact that it painted me as a heterosexual. Being someone who was morally questionable was a small price to pay to silence the questions and comments that had dogged me after the incident with the stripper on my eighteenth birthday.

With everything on base seemingly in line, I was free to explore the gay scene further with Scott. Our trips to Hide 'N Seek became a weekly occurrence. I got to know the other regulars and felt more comfortable with being in a gay atmosphere. It was on one of these nights that I ran into the man who would dominate my life for the next few months.

As I stood at the bar that at this point in the evening served only water and soda, I looked over to the dance floor to see a man gesticulating wildly to the thumping beat of the techno music. He was alone on the dance floor with no real sense of form or direction, and I tried unsuccessfully to stifle a broad smile. I cringed when I noticed that he saw my smile, but felt a little lighter when it was returned by one of his very own. His garish smile revealed small, spacey teeth that were a long way from a Colgate commercial. He closed his mouth and shrugged his shoulders, still smiling, and I walked over to join him on the dance floor.

It wasn't that Alejandro Rodriguez was even all that handsome, because he wasn't. He was average height and slight of build, with pockmarked skin and a fashion sense that recalled the last vestiges of late '90s grunge. He was certainly a long way from the build of the muscular studs that danced on the bars as well. He was gangly and paunchy, with an ever-so-slight paunch visible above his waist. His hair was cut in an unflattering style that left him nearly bald on the side with his thick hair tousled and spiked by what looked like an economy-sized bottle of hair gel.

Far from the typical gay boy uniform of tight T-shirts and jeans that all the other patrons of Hide 'N Seek emulated, including myself, he seemed very much out of place. His dress included baggy jeans and a nondescript polo shirt that could've easily been fished out of the bargain bin at the Kmart located not too far from the club. Whatever was going on with this person, he struck me as a bit different from the rest of the patrons of the club, most of whom seemed to be cut from the same cloth.

I moved closer to him on the dance floor and noticed that very few people were left at this point in the night. It was nearly 3:30 a.m., the time when most people have either found their company for the night or are staging their last-ditch attempts at it. I hoped that he didn't think those were my intentions. He smiled warmly as I approached. "Wanna dance?" I screamed over the pulsating music.

He smiled again. "What do you think I'm doing?" he said with a hint of a Spanish accent.

I exaggeratedly looked him up and down and cocked an eyebrow. "You really want me to answer that?" I teased.

"Hey, fuck you *pendejo*! I'm getting doooooown," he said, exaggerating his claims with a move that seemed to be straight out of the New Kids on the Block tour of 1989. An enormous laugh escaped me before I even knew what was happening, and soon his laughs joined my own. As the music changed, we switched up our dance styles and continued on into the night. It wasn't until the harsh lights of the club turned on that I knew it was time to go.

"So what's your name?" I asked as we walked to the parking lot afterward.

The sky was showing its first hints of dawn. I silently lamented another night of dancing into the morning at the club.

"Alejandro," he said. "But you can call me Alex. Everyone else does."

"Who's everyone else?" I asked coyly.

"My boyfriend," he replied.

"Oh," I said and immediately shifted to thoughts of getting back to base and going to sleep.

"*Dios mío*!" he said, catching me off guard.

"What?" I asked. "What did I do?"

"Nothing, man, it's just...you guys.... Everyone wants a boyfriend, you know?" he asked. "You guys find out I have a boyfriend and that's it, right? I'm crossed out. Done. *Finito*!"

"Well, what else is there?" I asked, curious as to where this was going.

"Well, there's friends, right? Like your boy in the club I saw you with earlier," he said.

"Who, Scott?" I asked.

Come to think of it, I hadn't seen Scott in a while. Maybe he'd gotten lucky or thought that I was about to. I'd driven that night, so it was no real concern.

"Yeah, him," Alex said. "I know you're not fucking him, but you still hang out, right?"

"Yeah, we still hang out, and how do you know who I'm fucking?" I asked.

Alex smiled, and I jokingly rolled my eyes. His smile and energy were warm and inviting, and I could feel the electrical current of attraction drawing me to him.

"Look, man. I already have a boyfriend. I mean, he's in Korea, but I have a boyfriend. Maybe a few more friends around here would be nice," he said.

"What the hell are you doing with a boyfriend in Korea?" I asked. Alex smiled and pointed to the Fort Carson Army decal on my car, which we were now leaning on.

"Same as you, bud. I used to be military, too. My boyfriend still is. He just left a few months ago, and I've been trying to put myself back out there, you know, but it's hard here. People just want sex. As soon as I tell them about my boyfriend, they're not interested," he said and sighed.

"Well, I've got no problem with friends, but I do have a problem with sleep. I'm fucking exhausted. Give me your number. Let's hang out sometime," I said before taking it and driving back to the base as the sun began to rise, illuminating the mountains behind me.

For the next few months Alex and I were practically inseparable. The burgeoning friendship provided a welcome respite from life at the base, which was becoming increasingly tense with continued attention placed on the war in Afghanistan. Into the late summer and early fall, I became a common fixture at his small one-bedroom apartment. He didn't seem to have many friends, so we became each other's best friend. I began to spend so much time with him that, when we started spending all of our time together, I barely noticed.

Alex had served five years as a tank mechanic at Fort Carson. He was using the transitional period after separation to figure out his next move in life. He worked full-time managing a gas station not too far away from base. I would sometimes stop by to fill up, teasing him about his engine-red Texaco polo shirt before I sped off to his apartment to meet up with him later on. I envied his life. It was simple and free of the demands of the military that were weighing more heavily on me as time went by. We did everything together, and he slowly replaced Scott as my go-to buddy to attend the gay bar with.

Within a few weeks, I noticed a pattern with Alex at the gay bar. He would flirt shamelessly with any man who crossed his path, entice the man in for a kiss, and then cut away at the last minute with news of his relationship, leaving the patsy in question stone-faced or irritated. I watched his behavior with an odd fascination at the way he wielded his sexuality. I was jealous from time to time when I watched the behavior from the sidelines. I would watch Alex do his private dance under the bar's blue and red strobe lights. One day it struck me that he needed the attention, craved it. However, I was filled with a smug sense of superiority about the whole thing. After all, Alex never slept with the men. He always went home with me.

I shared things with Alex that I'd never shared with anyone before. I memorized his different facial expressions and tics like a map in my mind that only I had access to. In those months I retreated further and further away from the realities of life at the base and more into the life I had with Alex. Sometimes we would spend entire days in his small apartment watching old horror movies on television, going to flea markets, or going to the mall.

One late Saturday afternoon, Alex told me he had something he wanted to show me. We piled into his dusty blue Honda Civic and drove to the outskirts of Colorado Springs to a point higher than I'd ever been in the city. We parked the car among many other parked cars. It was with some amusement and slight embarrassment that I realized we were in what seemed to be a very popular make-out spot among the residents of the city. As the sun went down for the day, the lights of the city started to turn on, and the entire nightlife of Colorado Springs came alive before my eyes. It was like nothing I'd ever seen before. Marveling at the view, I turned to Alex and unleashed a huge smile, which he returned before I noticed a shadow come over his face.

"Murphy and I used to come here," he said wistfully. He shared with me the details of his relationship with his closeted, active-duty military boyfriend

Alex and his boyfriend, Murphy, had served in the same platoon during their Army days, though unlike me they'd gone full-fledged into the closeted lifestyle. Alex described them as both being well-known fixtures at the strip club Déjà Vu and with the local girls. They had never suspected the other of being gay. That is, until they found themselves having drunken sex in the barracks one night after having a bit too much to drink. As he told me this, Alex pulled out a small wallet-sized photo of Murphy, as if to let me in on exactly what a stud this man was. The photo was of Murphy on what looked like a deployment. He was dressed in the sand-colored military desert uniform, and he wore a tight brown T-shirt and a wide grin. He was a fair-skinned Latino man, tall, broad-shouldered, and very attractive. Someone so stereotypically handsome seemed like an ill match for Alex's average looks. I had to admit that Alex had a magnetism to him that extended beyond his physical attractiveness.

After the two men had sex, they both clung to their "straight" identities. They would both date girls in the city while they continued to meet up for clandestine sexual encounters until something changed. Alex and Murphy began to feel as if they were falling in love. The concept of romantic love fascinated me. I'd never been in love. I had certainly never really felt loved by anyone outside of family, and even with some of them I wasn't too sure. My mother was distant, and my father was an aloof nonentity. For the first time I made the connection between my penchant for the sex that had dominated the first few years of my gay life and the disconnect I felt from others in my life who were meant to be close to me. I realized that I just wanted to love and be loved, but was unsure of how to go about it.

I'd stared out into the distance as he told me most of his story. When I turned toward him, he seemed a million miles away. His face was bathed in the glow of the moonlight, the pockmarks on his cheeks a reflection of the moon's craters.

"How did you know you were in love?" I asked with rapt attention.

"I don't know," he said, never returning my gaze. "I guess colors just seemed to be a lot brighter, and I finally understood what all those stupid love songs were all about."

They continued to see each other for two years without incident and remained very careful to keep their relationship a closely guarded secret.

"Two soldiers in the same platoon sleeping together? Are you fucking kidding me?" he asked. "God knows what would've happened if anyone had found out.

When he said this, I was again reminded of PFC Winchell. I wanted to ask Alex if he'd ever heard the story, but I thought better of it. I didn't want to destroy the mood. One time, they were nearly caught when their company commander ran into them at a restaurant off base. Alex didn't notice that his hand was sitting on Murphy's thigh under the table. Alex said that when the platoon sergeant approached, he immediately removed the hand but wasn't sure what the platoon sergeant had seen. The platoon sergeant had engaged in conversation and given them a few odd looks, but left to rejoin his family for dinner. Alex and Murphy had spent the rest of the weekend alone together sweating bullets about the incident, but it was never brought up again by the platoon sergeant. "You think he knew?" I asked him.

Alex smiled. "You know what? As crazy as it sounds, I think he did. I don't know. Maybe he didn't care."

Maybe he didn't care. I thought about that possibility a great deal as I negotiated my dual lives on and off base.

I'd had my own close call that made me reconsider the silent prison that I was living in back with the soldiers. Just a few weeks before I'd met Alex, I found myself alone in Hide 'N Seek one late Saturday night. Scott was pulling an all-night duty shift back on the base. I decided to go out to the club and do my usual thing when a cute redhead approached me on the dance floor. I danced with him relaxed and carefree like I did with all the others, but I stopped in my tracks when I noticed two very familiar faces through the neon-blue haze of the club.

Right next to the bar, standing beside two women, were Sergeant Kane and PFC Lopez, another soldier from my platoon. Though Hide 'N Seek was known mostly as a gay club, it was also one of the few after-hours spots in the city. It wasn't uncommon for straight couples to come if they wanted to extend the night past 2 a.m. I had no doubt that Kane and Lopez belonged in this category.

I froze in fear. My first instinct was to leave the club right then and there, but they'd already made eye contact with me. I cringed as they smiled, turned to each other, and started to laugh as if a long-held theory had finally been proven. I panicked, wondering how much they saw. I felt my entire body go slack. I knew it was over. I knew I'd return to base that Monday morning to find my discharge paperwork waiting for me because I'd been seen "telling" by two soldiers in my platoon. The DADT policy was sneaky like that. I'd recently done a little digging and learned that I didn't have to come out to anyone to get kicked out. If I was seen "engaging in homosexual conduct," I could have charges brought down upon me. I was quite certain that the amount of grinding that I was engaged in with the cute redhead easily qualified.

Unfortunately, there was only one exit from the basement, and using it required walking directly past Kane and Lopez. Maybe it was possible that they hadn't seen me do anything. I rushed past with my head down but heard the unmistakable "Smith!" booming from Kane's loud voice right before I hit the stairs.

My shoulders fell. I was caught. I turned around and looked in Kane's direction, everywhere but in his face, because I couldn't bring myself to look him in the eyes. In that moment I felt deeply ashamed. I felt as if everything I'd done thus far to try to be a good soldier was nullified. I knew I was an average soldier and nothing special in that respect. I knew that I just got the job done and nothing more, but I'd managed to stay out of trouble for the past three years. I'd avoided the legal pitfalls of other soldiers who got arrested for domestic abuse, DUIs, or public intoxication. Even after all of that work, my military career would be killed because I got caught in a sleazy gay bar in a desperate search for somewhere to express myself.

"Yes, Sergeant?" I asked.

"First of all, fucking relax, man," he said. "You come here a lot?"

I continued to look down, embarrassed and frightened beyond belief.

"From time to time," I said.

"Where you heading off to in such a hurry?"

"Home. Guess I gotta start packing."

He seemed perplexed by this, and he furrowed his brow as if trying to figure out a complicated mathematical theorem.

"Look, just calm down. I'm not gonna.... Look, man, just chill out, okay?" he said. "You wanna go, then go, but I'm not forcing you to go anywhere."

"Okay," I said.

I turned around to make my way up the stairs and out of the club. I felt deeply ashamed in that moment. I didn't know whether it was because I was gay or because I got caught. The rules made being gay such a punishable secret that it was hard to see the boundaries sometimes. If being gay were normal or natural, certainly it wouldn't be legally punishable in the military. In a place deep within me, I knew there wasn't anything normal or natural about what I'd been doing for the past few years. It wasn't because of the gay aspect but because of the lack of any type of real connection to the various bodies I'd become accustomed to giving myself over to.

I drove home in stunned silence. The traffic lights were blurry blobs of red, green, and yellow through my tears. I was just over a year from my end date, and this was how it was going to end? Caught at a gay club and railroaded out without a hope of seeing even a penny of the fifty thousand in college funds that I was contracted to receive. I cursed being gay, cursed the Army, and cursed the fact that I'd even decided to go out that night. Maybe my mother was right. Maybe it really wasn't what God intended, and I was getting what I deserved for being this way. It just seemed so deeply, fundamentally unfair. I had no control over my sexual orientation. I hadn't asked to be born like this, so why was it making things so hard? I stayed in bed for most of that Sunday, scared shitless at what the next day would bring.

That Monday morning after PT, I walked into the unit headquarters expecting to enter a sea of cutting glances and whispers, but heard nothing. I wasn't called into the company commander's office and wasn't reprimanded for anything. It was a normal day, just like any other day. Later on in the afternoon, I spied Sergeant Kane signing in some equipment, and I approached him. He looked at me sternly. "What's up, Specialist?" he asked.

"Uh, nothing much, Sergeant," I said.

His look relaxed a bit. "You have fun dancing? It was interesting running into you," he said, and I froze.

Another soldier from the platoon, PFC Conch, was within earshot, and came over to join in on the conversation. Conch was a young, jovial white kid from Kentucky, which was a source of never-ending teasing from some of the platoon members.

"Yeah, where were you guys at?" he asked.

At this, Sergeant Kane turned to him.

"None of your damn business!" he said jokingly in an exaggeratedly annoyed manner.

"Hey, my bad, Sarge, my bad!" Conch said in the same jovial manner and walked away. I looked at Sergeant Kane and smiled hesitantly. He cocked his head up and looked at me with a mischievous smile.

"Motherfuckers be so goddamned nosey at times," he said. "Ain't that right, Smith?"

I smiled widely, filled with a sense of relief. "Roger that, Sergeant," I said. "Nosey as shit." That exchange ended my fears of Sergeant Kane and/or PFC Lopez turning me in. Those two were thick as thieves. I knew that if Sergeant Kane wasn't going to say anything, Lopez wouldn't. I respected Kane a great deal for that and was glad that he didn't decide to make things hard for me. I wondered if it would've been any different had Sergeant Norman seen me at the club. I never wanted to find out. After the incident with Kane, I gathered that most soldiers wouldn't care much if they knew, but I still needed to keep my guard up.

I wondered if there would ever be a day when it just didn't matter. When I didn't have to do so much sneaking around, but I knew that day was very far away. Just like Alex's platoon sergeant didn't care when he caught him and Murphy together, Sergeant Kane didn't care when he found out I was gay. When I thought of the two situations, it confirmed my suspicions that whether we were gay or straight, we were all just guys trying to make the best out of a difficult situation. Most soldiers were too concerned with their own lives and promotions and relationships to get too involved in the petty dramas of trying to get a soldier discharged. Hell, it was possible that anyone who tried to get a gay guy discharged would possibly be looked at even more negatively than the gay guy himself. You don't fuck with someone's livelihood. That was a no-go.

Alex and Murphy were very careful after their brush with almost being caught. They stayed together for a few years, even as Alex decided to leave the Army and Murphy decided to do a year-long deployment to Korea before he exited. Deployments were a way of saving money for many young soldiers. The money was not only tax-free, but included all sorts of bonuses for war-zone pay and hazard pay. He sounded resigned as he spoke of it, as if Murphy would be sharing the enormous bed in the one-bedroom apartment right now if he had any say in it.

I looked at Alex as he finished sharing the memories of his relationship with Murphy. I was struck with an overwhelming desire to make it better for him in any way I could. Instinctively, without thinking, I reached over and placed my palm softly on his cheek. He turned toward me. I saw the wistful look on his face change to shock and surprise. As if jolted by an electric current of knowledge, I removed my hand from his cheek and sat quickly back in my seat. I tried to figure out what the hell had just happened. *What was I thinking?* It was with a sense of abject horror that I realized I was in love with him.

Suddenly it all made sense. Most days I slogged through the day just to get to the end of it to head back to Alex's apartment for dinner. I thought of him nonstop, and he'd attained a near-mythical place in my mind. I listened to him; he listened to me. I cooked him wretched concoctions of hamburger helper that he smiled at and choked down. I shared with him each and every thing that happened in my life. I loved his spiky hair, loved his knobby knees and his junky apartment. I spent so much time with him because he made me feel alive in a way that no one else in my life ever had before.

When I said so, it took nothing more than a look at the shock on his face to realize that he didn't feel the same way. The realization filled me with a deep sense of hurt, though I didn't blame him. We both seemed frozen in place, unsure of where to go or what move to make next. "Look...I.... " he began.

"I know," I said, cutting him off.

I didn't want to hear that he wasn't in love with me. I certainly didn't want to hear anymore about how in love with his boyfriend he was. I was still trying to process the whole thing myself.

"Just drop me off?" I asked.

"Yeah," he said, and we pulled out of the area and drove off.

I arrived back on base for the first Saturday night in a very long time. I couldn't get what happened between Alex and me out of my mind. There was a deep part of me that wished it had turned out differently. I walked into my building and ran into Lantos, who was carrying a bag of laundry that was almost bigger than he was. I realized that I hadn't spoken to Lantos since Scott outed him to me.

"Hey, man," I said.

"What's up, Smith?"

"Got a sec?" I asked, looking from side to side conspiratorially.

"Yeah, man, what's up?"

"Um, I wanted to talk to you in private?" I said.

He seemed confused. "Uh, yeah, sure. You can come up to my room. I think my roommate Conch is out with his girlfriend."

Lantos's room was relatively junky. Half-eaten cans of ravioli were strewn around the kitchen area, and old copies of *Maxim* magazine lay on the coffee table. He escorted me into his small room and closed the door. He sat on his bed, and I sat on a chair in the middle of the room.

"So how come I never see you at Hide 'N Seek?" I asked.

He looked surprised for a second, then relaxed and began to chuckle. "So I see Scott told you about me, huh?"

"Yeah, he did," I said, laughing a little myself.

"Hide 'N Seek is for desperate guys with no boyfriends," he said. I recoiled a bit. "I mean...do you go?"

"Yeah, only every damned weekend. So you don't go.... That means you've got a boyfriend?" Lantos smiled.

"Yeah, I do. He's up at the Air Force Academy. He's a captain there. We've been hanging out for about six months."

"Where did you meet him?" I prodded.

"Gay.com," he admitted sheepishly.

I laughed. "Oh, and I'm the desperate one? What does he look like?"

Lantos hopped up excitedly and went into a drawer, pulling out a small photo. In it was a stunningly handsome white guy in a full-dress Air Force uniform. He was tall and broad-shouldered, with a wide and bright smile showcasing a strong, angular chin. I looked from the picture to Lantos, who was so fair-skinned I wouldn't be able to peg him as Latino if I didn't know any better. I wondered what kind of relationship he had with this guy. I felt a wave of jealousy come over me. I pictured the two of them together, then Alex and Murphy together. I tried to add myself into the equation, and it simply didn't fit. One of these things was not like the other. I tried very hard not to feel my difference, but in the gay world it was hard to ignore. For every guy in the club who engaged in conversation, there would be three or four more who didn't even acknowledge my presence.

Right before I met Scott, I briefly dated a younger white guy I'd met at Hide 'N Seek. I was attracted to his lean, muscular body and a sexy torso that seemed to go on for miles. I had a great time just hanging out with him and getting to know all of his friends. I'd hoped I could get accepted into this circle of gay friends who did things like barbecue in the park and have *Queer as Folk* viewing parties on Sunday nights. We dated for a few weeks before I was abruptly dropped without any hint of a reason why. Through the grapevine, I soon found out that his friends had issues with him dating a black man, and thus a mountain of insecurity about how my race related to the gay world was born.

Afterwards, when I would walk around in Hide 'N Seek and see the white male couples, it occurred to me that even though I was gay like them, they were in a place different than mine. Although we were in the same room, in the same space, we were worlds apart. That was what I felt when I looked at the photo of

Lantos's boyfriend. Nice white guys like him went for nice white or white-looking Latino guys like Lantos, not dark-skinned black guys like me. Why was it that most of the men I slept with were white? Was it that I subconsciously hated myself? Could it be that the sea of white faces that made up the majority of the small Colorado Springs gay community had influenced the idea of what I wanted my partners to look like? My strong attraction to the very Latino Alex complicated things even further. When I would think of this, all the pain of my childhood teasing, all the times I'd been called "Bubba" in basic training, and all my insecurities would roar back to the surface with the strength of a volcanic eruption. I would feel sad, lonely, and unwanted. I again looked at the dark-skinned hands that held the photo and wondered if anyone would ever accept them and the human being who was attached to them.

"Nice pic, man. He's hot," I said and quickly excused myself from the room. Lantos rushed after me, grabbing me by my shoulder before I made my exit. I looked back at him, and he had a deep sense of fragility and fear in his eyes.

"Look Smith, don't tell anyone, alright?" he pleaded. Of course I wouldn't.

Over the next few weeks, Alex and I began to make tentative steps toward the normalcy of our previous relationship. We didn't talk about my feelings for him. He didn't ask, and I didn't tell. When we would interact and do all the things we usually did together, I wondered if I was a pawn to him, just another toy like the men he teased in the club.

During long weekend days running errands in the city or the cold winter nights we spent huddling in his apartment, I would feel his eyes on me when he thought I wasn't paying attention. I wondered if he was studying me, perhaps trying to determine whether or not I would be a fun plaything for him. Though there was a part of me that knew he thrived on the attention, I was powerless over my unformed and immature emotions. I loved him. That I knew. I knew it as well as I knew that he would never, or could never, love me, despite his professed sexual attraction to me.

Through a stolen glance under the lights at the movie theater or a seemingly innocuous brush of his hand against my inner thigh as he left the couch to refill a drink, we danced a subtle waltz of sexual tension. That tension between us would simmer just beneath the surface of our interactions for months before exploding due to a combination of stress and fear.

There had recently been more and more talk about a potential war with Iraq, not only in the news, but within the base as well. As a result, our training increased exponentially. Brutally cold winter days were spent becoming more proficient with our weapons than ever before. Several nights were spent out in the field during weeklong training exercises. The squad members whom I'd become so used to over the past few years were restructured. Sergeant Brandon, Sergeant Norman, and PFC Wilton exited our platoon for another. A new sergeant took over the squad and brought with him three new members.

Sergeant Stanton was lean and wild-eyed. His bright blue eyes were dotted with pupils that always seemed to be dilated, as if he'd just been caught off guard in front of a bright camera flash. He was bursting with energy and would lead us through the training energetically, as if we were running out of time. Specialist Thompson was a tall, broadly built black guy with a low-key attitude, and Sergeant Thornden was a tall, jovial white frat-guy type from Georgia. He had a crooked moustache and always seemed to be smiling, just happy to be invited to the party. In addition to Lantos, Howard, and me, this made up our squad. As the time passed and the training became more intense, it occurred to me with more certainty that these were the men I would be heading off to war with.

The thought of having to put our training into action filled me with a fear that came from a place so deep and dark that I didn't even know it existed. As hard as I tried, I couldn't imagine myself in Iraq fighting in those battles in the same way that I'd seen the soldiers deployed in Afghanistan do. Something didn't seem right about Iraq, and it was a sentiment that was covertly shared between a great many of the younger soldiers.

Afghanistan was a necessary and needed war. It was fought because of a madman who'd attacked us on American soil and succeeded in killing thousands of people, but Iraq? This topic seemed a bit harder to define. Howard still remained my closest friend in the platoon. We would discuss the possibility of going to war in between going to the target range and during our lunchtime breaks on base. Howard was as afraid as I was, and we both knew that we could share opinions with one another. "Guess it's time to send more poor folks and black folks off to die," he'd say with a bitterly sarcastic tone that was much darker than usual. It made me think about exactly what I was sacrificing for this college education I wanted so badly.

I'd never thought too much about money. When I looked around at the other soldiers, regardless of what color they were, it was pretty clear that most of the guys on the ground didn't come from a lot of money. The only ones with college educations were the officers, and they were treated with contempt and a subliminal lack of respect. A common joke among the enlisted men revolved around the difference between the officers and enlisted men.

"What's the difference between a second lieutenant and a private first class? A private first class has been promoted."

Both privates and sergeants alike would share a laugh at the officer's expense, bonded by the shared struggles.

During the years, the prospect of going to college had begun to dominate my thoughts. I'd started to think about what I was sacrificing to do so. *Why me?* I thought. *Why do I have to risk so much just to go to college when there are so many people out there who'd never have to do this to go?*

Day in and day out, I was terrified at the prospect of going to war. I was also disturbed by how cavalierly the subject was broached by people in my platoon.

Sergeant Stanton would routinely comment that we were "probably gonna be parachuting into Baghdad."

The other soldiers would cheer and laugh at this, slapping him on the back. I was getting more terrified, not only by the prospect of going to war but by the excitement that the prospect seemed to engender in others. I wondered what it was really going to be like to serve in a wartime situation with these soldiers.

Checking the news became a daily ritual for me. I began to hear more chatter about weapons of mass destruction and the UN inspectors being allowed into Iraq to look for them. I prayed that they would be able to do their job and that they would find what they were looking for. I was deathly afraid of going overseas, and in those months I could see my fear reflected in the eyes of the others in the company, particularly the young ones. We seemed lost and afraid. We were all grappling with issues of life and death and war and peace. Very few young twenty-somethings would ever have to face this madness, but we were expected to do it with grim determination because it was the right thing to do.

As we continued the physical and mental march to war on the base, I found myself spending more time with Alex off base. He became more tender and understanding. I foolishly found myself falling deeper in love with him. His warm brown eyes had a way of calming my anxieties about the impending war as I shared them with him. In a move that surprised no one, the unit was notified that we would be deploying to Iraq in just a few short months. The intense period of unit restructuring and training that we'd been going through for the past few months had been undertaken to prepare for the deployment.

The days of training, fear, and doubt became like a blur to me. There was only one thing to distract my mind from what my body was about to do, and that was Alex. In those days and weeks I got lost within him. It was three weeks before we left for Iraq when I finally confessed to him how I felt.

We sat cuddled up on the couch, me innocuously laying my head on his lap as we awaited a press conference with President George W. Bush, who was rumored to be making an important announcement. I watched him as he stumbled over his words and looked nervously from side to side while announcing the commencement of combat operations in Iraq. I felt a deep contempt for him. I didn't know much about politics, but I knew that this was his doing. Though I was frightened, nervous, and angry, going AWOL never factored into my mind. I knew that I'd made a decision and that there were sacrifices in store in pursuit of my education. I never had an idea quite how grave they would turn out to be.

I looked up at Alex, and he looked at me. I could tell that he was nervous for me. He gave me a half smile, trying to provide some comfort and reassurance. I sat up and muted the television. I wanted to say so many things to him. I wanted to tell him that I loved him and that I wanted to spend the rest of my life with him. I wanted him to ask me to run away with him and be free. I wanted to say so many things, but I could get no words out. What I could do was take action.

I grabbed him by the back of the neck and kissed him more forcefully than I had ever kissed anyone. I felt a feeling deep in the pit of my stomach. It was new and foreign to me, like an internal earthquake that started from my insides and came roaring out in a breathy moan. At first I felt him resist, then he stopped doing so entirely. I broke away from him, looking him directly in his eyes as I positioned him under me, cradling his neck in my arms.

"I'm in love with you," I said in a voice only slightly more audible than a whisper. He looked at me with an expression that was at once both flippant and contrite.

"I'm sorry," he said.

My heart sank, but I was determined to stay in the moment.

Alex and I kissed that night. I reveled in the feeling of his lips on mine and the warm taste of his soft tongue against mine. My body was a bottomless pit of need, and he was giving me what I needed. I needed to be kissed, held, and loved. He tried to deny it, but I knew there was something real in the way he kissed me and held me that night. I fell asleep and woke up in the middle of the night with my head on his chest. I looked up at him, and he was sound asleep. I wanted to get up and turn the lights off and perhaps move into the bedroom, but I didn't. I just rested my head on his chest and inhaled as he squeezed his arms tighter around me. I watched the muted television that still played in the background and saw the first explosions that signified the official beginning of the invasion of the war in Iraq. Outside we were at war, but at home in his arms, I was safe.

## PART THREE

# THE WAR
# WITHIN

# CHAPTER 9

# SHOCK AND AWE

Though we were briefed on the necessity of making a "dark" landing, it still came as a nasty shock when the lights of the cabin went out, leaving the entire company in the darkness as the plane careened toward its midnight landing in Kuwait. Since there was nothing visible outside, the heavy double-thump of the plane landing was an unwelcome surprise, causing me to bite my tongue. I grimaced as I tasted the bland thickness of blood in my mouth. I inhaled deeply and swallowed it. If that was going to be the only injury I would sustain here, I'd consider myself lucky.

The last forty hours had been a blur of waiting games. We'd reported back to base at 6 a.m. the previous morning with all of our equipment, then were shuttled to a field house on the base where our family members could say their last goodbyes. I watched as husbands blinked back tears while hugging their wives and children. We were about to be sent halfway around the world for an undetermined amount of time, understandably heightening my emotions. If those in charge knew the time frame, they weren't telling us. What we did know was that the plan was to head to Kuwait first and then to Iraq. It had been nearly a month since the initial invasion. We had a decent handle on what was going on there, and the news seemed to be promising.

The various news anchors in the media seemed to be convinced that we would be greeted as liberators. By all accounts Saddam Hussein would be found soon, and none of us had any reason to doubt them. The images that were flowing out of Iraq were ones of explosions and bombing, yes, but also of stability and hope. When I watched footage of liberated Iraqis taking down a statue of Saddam Hussein at a busy intersection, I hoped we were doing the right thing, regardless of my reservations about the reasons we were truly there.

Kuwait was the same dusty sandbox that we'd left several months ago. I was again struck by how brown everything was. Brown vistas were visible from all directions, and the overpowering color of the sand seemed to be sucking the color out of even the sky. It was as if we were trapped in an *Arabian Nights*-themed version of a snow globe, but instead of snow, we were greeted by the sting of hot sand that blew through the merciless gusts of warm wind.

We were scheduled to train in Kuwait for the first three weeks. After the training we were to convoy into Iraq through Baghdad and up to a point that would be determined later. In those first few weeks, the new squad members got to know each other. We joked and laughed about where we were in order to cut the tension regarding why we were there. Regardless, I stuck more to my relationship with Howard than any of the other soldiers. He was always my best friend in the unit, but now, inching closer to war, he was something more. Howard was now my confidant. He knew I was gay.

In the weeks leading up to the deployment, I found myself falling deeper and deeper for Alex. He remained vocal about the fact that he didn't share my feelings. I didn't care. I was finally experiencing what love was, and though something felt incomplete about the lack of reciprocation, I was intoxicated nonetheless. Ironically enough, my feelings were just as he'd described when we talked about his love for Murphy. I thought of all the love songs I'd heard and how I never quite understood them until I fell for him. In fact, they all reminded me of him. During pre-deployment training operations, I thought of nothing but Alex. The feelings I had for him in my heart would brighten even the most gray and dreary days on base.

We continued to play around with each other in those weeks. When I would look into his eyes for a connection, I noticed that he would look away in a somewhat embarrassed manner. It didn't matter to me that Alex didn't return my feelings, because the sex was more enjoyable and meaningful than it was with all the other men I'd had sex with in the past. This wasn't just any stranger I was sharing my body with; it was someone I loved. It had to mean something that he had sex with me, even if he was adamant about not being in love with me as I was with him.

Soon enough, the time to deploy came. The night before, he dropped me off back at my barracks room, as I'd already turned my car in for storage during the deployment. We sat in the car outside of my barracks for what seemed like hours as I watched the sun fall on Colorado Springs for the last time for a long while. I was again struck by how perfectly aligned the colors of the sky seemed to be. It was a brilliant milieu of orange, blue, and a hint of purple as the two mixed and day became night. I was in love with Alex, yes, but what I was unprepared for was how hard it seemed to be to say goodbye to him. I knew when I left the car that I'd be leaving him, with our next meeting at a date and time that was yet to be determined.

I looked over at Alex, and his face was filled with a knowing kindness. He didn't love me like I loved him. That I knew. I knew that the man who owned his heart was an entire world away in

Korea. He knew that I loved him, and yet he was still here. Why? Was he supporting the troops or soaking up the attention? Or, perhaps, he loved me just a bit. I thought that maybe the truth lay somewhere in the murky middle of all these possibilities. Day had officially turned to night, and as we sat in his beat-up old Honda Civic, I couldn't find any words to say. I knew I had exhausted them all and said all that I needed to say and possibly far too much. He knew how I felt, that I loved him. He knew that I was going to be a scared gay soldier in Iraq who was going to be holding onto that love for dear life, because it was all I had.

"Promise you'll write me?" I asked him, and he smiled.

"Of course," he said.

The sun had gone down, and the car was shrouded in darkness. I could see his face only via the glow of the streetlights that were now starting to turn on around us. In an impulsive, reckless instant, I leaned over and kissed him tenderly. At that moment I didn't care if my entire platoon were to happen upon us. I couldn't control myself and knew that these final precious seconds were not to be wasted with fearful warning glances. I was sick of the glances and sick of the split-second questioning that had to go into every move I made when we were together in public. I relished the moment, trying my hardest to make a mental imprint of the feeling of his lips and the soft brush of his eyelashes against mine.

"I love you, Alex," I said and exited the car as if it were on fire. I didn't look back. I walked back into the barracks that night utterly destroyed, a bundle of exposed nerves and emotions set to be frayed at the slightest provocation. All of the pressures that had been building up over the past few years seemed to boil within me, and I wanted to scream, yell, and cry. I hated that Alex didn't love me, but I hated myself more for loving him in spite of that knowledge. What did that say about me? The situation brought up dark questions that had always lain within me but that I'd been too afraid to ask. Did anyone love me? Did I deserve to be loved?

My family's aloof reaction to my impending deployment provided an unwelcome answer to that question.

My mother was well into her recovery from the surgery to remove the tumor in her colon, as well as the rounds of chemotherapy she was forced to endure. Her once thinning hair was starting to grow back. She had gained a great deal of weight since being officially declared in remission by her team of doctors. Husband number three was out of the picture, and she was living life as a single woman once again while trucking all across the country in her eighteen-wheeler. Whatever emotional walls were broken down by her near-death experience were built back up again though, seemingly with reinforcements. Our conversations were biweekly at best and never lasted longer than a few minutes at a time. I never talked to her about my fears of the deployment or of the potential to lose my life at such an early age. The perfunctory last call with my mother ended only with a lukewarm "Be careful Robert, and promise to send me your address so I can write you."

As the words were being said, I knew it said something about that particular relationship I was happy and satisfied with, even the small bone of parental concern that was thrown my way. *Be careful*, I thought. *Your twenty-year-old son could possibly get his head blown off, and all you can say is fucking "be careful"?* My father was my father, too concerned with his impending retirement and his finances to muster up any concern for me. After trying unsuccessfully to build at least a solid phone relationship with him, I gave up in frustration, waiting to see how long it would take for him to call and check up on me. I waited for a call that never happened.

As fucked up as I knew the relationship with Alex was, it had nothing on the one I had with my parents. I knew that all three were interlinked, the common denominator was being constantly unfulfilled. I needed love and acceptance. I knew that the time for analysis was over. I had a war to go fight.

As I walked into the barracks, I was afraid and nervous. I didn't want to be alone. I soon found myself outside of Howard's door. I knocked tentatively and was relieved to see him open the door. As always, he was a soothing, comforting presence, and I remained thankful for our friendship. His room was an absolute mess of half-packed bags and equipment. I assumed that in typical Howard fashion, he'd waited until the very last minute to start packing. It was only 8 p.m., though, and we weren't scheduled to report to the unit until 6 a.m., so there was plenty of time.

"What's up, Smith?" he asked and smiled that reassuring smile of his.

"I'm all packed. Didn't have anything else to do. Don't want to be alone," I said truthfully and was relieved as he smirked and let me in.

We sat for hours and talked while he packed and repacked his bags. He eventually whittled the large mess down into three tightly packed duffel bags, ready to be shipped via cargo plane to the Middle East. Neither of us could believe what we were about to do, and it remained the elephant in the room as he packed up. I looked at the clock and realized it was nearing midnight. The weight of the deadline crashed down on my shoulders in a way that it never had before. In twenty-four hours I was going to be fighting in a war. I was about to be issued real ammo for my weapons and expected to use it in enemy fire.

I thought back to all the war movies I'd ever seen. I knew none of them were going to prepare me for what was about to happen. This was going to be modern city warfare, not the WWII-style trenches of *Band of Brothers* or the forest warfare of *Full Metal Jacket*. It was becoming more real by the second, and I wasn't sure if I was ready. The room got very silent as if my thoughts of war and life or death were being telegraphed from myself to Howard. I looked over at him, and his already heavy face seemed even weightier. I could see the stress of the impending deployment all over his face. It was in the deepening cracks of his laugh lines and the lines in his brow. The mental shadow seemed to make his already dark skin even darker, as if his skin was changing shades like a mood ring to reveal the happenings beneath the surface.

"Do you think we're gonna die?" I asked him quietly. He looked up, and it was as if he'd aged fifteen years in the last fifteen minutes.

"Don't know, Smith," he said.

"I'm...not heterosexual," I said suddenly.

"What?"

"I'm gay."

"Oh, I know."

I couldn't believe what I was hearing, but not because I was afraid that he would turn me in. His revelation meant that I hadn't been as careful as I thought for the past three years.

"What? How?"

He looked over at me as he sat on his duffel bag and immediately and mischievously cocked one eyebrow and chuckled. "Come on, Smith."

Couldn't argue with that logic.

My admission and his surprising reaction brought about so many questions that I bombarded him over the next hour.

"Does anybody else know?" I asked.

"I doubt it. I knew something was up when the stripper story got around, but that was so long ago, and so many transferred soldiers ago, I don't think it caught on with the newer guys," he said. "Plus, of course I would know. I'm the only one you ever talk to when you're around, which isn't often. If the others thought you were gay, they'd probably think the two of us were fucking."

I thought about what he said, and he was definitely right. There was a reason why I wasn't around. I thought that perhaps it was time to let Howard in on it.

"There's someone I've been hanging out with. I'm kind of in love with him," I said, and Howard looked around a bit nervously.

"Look, you don't have to hear this if you don't want to," I said.

"Goddamn, Smith, where the fuck else do I have to go?"

I smiled and launched into a babbling litany of the Alex situation. My first love had made my life a living soap opera for the past few months. I told Howard everything, expelling the story like vomit. I needed to get it out of my system. Howard nodded and listened to the entire story. As I talked, I heard myself; I sounded like a love-struck kid. For the first time, I started to question why I was putting myself through this. I could tell by the look in Howard's eyes he was asking the same question. When I finished the long, drawn-out story, I looked at the alarm clock. It was nearly 2 a.m., and I was tired. When it was all over, I looked over at Howard and knew that he was a true friend. Anyone who'd patiently listened to my teenage girl ramblings for the past hour could honestly be classified as nothing less. I was glad to have him and especially glad that we were going on this deployment together.

"So do I sound stupid?" I asked him.

"No, man," he said. "You just sound like you're in love."


Upon our arrival in Kuwait, we had absolutely no access to media of any kind. Our vision of what exactly was happening up north in Iraq depended completely on conjecture and hearsay. The commanders and sergeants took that as license to conduct gritty and grueling training. They felt it was a good way to pass our time while awaiting deployment orders in Kuwait. The days were long and hot. We were weighed down with seventy pounds of armor and equipment while we did our training. We did trench training as well as urban warfare training, learning how to enter and clear rooms and areas with a five-man stack formation.

The five-man stack was a tried-and-true method of fighting urban warfare. We'd spent a great deal of time training this method back in the states pre-deployment. The five-man stack consisted of the rear man running to the front of the line and kicking down the door. They would then pull rear security as the rest of the men piled in, each focused on different directions that the threat could be coming from. We knew that doing this in reality was what would be required in a few short weeks, so there was no half stepping or complaining. We repeated the movements with a grim determination to get it all right. Soon, we weren't going to be training; we would be fighting for our lives. The time for weak links or bullshit was over. I looked at the faces of my squad members and saw the same determination and fight that was in my heart. We were sweaty, grimy, and filthy, but we were soldiers, and this was our job. There was no running water or hot shower where we were. Every five days or so we would take a bottle of water and give ourselves a scrub-down, usually under the cover of nightfall.

The weeks in Kuwait were dedicated exclusively to honing our skills. We would only stop for food, water, or to turn in for the night once darkness overtook the sky. I noticed the crippling fear that enveloped me slowly starting to dissipate. I was becoming more comfortable with the movements required of me. I was certainly comfortable with my machine gun. What I was carrying in my hands was enough to take a lot of men down should the situation arise. Even I wasn't immune to the charms of that much power in my hands. What was within them could save lives...or bring death.

I silently prayed at the end of every sweaty, hot, tiring day that I wouldn't have to kill anyone. As time drew closer, I became more sobered by the nature of what I was there to do. I knew that

I wouldn't hesitate if I needed to engage. The feeling was all-consuming and frightening in its power. I thought about all the soldiers I was there with, the sergeant-level family men and the younger soldiers like me. I hoped and prayed that all of us would make it through this intact. I was again angered that we were the ones who were forced to do this. My mind was not yet sophisticated enough to piece together the myriad inequalities that pushed some people into military service while others had rich families who sent them to college. I was puzzled by a murky and unfocused sense of unfairness. Why should any of us have to die, and what exactly is it we would be dying for? Even with all the articles, news stories, and briefings from our company commanders, I still found myself with unanswered questions. Did we really let the UN weapons inspectors do their jobs? Was Saddam enough of a threat to America to risk our lives? Were there really weapons of mass destruction?

I thought back to my conversation with the first sergeant that dark night during the first Kuwait deployment. He looked on and talked about "that motherfucker to the north." I had serious doubts in my mind about whether picking a fight with Iraq was really about WMDs and their threat to the American public. I truly believed it was about George W. Bush finishing what his father started with Desert Storm. He was playing with the lives of the soldiers who would have to risk everything for him to settle an old score. I knew he was getting what he wanted, and it was all of our lives that were going to be on the line for it. Whatever I felt then didn't matter, because I was there, and I needed to focus on my training if I wanted to get through this alive.

The motor pool where the tanks were held was a hot, dusty sandbox. I stood with my fellow squad members as we took in all the chaos that unfolded before us. Helicopters took off and landed less than a mile away, and tank mechanics ran around furiously making last-minute fixes on the vehicles while the drivers struggled to secure the gear on the outside of them. My squad members and I were the muscle, the hired guns, and we made sure to just stay out of the way while everything was getting set up. I looked to my left to see Howard with his same expression of bemused contentment and to my right to see Sergeant Stanton. For the past three weeks of training, he'd taken on a gung-ho persona that felt reminiscent of someone who'd maybe seen one too many war movies. He always seemed jittery and on edge. His eyes were filled with an unwavering intensity that was unsettling and a bit scary. His teeth were spacey, and his gums jutted forward prominently when he spoke. I wondered if it had anything to do with his Russian lineage. He had a lean frame and lacked any fat on his face. It gave him a look that was almost emaciated, and when he smiled, he reminded me of a department store skeleton mask that one would find during Halloween.

When practicing the five-man stack in the makeshift urban-warfare area, it was always Sergeant Stanton who pushed us to go again, ensuring that we got it right.

"C'mon, Smith, do it again!" he'd say while pacing furiously if I missed a step or if I was too slow getting back to my position as rear guard after kicking down the door. Sergeant Stanton was a new addition to the platoon just weeks before we deployed. I knew he felt tremendous pressure to succeed and for us to be successful soldiers.

I couldn't shake the fact that he seemed to be enjoying the experience. The excitement that came across when he would talk about our future missions in Iraq was disturbing.

"I just want to find that motherfucker, Saddam," he'd say, grinning that crazy grin to all of us during chow in the makeshift cafeteria. Howard and I would look at each other knowingly. In private, one night after a long day of training, Howard confided in me his thoughts regarding Stanton during our early evening walk to the cafeteria.

"Now that," he said, "is the kind of motherfucker who will get you killed."

Whether that was true or not remained to be seen. As we prepared to cross the border into an unknown, hostile war zone, I tried my best to put my suspicions about his behavior on the back burner and focus on the job at hand.

The squad piled into the tank that we'd be riding up in. I felt the weight of all the gear as I moved up into position. I was carrying my M249 machine gun, body armor, a supply belt, and a Kevlar helmet. We were going to pull side security for the convoy while riding on the top of the tanks. I felt deeply uncomfortable with that amount of exposure. We were in the middle of fifteen various tanks and cargo trucks, and I could imagine my head in the crosshairs of an insurgent's sniper rifle. As we piled into the tank, I could see that Howard and even Stanton shared my worry. We were first up. As a squad we would rotate pulling outward security through the roof of the tank while the others stayed in the back of the tank and rested. I heard the roar of the various tank engines as they started. We pulled out of the staging area in Kuwait in a cloudy blast of hot sand. It would be a long time before any of us returned to a non-hostile country.

When we crossed the border into Iraq just a few hours later, I noticed an immediate difference in the scenery. The streets of Iraq had a look of war-strewn desperation to them that was hard to stomach. Everywhere I looked, I saw Arabic language that I couldn't understand. The roadsides were littered with abandoned fighter vehicles that the Saddam loyalists had used in their futile attempts to defend themselves against the American invaders. Small, brown Iraqi children would come out of nowhere sometimes, running and waving at the tanks. We were moving slowly enough in the fifteen to twenty vehicle convoy for them to keep up with to a point. They wore tattered pants and T-shirts with logos and brands on them that were distinctly from the 1980s. Their high voices were filled with joy and hope as they chanted, "America! USA!" with bright smiles and hands extended in the thumbs-up position. Many times they were alone, but sometimes older, hardened Iraqi men who looked at us with contempt and distrust joined them. I smiled and waved at the children. They were ignorant of the fact that I was doing so with a semi-automatic weapon positioned directly in front of me.

When I saw the faces of the adult men, I gripped my weapon just a little bit tighter. I pressed the butt of my weapon deeper into my shoulder in case any unforeseen events required me to have it in position immediately. I would look each man in his eyes above the heads of the small, simple children they were protecting. I matched the contempt in their eyes with steely resolve in mine. They needed to know that I wouldn't hesitate to pull the trigger in case they wanted to try anything. I found myself locking eyes with most of them until we were safely out of view.

I wondered what they thought of us, American infidels who'd come to violently overthrow the regime. I saw a lot of children and a lot of angry Iraqi men during those days on the convoy. I thought a lot about how I would feel if the situation were reversed. What if my country had been bombed into submission for reasons that were still murky? What was it about America that determined we were always right in using force? If we were to listen to what was told to us by the government and our leaders, Saddam Hussein was a bloodthirsty tyrant. He was out to unleash weapons of mass destruction onto an unsuspecting American public. I just couldn't allow myself to be convinced. Were the 9/11 attackers not based in Afghanistan? The shift from talking about Afghanistan to focusing on Iraq was so swift and smooth, I didn't even realize it happened.

All I knew was that after returning from the first six-month deployment in Kuwait in mid-2002, all talk had suddenly shifted to Iraq. I wanted to trust what was being told to us, but the questions in my head wouldn't allow me to do so fully. Was blind trust a prerequisite for serving the country, or did it just make it easier to do the job?

My days were spent asking a lot of those questions in my head. Being in Iraq had turned the mood somber for all of us. I looked into the faces of my fellow soldiers and could tell they were lost in their own thoughts as much as I was in mine. After four days of convoying through the cities and fields of Iraq, we finally arrived at our first destination. The small city was named Samarra, and we came right on the heels of a firefight that was happening between Marines and Iraqi insurgents in the city.

As my squad members and I dismounted our vehicle and walked into the city, there was a faint air of chaos around. I knew that we'd just missed a hell of a battle. We gathered up as a platoon right outside of an abandoned building that had been taken over just hours before. We were briefed on our first mission. The company had received reliable intel that the insurgents who were responsible for the attack we'd just missed were holed up in a mosque on the outskirts of town. We were going to attack right after dawn. As the company commander briefed us, he motioned to a mosque just behind him in the distance. I could see the roof of it against the backdrop of the hazy Iraq sun. It looked a bit like the Capitol Building, only with a purple metallic color and a very distinct point coming out of the roof. That building was where it was going to happen, our first mission.

We pulled the platoon's vehicles and equipment into the area we were to sleep in. It was an abandoned, bombed-out building that was rumored to have once housed a private school for the children of Samarra. I walked to the gate for my first guard shift with Howard. We stood on either side of the concrete double doors, hearing the faint sounds of the life that went on in the city as we were in the planning stages of executing an attack on it. We could hear the faraway sounds of children laughing and of mothers admonishing their children in the Arabic that neither Howard nor I spoke. I could feel the tension between us as the gravity of what we were to do in just eight short hours sank in. We were scheduled to get up at 4:30 a.m. to execute our attack. I looked over at Howard, who wore a grim, frightened expression on his face.

"Are we gonna die tomorrow?" I asked nervously.

He looked over at me cautiously. I realized in that moment that I didn't want the truth from that question. What I wanted was for him to reassure me that everything was going to be all right and that nobody was gonna die here, least of all the two of us.

"I don't know," he said.

He started to say something else, but the silence of the moment was shattered by a screech. It was brakes on an old Toyota truck barreling toward the gate. Howard and I brought our weapons to the ready with lightning-fast speed. My right index finger cupped the trigger on my machine gun. The car stopped suddenly as Howard and I approached.

"Stop right there! Get out of the fucking car!" we both yelled nearly in unison. The figure in the car sat silent and did nothing. I thought about the suicide bombers who were popping up in cities all over Iraq. I felt the weight of the trigger on my right index finger comforting me, goading me. I wanted so badly to squeeze it and eliminate the perceived threat. If I were to kill this man, would anyone blame me? How on earth did people make these decisions at the spur of the moment? I knew that I'd come very close to firing on the vehicle.

"Get out of the fucking car!" I yelled again, and at this point I realized that my heart was beating through my chest.

My blood seemed to be racing, and I could literally feel my body getting warmer. The feel of the trigger on my finger was becoming more and more inviting. I would have to shoot. It was only the door swinging open that stopped me. I followed the man with the barrel of my weapon as he stepped out of the car. He was old, frail, and disoriented. I did a quick visual scan of his body for any lumps in his clothing that could be indicative of explosives, and I found none. When I looked at his face, I could tell that he was frightened. He raised his hands in deference to us and continued to move forward. "Stop right fucking there!" I screamed, and shook the weapon and its barrel in his direction to make my point.

He started to scream in Arabic. I didn't understand what he was saying, and both Howard and I continued to shake our weapons at him.

"Cover me," Howard said as he went over to the man, forced him down to his knees and gave him a pat down.

"He's clean," Howard said and looked at me. "I think he's lost."

I looked at Howard incredulously. "Get him the fuck outta here, then!"

Howard took his weapon down and looked the man in the eyes. He pointed in the direction of the road. "Go! Go!"

The man seemed to get an idea of what Howard was saying. He hurried to his car and sped off down the road. Howard and I watched the truck careen into the distance until it was a mere speck obscured by the dust that it kicked up in the road.

I was sweaty, and my eyes were wild. The man was long gone, but my heart was still beating out of my chest. Howard and I looked at each other in shock. I was breathing hard, as if I'd just run a marathon.

"I almost fucking shot him," I said, almost to myself. "I almost fucking shot him."

After my guard shift I laid my sleeping bag out on the hard granite floor of the building that we'd taken over. The other guys in the platoon were spread out in the same area. Everyone was struggling to get even the most minuscule amount of sleep before it was time to fulfill our duties in the morning, but I was wide awake. I was on my back, and when I looked to my left, I could see the night sky through a hole in the wall that was at some point long ago a window. *I could've fucking shot him,* I thought as I struggled to find sleep. The thought of taking a life was terrifying to me. I knew just a few weeks in that I would never again be the same person I was before crossing that border. I was fearful of who I would become if I was forced to take a life. I wasn't afraid that it would break me, but that it would perhaps unlock something in me that I didn't want unlocked—the desire to kill. I was in the only place on earth where it would be allowed, perhaps even championed. If that person existed in me on some level deep beneath the surface or within my subconscious, I never wanted to meet him. I never wanted to turn into that monster. I realized I was afraid of Sergeant Stanton because I knew that a killer lived inside of him, just waiting for the opportunity to come out. Eventually I managed to banish the thoughts and slip into a thin sleep. I needed all the rest I could get. We had a long day ahead of us in the morning.

# CHAPTER 10

# DAYS OF BLUNDER

An ancient glass bottle cracked beneath my boot, breaking the silence we'd tried so hard to maintain on the early morning streets of Samarra. Lantos was directly ahead of me in the stack against the outside wall of the complex we were invading. He whipped his head around toward me in anger, silently admonishing me as he raised an index finger to his lips. I shot him a look of contrition and continued my slow, steady movements against the wall. The sky was pitch-black, though dark-orange hints of the early morning sun could be seen in the distance.

We were briefed upon leaving our staging area that we would attack directly at sunrise. We'd walked through the streets of the city for forty-five minutes in darkness. I jumped at every little sound I heard from the streets. I was consumed with a pathological fear that insurgents would be prepared to jump out at any moment to slaughter us all. We would become casualties in the Iraq War, reducing us to names to be scrolled on the bottom of the television screen during the evening news.

I looked directly in front of us at the other squad that was moving against the wall opposite us. I wondered what they were thinking. Were they going through the same things as I was? Did they fear death, or was it something that never crossed their minds? I had seen fear in Lantos's eyes when he'd looked back at me earlier. I knew that Howard and Thompson were afraid, but what about Stanton? I got the feeling that he loved this, and he couldn't wait for what lie behind the enormous gates that led into the complex. He looked back at us and gave us the signal to crouch. We stayed that way until the sun started to come up. Stanton had control of the radio and communication with our tank drivers and gunners. The plan was for the ground squads to attack first and then for the tanks to come roaring in behind us. They were to secure a perimeter as we cleared each individual building.

It was time to go. I felt a now-familiar sensation come back to me. My heart started to race, the blood started to flow in my veins, and I was ready for action. It was a peculiar feeling. I didn't want to be in the situation, although I was completely committed to it. The fear of certain death seemed to override the fear of inaction. I couldn't for the life of me understand why some people just physically shut down when it is time to go into battle. How could you when there is so much at risk, least of all your own life? Sergeant Stanton and the opposite squad member gave themselves the countdown, and we were off.

The complex was enormous. I was thrown off by the sheer size of it. There had to be at least ten buildings within it, and some had multiple levels. We started out on the right, and the first building was located to the left. Our squad pulled security as the other squad cleared the first building. It was a small building that had been an original target of the "shock and awe" campaign. Shattered glass and bricks lay all around the complex. From what I could see of the building, it had been looted for all supplies a few days before. I watched the squad do their stack as they cleared the building and felt a sense of pride as they executed it flawlessly. We heard an "all clear" come from inside the building, and it was time to head on to the next one. I felt like a mouse in a maze as we headed toward the next building, a multilevel office building. I looked back as a flurry of other soldiers from the company scattered into the area, each clearing one of the buildings that made up the massive complex.

Since there were so many soldiers in the area, there was no need for me to pull rear security outside. I followed my squad into the building. We walked in to see a long hallway that led into what seemed like at least ten to fifteen rooms. Sergeant Stanton looked back at me, his usual wild-eyed intensity replaced by a quiet focus that I found oddly comforting.

"Smith, we're gonna do the four-man stack in these rooms, okay? I need you to keep eyes on the hallway out here. If you see anything, shoot it," he said.

"Roger that, Sergeant."

As rear man, I kept eyes on the hallway, ensuring that there were no surprises in store for the squad. If I saw anything, I wouldn't have hesitated to shoot for even a second. The squad quickly cleared the room, and they moved from door to door, clearing out every room while I kept eyes on the hallway. It was an old office building. The doors all led into one-room offices, so it didn't take long for them to be cleared. After an hour of this, we'd cleared all fifteen rooms and made our way to the exit of the building at the other end. The building was all clear.

When we exited the building, the morning sun was in full effect. I was taken aback by the sheer amount of soldiers that were roaming around the complex at all points. We continued this way for a while as we cleared each and every one of the buildings. The longer we continued, the more we realized that the complex was empty. Whatever intel had been received about insurgents camping out here was obviously wrong. We were very much alone.

When we got the final all clear, the soldiers all relaxed a bit as the tanks roared into the complex. They took their positions at the front, near the gates. We sat in a half circle as a squad, took off our gear, and dug into our MREs. They were bland and tasteless, yet filling and medically stacked with protein and nutrients that were designed to keep our strength up. As we devoured our food, we shared the kind of foolishness and jokes that could only come from soldiers who were greatly relieved at not having seen any action for the day.

"This motherfucker was in the hallway just shakin'," Thompson said through a mouthful of food, motioning toward me with his spoon and grinning warmly.

"Man, I bet you would've lit up a thirty-five-round burst if you saw a fuckin' rat." I smiled and laughed it off.

The truth was he was probably right. Thompson finished his one-man comedy routine. He remained blithely unaware of the flecks of food being expelled from his mouth. I looked over at Sergeant Stanton, who remained grim and wordless. I felt the smile leave my face when I realized that he was disappointed for the same reason the rest of us were relieved. I wanted to say something to break his mood, but I realized I had nothing to say. At that moment, Stanton officially started to give me the creeps. I wondered what kind of man would be disappointed at the lack of a near-death experience, but the thought was so disturbing I immediately put it out of my mind.

"Would you take a look at this!" someone screamed, and immediately we all jumped up with our weapons at the ready. We walked over and were greeted by a sight that inspired large smiles on all of our faces, even Sergeant Stanton's. One of the soldiers had uncovered a makeshift shower, complete with running water from a hose that had been jerry-rigged to resemble a showerhead. We were all glad because we hadn't showered in weeks.

The combination of sweat, dirt, and sand had created a thick film on my body that was becoming increasingly hard to scrub off. I'd done the best I could to stay clean, but our "whore baths" consisted of nothing more than splashes of cold water on our face and underneath our arms. Crotch rot was also a concern. We rarely removed our underwear or pants, and the sweat mixed in with the friction between the inner thighs resulted in extreme chafing of the skin. Though we joked around about the fact that we hadn't showered in so long, it felt disgusting and was made worse by the fact that we had no clue when a shower was coming. We smelled, no doubt, and I would imagine little cartoon stink lines coming from our bodies, like the character Pig-Pen in the *Peanuts* comics

The platoon members excitedly rushed over to the makeshift shower as if their favorite *Playboy* playmate was giving out free handjobs. I dutifully stayed back to watch the gear as I watched the guys strip down. Pale white bodies stood in line in various stages of undress. I noticed immediately that the dirt and grime was much more noticeable on them than it was on me. Some were so dirty it was as if they'd literally wallowed around in dirt right before getting in line. Everyone was excited to be getting a shower, however random the location.

When it was my turn to use the shower, I happily stripped and ran in. It was little more than a hose over a pile of rocks in an enclosed shed, but it was running water. Someone had rustled up some soap from a care package. I giddily rubbed it all over my body, acutely aware of the fact that countless guys in the platoon had probably used this same bar of soap. The water was ice-cold, and my body broke into gooseflesh and involuntary shivers as the mid-morning air hit me. I relished the feeling of the soapy foam all over my body. I looked down as the dirt from my body mixed in with the water to create brownish-gray splashes on the white rocks. For just a moment as the cool water washed over me, I felt far away from all the stresses. I was thankful that the morning's mission had been successful. I could've stayed in that place all day, but loud banging on the sheet metal door of the shed let me know that my time was up.

For the next three weeks we stayed at the complex and made it a makeshift home. We trained, pulled guard duty, and took time to explore it. Different platoons took over different buildings, and our squad took over the first building that we cleared. We spent lazy days laying out in the different rooms, speculating on what they used to be, and talking about life back in America. We spoke of America a great deal. We wondered if people still remembered that we were overseas. It struck me as somehow unreal that Americans could be going about their daily lives without giving a thought to those of us fighting for the country a world away. It was a feeling that we all shared, though letters and care packages helped to alleviate the fear of being forgotten. I had not gotten a letter unlike some of the soldiers in my company, who'd started receiving things practically upon arrival in Kuwait. I hoped to get one soon. I'd taken extra pains to make sure that Alex, my parents, and my extended family got the basic mailing address. I was looking forward to corresponding with Alex and perhaps rebooting some of my other relationships. Maybe I just needed to be in a life-or-death situation for people to realize how important I was to them. On those days when we sat in the room talking about life and our hopes and dreams, I felt closer to the members of my platoon than I had in the past.

When the squad members started to discuss women and sex, I'd let them go on and remain silent. Lantos and I would exchange knowing looks, then as a joke between the two of us we'd join in the conversation. We would pick the most random female celebrity and try to outdo one another with filthy and graphic depictions of what we would do to them. Howard sometimes laughed out loud at this, and I would continue on, grinning at him the whole time with a twinkle in my eye.

Those days were calm and almost serene. Samarra had calmed down considerably since we'd come to the city. The nights were silent, unmarred by gunfire or sounds of battles in the distance. We'd even set up communications with a larger base nearby and were treated to one hot meal a day for the first time in weeks. The first meal was breakfast, and although there was a part of me that knew the food was bland and mediocre, I still relished it. The scrambled eggs, potatoes, and bacon were real food, comfort food. Everyone devoured it, afraid it would disappear at any moment. It was in those days that we came together almost like a family. The bombed-out complex in Samarra, Iraq, was our home.

A few weeks later, we found out that we would stay at the complex for a few more days before we moved to our final destination. We were going to a small city just outside of Kirkuk where a larger military base had been set up. The news was met with overwhelming enthusiasm. We'd been on the convoy for weeks. We were starting to tire of the constant travel, lack of stability, and the constant tension of being exposed in unfamiliar territories. I wondered if anyone at the top really knew what was going on.

Before coming to Samarra, the platoon had spent nearly two weeks at a checkpoint we'd set up on a road in the middle of nowhere. The rest of the company was further back where they'd staged at abandoned palaces previously owned by the Imperial Guard. We had contact with them only via radio. We created a break in the road via a thin strand of razor wire that was joined in the middle by small hooks that could be easily separated by the soldiers stationed on either side of the street. If a driver really wanted to pass through, he could have done it without much of a problem. We wouldn't have had much recourse but to go after him. Though that never happened, I felt the same fear in my legs and tightening in my stomach with each car that we stopped and searched. Each car was a potential ticking time bomb, as was I.

For ten days we stayed in this position at the checkpoint, and after a few days it became a source of visible tension among the lower-level soldiers. No one really knew what we were doing there. We knew not to ask our sergeants, not only for fear of being insubordinate, but because we knew they didn't know either.

"Why don't you worry about doing your fucking job, soldier?" was Stanton's typical response when I dared ask a question about our next steps as a platoon.

I should've known; my job as a specialist-ranked rifleman was to be seen and not heard. I felt if I knew what was in store for us, it would help alleviate the almost unbearable tension within me. We eventually hit the road again and continued north. The lack of direction and communication about what was happening was a common occurrence that would continue through the rest of the deployment.

It was early evening when we finally pulled into Riyadh after yet another full day on the convoy heading north. The sun was setting rapidly in the west. I stared blankly out into the open fields as the stuttering motion of the vehicle made my Kevlar helmet shake loosely on my head. We were informed that the company would be taking over three different locations in the town. We would be stationed at an abandoned school, an abandoned train station, and an abandoned grain factory. My platoon was scheduled to take over the grain factory. As we approached, I got a bird's-eye view of the complex.

It was roughly the size of a football field, surrounded on all sides by a thick concrete wall that was about fifteen feet tall. There were different buildings for living located on one side, and the nuts-and-bolts factory equipment was on the other side, separated by a long field populated with dead grass. I watched the wind whip the sand up into a mini tornado, sending grains of sand crashing against the buildings and onto the stairs that led into each of the buildings. The all-consuming fear that had preceded previous missions wasn't present here.

After being given the all clear, Lantos and I jumped off of the tanks and pushed the gates open from either side. The three tanks that comprised our platoon roared in behind us. The remaining platoon squads scurried out of the tanks and into position on the ground. We cleared the buildings in record time, finding nothing as I assumed we would.

As the sun set on another long day in Iraq, our squad settled in a building closest to the gate. We unloaded our gear off the tanks and set up in the two rooms that were adjacent to one another. Lantos, Howard, Thompson, and I were in one room, Thornden and Stanton in the other. We were told not to get too comfortable though, as we were to have a weekly rotation through the three areas as a platoon

The company's communications base was set up at an abandoned train station closer to the center of town. The revolving week-long rotations were a respite from our long, dreary days spent not doing much of anything. The train station was massive with a shower area and a satellite television. Word spread around the company that the higher-ups didn't like the soldiers watching CNN International, so it was banned. The television was always tuned to one of the international video channels, where Beyoncé's video "Crazy in Love" dominated the airwaves.

When the video would come on, everything happening with the company's functions would stop. Privates, sergeants, and captains alike would be transfixed by the aggressive sexuality of her movements. While it was doing nothing for me, I found it humorous that the female form held so much power over the other men. I wondered if there was something that I was missing out on. Then, 50

Cent's "21 Questions" video would come on, and I would forget all about Beyoncé.

We finally got our first real mission. We had gotten up just before dawn and were told to gear up. We loaded back up the platoon's tanks and headed to the train station. We were briefed from the captain concerning WMDs. There were suspected caches in the area, and it was our mission to root them out. At this point, I did a mental eye roll, as this development seemed to confirm my suspicion that the people at the top had no idea what to do with us.

Some soldiers were starting to lose morale as a result of disappointment and lack of information. As rumored withdrawal dates from Iraq came and went, I found myself sinking into a deep depression about the state of my life. I had never experienced living life just to get from one day to the next. I shuffled around like a zombie, feeling no excitement each morning when I was awoken from various dreams. I'd shuffle outside of the building we slept in and piss into the makeshift urinal we made from an old pipe we'd buried deep into the ground. The brown sky that I looked up at remained a sobering visual reminder of where I was. I started to become disillusioned with our mission and found myself questioning our purpose in Iraq more and more every single day. The lack of an end date or any kind of real information made us all moody and unmotivated. The scales had fallen from my eyes, and I became harder and more easily irritated.

As I sat and listened to the captain, though, I noticed the soldiers around me tittering with excitement like schoolgirls. There were talks of "getting Saddam" and Charlie Company going down in history for finding the WMDs. I looked at them contemptuously, almost wishing I was dumb enough to get excited over this foolishness. I was interested in exactly what was about to happen here. I was relatively certain that if there were really WMDs around, they would most likely not be hidden in the small town of Riyadh. It was at least forty minutes north of Kirkuk, itself hundreds of miles north of the center of the war in Baghdad.

It was just after 8 a.m. by the time the briefing was finished. A palpable sense of excitement in the air indicated that Charlie Company's commanders had done a good job of hyping the soldiers up for the mission at hand. We filed into our vehicles, bodies dripping with sweat from the combination of the gear and the already hot Iraq sun. It didn't make me happy to know we were most likely in for a full day of doing various tasks with seventy-five pounds of gear on in over one-hundred-degree heat. My chest armor dug uncomfortably into my shoulder, and the skin on my hips continued to be rubbed raw by a too-tight utility belt.

I looked past the woods and houses that faced the train station. It was extraordinarily bright, simultaneously mocking and oppressive. I could see the surroundings of the train station reflected through the rays already being generated by the heat. The various houses and a flat skyline all seemed to be the same shade of hazy brown. As we got further into the summer, the heat was escalating from a mild annoyance to virtually unbearable. Today was different though, because instead of relaxing in the relatively cool respite of our room at the grain factory, we would actually be working in it for countless hours. We loaded into the back of the tanks and sped off as if our lives depended on it.

The fit was even tighter than usual. The five soldiers in my squad were crammed into the back of the tank with four from another platoon. It made the air even thicker with the steaming morning breath of nine people. I bemoaned the obvious lack of oral hygiene within most of the group. The morning breath and the body odor that comes with only showering once per week combined to create a ghastly, eye-watering aroma. I could feel my stomach dropping. The constant shaking of the vehicle, plus the watery, runny eggs I had consumed for breakfast at the train station convinced me that I just might puke all over these guys. It was making a bad, smelly situation even more disgusting.

I closed my eyes and tried desperately to mentally remove myself from the situation to regain some composure. I thought of life back home, good food, warm beds, and nights of sleep that weren't interrupted by guard duty or the ominous rumblings of distant gunfire. After a few moments, the urge to vomit receded, and I opened my eyes. Everyone else was asleep. Black, white, and brown bodies slumped over in various positions. Everyone's mouths were open to keep that bad breath smell pumping. I looked over to the small, rainbow-colored slat windows that were our only view to the outside world. As the ride went on for what seemed like ages, I noticed civilization being gradually left behind. The houses became fewer and farther between. Eventually, I fell asleep too. I was startled back into reality only when the tank jerked to a sudden stop.

The back door immediately came down, filling the tank with sunlight. Stanton had put camouflage paint on his face and resembled an extra from *Apocalypse Now*. He looked at us intensely and motioned for us to exit the vehicle. The four guys from a neighboring platoon went to meet up with their squads. I looked at my squad mates and smiled. We had big, dumb Thornden, skinny and geeky Lantos, warm and supportive Johnson, and dark-skinned, chunky Howard. Howard's thick Army-issued glasses seemed deeply uncomfortable as they pressed against the tip of his Kevlar helmet. I noticed that he was the only one who looked as confused and apprehensive as I did.

The field was vast and grassy, and went on as far as the eye could see. There were no houses or people to the north, just grass and sky, the same bland, boring brownness that was so characteristic of most places I had seen in the country. Our tanks were lined up facing all directions, the huge guns on the tanks spinning around 360 degrees, which meant that the gunners inside were scanning the area for any potential threats. I wondered what on earth we were doing in the middle of nowhere when we had been prepped for a huge mission. I looked over to my right and got the answer to my question.

The other platoons were moving out in formation, side by side, scouring the big, empty field for weapons of mass destruction. They were intensely engaged in the search, knocking over bales of cut grass that were so dry and brittle that they resembled hay more than anything else. The planned activity for the day came into laser-sharp focus. This was where we were to look for the WMDs. This was where Saddam Hussein had apparently hidden the powerful and destructive nuclear weapons that he would use to carry out his jihad on his foreign enemies in the USA. Either that or the higher-ups really wanted to find something for us to do that day.

I looked dejectedly at the endless field, and as if on cue the sweat began to accumulate on my forehead. I felt the distinct, slimy drag of a sweat bead rolling down the small of my back. Stanton came over to the rest of the squad and looked at us as if to give us direction. We were standing in a half circle as he looked at us. I could see the disappointment in his eyes. He started to say something but then stopped. We looked at him, then at the remainder of the platoons who were walking in formation across the vast field searching for the WMDs we all knew we weren't going to find. Without saying a word, we got into formation and proceeded to do the same.

# CHAPTER 11

# SHARP EDGES

The days seemed to run into each other, like some sort of warped version of the movie *Groundhog Day.* There was a noticeable lack of real missions to carry out daily. Most days we would bullshit, play cards, and eat. We would trade snacks from the various care packages our families had sent us and talk about life back home. There would be talk of food, wives, girlfriends, movies, and what people must be doing at this very moment half a world away. There were always various, increasingly bitter, complaints and questions about exactly what it was that we were doing there.

It was in those lazy days that my thoughts would drift back to Alex. I was still very much in love with him. Some nights as I curled on the hard cement floors to go to sleep, I would curl over to my right in the fetal position and fantasize that I was laying in his arms. We would receive mail and care packages roughly once a week. Whenever the boxes or letters came, my heart would stop in the anticipation that Alex would finally fulfill his promise of writing me a letter. I imagined that he missed me so much he couldn't stand it, and that my absence would make him realize that in fact he did love me as much as I loved him. I imagined I would open the letter from him and read the words declaring his love for me. I would spend the rest of my days in Iraq fantasizing about when I could leave and we could finally be together. As the weeks passed without a letter from Alex, that dream slipped further away. I found my feelings for him slowly decreasing in their intensity.

My twenty-first birthday came, and with it a huge care package from my mother that was filled with my favorite snack foods and a few magazines. Within the package was a birthday card from her with a message that was short and sweet.

*Be safe, I love you.*

I appreciated the gesture, though I still had residual anger toward her for how she continued to ignore my sexuality. In fact, I felt myself becoming more angry and frustrated with several things. I felt ignored. I was out of touch with my family and friends. I know it was a feeling that was shared by most of the soldiers. Here we were, fighting for the rights of the people over on American soil. It was like we were on our own little planet removed from the rest of the world.

The days got longer and hotter, and we were taken over by a sense of cabin fever. Each day was the same as the last and sure to be the same as the next. When my eyes opened in the morning each day, I was filled with dread when I realized where I was. We continued with the rotations. I could feel myself becoming repulsed with the country and the people within it. Man, woman, and child were all potential threats, ticking time bombs that we had to keep our eyes on to ensure our own survival. We would sometimes do patrols in the town, driving our tanks through narrow roads and villages with houses that were little more than shacks. The smiling children, whom I'd once looked at with smiles, I now dismissed coolly. From my vantage point atop the vehicle, I would look through them and past them to ensure there were no threats coming from any unknown sectors.

I knew that these children and these people were why I was here, why I couldn't be back in America with my friends and family. They knew no better way of life than the old shacks and oppressive heat of Iraq. They knew nothing of the luxuries that I'd left behind to fight for their freedom. They knew only survival, and survival was a way of life that I was becoming accustomed to with each passing day of the deployment.

Survival meant there was nothing to look forward to, that there was only getting through the day. Survival meant trying not to get killed or go insane in the process. The days are not lived or enjoyed. They are just another slash mark on the granite wall. We'd never been in any real danger physically, but I could feel myself changing mentally. I was becoming hardened and cynical as we went through days of doing nothing, while the rest of the world was moving forward and leaving us behind.

One evening, I sat atop a tank with Howard while the sun set on another day in Iraq. We had returned to the abandoned school, which we'd proceeded to make a home out of like the other rotation areas. The rotation at the school always unsettled me because it was so exposed. The multilevel building sat in the middle of two small towns with a large road dividing them. It was less finished than the grain factory or the train station. The rocks and gravel debris from the recent bombings remained. The inside of the building was less habitable than the other locations. We slept on the rooftops of the buildings while soldiers in the platoon pulled guard duty on each corner.

We would be rotating to the abandoned factory again in the morning, and we were killing time before dark. The air was thick, but the sky was calm and serene as we looked past the razor wire that had been set up around the perimeter and out to the town surrounding us. We sat in silence for a while, just appreciating the calmness of the moment as day turned into night.

I looked over at Howard, steaming. "What the fuck is going on with this place?" I asked. "This place is so fucking stupid, and I can't stand it. How long has it been?"

The side of his mouth curled up in a half smile so faint it was almost hard to catch. He was only a few years older but always seemed so calm and serene, which was in direct contrast to my restless, hyper energy. He looked over at me.

"Four months, Smith. We've been here for four months."

I sighed petulantly.

"Yeah, four months, and nobody ever knows what the fuck is going on here. It's like, why are we even here? They don't want us here. You can tell they don't." As I said this to him, I thought of the men who would look at us with thinly veiled hatred in their dark eyes and the women wearing hijabs who were unsure who to be more afraid of, their husbands or the American invaders.

"Yeah, I guess they don't, huh," he said.

I shook my head and gazed off into the distance. "So what the fuck are we doing here, Howard?" I looked over at him inquisitively, as if I were expecting an authoritative answer to the question that had a constant presence in the back of my mind. It nagged me, bothered me, and frightened me. The thought that I could possibly die here without being able to completely and honestly answer that question was one that was deeply disturbing to me. He turned toward me, the pools of his dark brown eyes gazing firmly into mine.

"Trying to get back home, Smith," he said.

There was a hint of sadness in his next words.

"So that you can go to school, and I can get the fuck outta here and go home."

I was struck by a familiar sense of guilt when he said those words. In my heart I knew that the all-consuming desire for a college education was really what this was all about. I knew it was what I wanted. I wondered if it made me somehow less genuine than the other soldiers. I'd stopped talking to people in the platoon about my college aspirations. My goals always seemed to bring up a sense of revulsion in them.

"You're supposed to be here because you love your fucking country, not because you want money for fuckin' college." This was the opinion of a platoon member who was now back home. I found out later that that particular ball of sunshine was a racist. He had a reputation for sprinkling his opinion that "niggers should know their place" in casual conversation among other white soldiers. I found that his opinion on the college issue was shared by a large cross section of soldiers. Being vocal about wanting a different life for yourself after your time served in the military was frowned upon. I learned very quickly to keep my aspirations silent.

I started to say something else to Howard, but he turned away and stared off into the distance. There was nothing more to say, no point in trying to analyze or comprehend the unexplainable. The truth was that we didn't know why we were in Iraq anymore. Information was kept from us so skillfully that we didn't even realize what was happening. We knew just enough to get from one day to the next. It was just how the people in charge liked it. It was better for them to avoid more questions, I supposed, but it still didn't comfort me. Howard and I sat on the top of that tank for a while after that exchange, the heaviness of the question hanging in the air like an ominous cloud destined to bring rain at any moment. *Why are we here?* In the sky, the dark blue was overtaking the orange. Day was turning into night.

The next morning while Howard, Thompson, and I were finishing up breakfast, we were approached by an unusually manic and excited Sergeant Stanton. His wild eyes darted furiously from side to side. He hopped back and forth, as if he were a child bursting at the seams to open a long-desired Christmas present.

"Load the fuck up men, we're going out!" he said. He ran past us to gather his equipment.

The three of us exchanged knowing glances as we moved to secure our gear. A sharp pain shot into my right shoulder, and I grimaced as I put the heavy flak vest on. I gave a quick dust-off to my weapon, and double-checked the chamber to ensure that it was free of debris or dirt that would affect its firing. A weapon jam during a mission was not what I wanted. I looked around and noticed that we were the only squad gearing up to go. I walked over to Sergeant Stanton, who gave me an excited grin as he turned to face me.

"What's going on, Sergeant?" I asked.

"Some shit is going on downtown," he said, grinning. "They needed a squad to go down and keep the peace, so I volunteered us, Smitty."

He clapped me on the back as if we were old friends. I felt resigned and nervous to be doing the mission, but it beat spending yet another day doing nothing.

The squad loaded up into the back of the tank, and again my worldview was shut off as the door closed tightly behind me. I was always deeply claustrophobic. I had disturbing visions of the tank hitting an IED and somehow trapping us inside and effectively burying us alive. I heard the roar of the tank taking off as I felt the stutter of its jerky movements. I knew we were well on our way to our destination. I looked around at the squad members and noticed that, with the exception of Sergeant Stanton, they all wore glum expressions. We seemed to be worn down from the process of everyday living. As the summer got hotter, it became harder and harder to maintain energy and focus. We arrived at our destination, and the tank door opened to absolute chaos.

The first thing I noticed was the noise. Dozens and dozens of voices screamed unintelligible gibberish in a language I couldn't understand. What I did understand was that they were frustrated and upset. We exited the rear of the tank and realized that we were at the Riyadh downtown police station. A near-riot seemed to have broken out at the gas station next door. Dozens of Iraqi men were struggling against one another to gain control of the only four gas pumps that were available. A thick feeling of fear and claustrophobia overwhelmed me. Even with our weapons and gear, we were easily outnumbered by the amount of men. The Iraqi security force that greeted us at the front door provided little mental consolation. The American soldiers remained distrustful of the Iraqi police. There were only two sides in this war, them and us. Without an interpreter by our side, we were forced to trust the word of an English-speaking Iraqi policeman. He filled us in on what was going on, as if we couldn't already see for ourselves.

We stationed ourselves around the tank as Sergeant Stanton spoke with the policeman. I couldn't hear their conversation over the roar of the unruly crowd just a few feet ahead of us. I was too afraid to take my eyes off of the many buildings that surrounded us. I felt exposed. I watched as the figures darted in and out of the windows of the buildings around us. I was paralyzed with the recurring fear that any one of them could be home to a sniper, and my head could be in a sniper's crosshairs at that very moment. Iraqi men and children lined the streets around us, watching the chaos unfolding at the gas station. The children who watched us weren't sweet and innocent like those who would run alongside the tanks selling bottled sodas when we patrolled the city. They couldn't have been any older than twelve or thirteen. Their eyes were hardened, and they shared the steely gaze that was generally found in men two and three times their age.

When I looked at their expression, I realized that they could be a threat. I told myself that I needed to see them not as children but as potentially dangerous adults. I had to look at them that way, because I needed to be responsible for my safety and for that of the rest of the guys in my squad. If one of these boys or men were to do anything other than stare in hatred, there would have to be consequences. It was when I looked into their eyes that I knew it was all a lie. We weren't being greeted as liberators. We were seen as invaders who would be hated more for every second that we spent as uninvited guests in this country.

Stanton signaled at the gunner, Sergeant Kane, posted atop the tank to pull security as he pulled us in and gave us the details of what was going on.

"They're getting out of hand," he said with a focus and intensity that he'd never shown before.

"We need to contain this situation. Fix bayonets."

With that, the other squad members attached their bayonet knives to their rifles and moved in. My machine gun wasn't bayonet-compatible, so he gave me the direction to move in front of the other soldiers, using my weapon to try to push the Iraqis back and maintain order.

The soldiers lined up behind me in a reverse-V position. I felt the physical presence of the Iraqi men as they swarmed us while we tried to move forward. I held my machine gun up at the ready, pointing it in their direction and yelling "Back, back!" at the top of my voice so that they knew I meant business.

I realized then that the Iraqis had closed in on us, and though their ire wasn't directed at us, it was utterly terrifying. I felt strong, sinewy bodies pushing and pressing against me from all directions, engulfing me in a sea of angry people.

I looked behind me and noticed that Stanton, Lantos, Thompson, and Thornden were succeeding at pushing some of the Iraqi men back toward a small fence that was adjacent to the police station.

"Calm the fuck down! Move back!" they screamed as they shoved some of the men back. Their bayonets were wild and unwieldy. The Iraqi men looked in fear at their razor-sharp points as they were waved in the air. I heard the distinct swoosh of one of the blades going through the air beside me. I noticed that Lantos had brought his weapon out diagonally in front of him and was waving it wildly as he tried to get the men to move back. The men backed up in fear. He was only a few centimeters away from slicing their faces wide open.

The roar of the crowd was deafening, but I started to notice some progress. We were getting some of the crowd to retreat. The men who'd enclosed us before were moving back into the more orderly line to get gas. I looked back at Sergeant Kane, who was acting as security man atop the tank, which was now fifty or sixty feet behind us. He seemed determined and focused with his weapon squarely focused on the crowd. His driver scanned the buildings and streets that surrounded us. It seemed very dangerous for him to have to shoot into the crowd that we were in the center of, and I just wanted to get out of the situation as soon as possible.

"Get the fuck back!" I screamed.

I pushed the group of forty or fifty Iraqi men in front of me farther and farther back. The reverse-V formation was working, as the men who'd enclosed us from behind had all but disappeared into the streets or into the line for gas. We pushed those remaining up against the fence. The crowd started to calm down and relax.

We had gained control of the situation. The Iraqi policemen came out of the station and thanked Sergeant Stanton for his help. I noticed that there were at least six other Iraqi officers who had simply stood guard while we diffused the situation. The situation lasted only twenty minutes or so, but it seemed like it went on for hours. The squad was tired and shaken up as we loaded up into the tanks. We returned to the abandoned school. It would be lunch-time soon.

We were a little shaken up from the experience, but determined to put it behind us and move forward. What had happened at the gas station terrified me, because it seemed like a situation that could've gone very wrong. For the rest of the day, we did nothing much and didn't speak of the mission downtown. As night fell, I settled into my usual spot for sleep on the roof of the school. I looked into the night sky but found that I had trouble closing my eyes. I lay flat on my back, stiff and rigid. It was an unfamiliar, disturbing feeling as I replayed the day's events in my mind.

Instead of the safe ending that had occurred in real life, my mind went through the many ways the situation could've gone wrong. I saw one of the figures in the window start shooting. I thought about Lantos's bayonet making contact with one of the men, slicing his face open. I imagined Sergeant Kane being forced to open fire into the crowd, killing some of the Iraqi men and injuring us. I was afraid to close my eyes, because I knew the faces of the Iraqi men, so filled with fear and loathing and hatred, were what I would see. Eventually, my body and mind gave over to a heavy and dreamless sleep. I was thankful for the lack of dreams.

Over the next few weeks, Sergeant Stanton was on fire, unaf-fected by the situation at the gas station. In fact, he had more energy than ever. We continued our rotation and our day-to-day lives without any real missions. Stanton would take it upon him-self to devise mini missions for us to do, leading to grumbling and frustration from the rest of the squad members in private. His be-havior became increasingly unbalanced and disturbing. I became more and more uncomfortable with his mini missions. Most of the missions consisted of us exposing ourselves outside of the confines of our rotation stations for no real reason. We would sometimes spend hours stationed in the vast fields that surrounded the thick concrete walls of the grain factory. We would lay in position with our weapons pointed north at absolutely nothing while the brisk night winds cut through the thin flannel of our Desert Camouflage Uniforms. We would always pick up and move back to the relative safety of our station, saying nothing about what had just happened for fear of angering him.

Stanton was becoming a wild card. His increasingly bizarre behavior in the pursuit of filling time was starting to put our lives at risk. I felt impotent and powerless because I could do nothing to stop it. I was a specialist, and specialists weren't in the US Army to have opinions; we were there to point and shoot. I had long since gotten through any fear of using my weapon when necessary. However, it made me deeply uncomfortable to be put in the position of having to engage for no real reason. When the reason behind Stanton's behavior finally dawned on me, I felt truly frightened. It occurred to me that it was almost as if he was looking for a fight.

# CHAPTER 12

# MONSTERS

The first night I almost died in Iraq, I had retreated to my bed on the rooftop of the school. I was looking into the clear night sky as my eyelids grew heavier. Just before I hit sleep, Sergeant Stanton's head popped up in my field of vision like a jump scare from some awful horror movie. He had a devilish and excited glint in his eye.

"Hey, hey, wake up, Smith," he said.

I looked at him like he was crazy.

"Hey, Sergeant Stanton, I was just trying to get some sleep before my guard shift at 2 a.m. What's up?"

"We're going out, man. I'm gonna take the team out on patrol."

My heart dropped. This motherfucker was about to kill yet another night of sleep for me.

"Why? Is something going on?"

"There's nothing going on, and we're gonna keep it that way. And since when the fuck do you ask questions, Specialist? Be down at the gate in five."

"Roger that, Sergeant."

As soon as Stanton was safely out of earshot, I privately grumbled to myself. If there was no trouble, this asshole was sure as hell gonna try to find some. I put on my gear and headed out to the gate.

The night was calm and eerily quiet. I couldn't allow myself to get too comfortable seeing as how insurgents could always come from anywhere at any time. When I thought about that, the insurgents striking, it made me curse the utter ineptitude of the entire operation. I mean, here is an entire company of American soldiers in a violent city in a hostile country, and every one of the locals knows exactly where we're all staged. You could set a clock to the rotation that we do between the school and grain factory, and of course we all stage at the train station for meals at virtually the same time every day.

There were five of us out that night, with Stanton, of course, leading the way. The evening was deathly silent, punctuated only by the steady clop, clop, clop of Howard's gear moving and shifting around his substantial frame as he walked down the street. I was rear man, and I made sure that I covered the back as we moved through the streets. After about an hour of walking, we turned around. I felt a deep sense of relief because it seemed like we were heading back. Instead, we copped a squat in the middle of the street, with Stanton and Thompson at the lead, and myself and Howard bringing up the rear. I looked around at all the houses that surrounded us on this desolate street and again felt exposed. Every shadow that passed by a window seemed like a potential threat. The rustling of the bush around us had the potential to be an insurgent who could send a grenade into the middle of our formation, killing us all. I looked over at Howard. I could see the pained look on his face by the light of the moon's reflection. He looked over at me, fuming.

"Man, I'm so fucking sick of this shit," he whispered, barely audible.

"You know what I wanna do? What I really want? I just wanna get the fuck out of here and go back to Texas, man. I could get a good fucking job back in Texas, especially with four years in."

I looked at him and saw in his eyes that he was both furious and frightened.

"I know you wanna be a college boy and shit, but I just wanna go back to Texas," he said. Thompson looked back at us.

"Hey, guys, come in. Sarge wants to talk."

We all moved in. Stanton leaned in, presumably doing his best impersonation of whatever action movie he wanted to reenact this week.

"We're gonna move out across that field right by the school. One of the informants says there may be an insurgent over there in that apartment building. They may be running weapons and shit. We're just gonna go and check it out, then we'll go back. Roger?"

I shot a worried glance over to the desolate building that overlooked the dark field just down the road from us. I looked back at Stanton, who to my surprise was looking directly at me. His expression was disdainful and resentful. He couldn't imagine why the potential exposure to some action wouldn't be as exciting to me as it obviously was to him. Stanton stood up and rearranged his gear, poking his chest out in an odd gesture of defiance. He headed down the road as Thompson, Lantos, Thornden, Howard, and I hurried behind him.

The grass in the field was long and thick. The silence of the night was punctuated only by the small crunching of various branches under our feet. We moved closer to a medium-sized block of houses surrounded by a huge wall. I noticed people going about their business in their homes with no idea that a squad of infantrymen was moving in on their location. It was late, so very few of the lights were on. I could faintly make out the ones who were still awake moving around the house, perhaps getting a midnight snack or watching a little TV before bed. There goes stupid me again, humanizing them. When I first got to Iraq, I overheard one of the COs saying something I never forgot. He was about twenty years past his glory days and took it upon himself to bestow some wisdom upon the sergeants and squad leaders whenever he got a chance.

"Now don't you be one of those 'we are the world' pussies that thinks *hajji* is a fuckin' person and shit. That motherfucker—all those motherfuckers—would slit your fuckin' throat just as soon as they would look at you, and don't you ever forget it."

I instinctively knew that humanizing them made me weaker, but I couldn't help it. I knew there would be something in me that would be lost if I didn't. I wondered if it was easier for the white soldiers to see them as less than because they'd never had the experience of being seen that way themselves. It was hard for me to call them *hajji* to dehumanize them, because I knew that people had once called those who looked like me "nigger" to do the same.

I was jerked back into the present when I saw Stanton's arm shoot up with his fist enclosed. It was the stop signal. We all took a knee, and Stanton leaned in.

"Cover me. I'm gonna hop up on this wall and take a closer look," he whispered.

We all took our positions covering Sergeant Stanton as he shimmied his lean, muscular frame to the top of the seven-foot wall. As I looked above him, I could see the house maybe fifteen or twenty feet just past the wall. There was a figure moving on the roof. I could see the shadow pacing frantically, illuminated only by the brightness of the moon and the reflections of the other lights in the adjacent houses. Flashes of gunfire lit up the night, and the idyllic silence was shattered by their deafening shots. It sounded like a shotgun fired in rapid succession over the wall and over our heads.

Everything was happening at a rapid-fire pace. I felt beads of sweat dripping down my forehead. My first gut reaction was to aim my M249 machine gun over the wall and Sergeant Stanton's head to return fire. I didn't because it was too dangerous, and I couldn't see him. I noticed Sergeant Stanton running rapidly in our direction as we moved up into line formation to fire. He dropped immediately to the left of Lantos, who was the last man on line. Stanton was sweaty, exhilarated, and insane.

"Return fire! Return fucking fire in that direction!" he screamed.

I cleared my chamber and began firing ten to fifteen-round bursts in the direction of the target. The sounds of weapons firing filled the air as the entire squad was firing. The smell of the weapon fire burned my nostrils like strong-smelling salts. It caused my eyes to water. I could hear the sizzle of my own burning flesh as the white-hot bullet casings bounced off of the backs of my hands while I fired multiple bursts. I wondered if this was what every night was like for the soldiers stationed in more hostile sections of the country.

All the days we'd spent watching the sun set and all the great talks I'd had with my platoon mates shifted sharply into another focus. We were at war, and no amount of daydreaming could take me out of this reality now. I heard something ricochet from the ground to the right of me. I couldn't tell whether it was an enemy bullet or one of my empty casings. Everything was happening simultaneously. I felt the adrenaline flowing through my body, tightening my bones, and setting my eyes in the direction of the gunfire. It was coming from the building we were watching.

"All right, cease fire, cease fire! We're gonna move back and cover each other when we go. Smith, Lantos, and Howard go now!" he screamed.

Though I couldn't see his face, I heard the smile in his voice. Howard, Lantos, and I remained as low to the ground as possible and ran back about twenty feet while Stanton and Thompson fired. To my right, I saw tanks roaring out of the gate at the old school where the rest of the platoon was staged. Their headlights bounced up and down as the tanks moved recklessly across the uneven terrain. In the neighborhood just beyond them, lights were starting to flicker on in various houses. Howard, Lantos, and I plopped down in position, weapons aimed squarely at the direction of fire.

"Go, go!" I yelled to Stanton and Thompson.

I fired more bursts in the enemy's direction. As they ran toward us, I saw the insurgent staged at a higher point in the house. I took aim and fired. I grappled with the fact that I might kill him as he certainly tried to kill me. Maybe it wouldn't be so bad to take his life.

One of our platoon's tanks roared into the field and parked less than ten feet behind us, lowering the back door so we could enter. Stanton and Thompson plopped down. Stanton motioned furiously toward the tank. We all rushed in, and the door closed behind us. We all sat crammed into the back of the vehicle. I was stunned. My helmet was cocked halfway on my head, and my eyes were focused directly forward. They were stinging from the sweat that was pouring into them. Voices shouted around me, but they sounded muffled, distorted, and distant. I was trying to make some sense of what had just happened, but it wasn't coming to me. All I knew was that it was over for now. The next thing I knew, Sergeant Stanton was on me, pushing into my chest with what felt like the weight of a Mack Truck. We were face to face, the distance in my eyes no match for the focused intensity of his.

"Smith! Christ, wake the fuck up! Are you hit?" he screamed. As I looked into his eyes, I felt disoriented, as if I'd just awoken from a nap. Not waiting for an answer, he continued to pat me down roughly, checking my arms, chest, and legs for any signs of being shot. I could see Thompson doing the same to Howard, who looked as equally shaken up. Lantos and I locked eyes briefly, and his fear mirrored mine as he lifted his hands up, giving everyone the all clear.

I realized that this was real life, not *Band of Brothers* or another one of those war shows or movies they seemed to show endlessly during basic training. On TV, there were always winners and losers, heroes and villains. Things were cut and dry. They were always simple and easy. You would never put your brothers in harm's way. You would be willing to nobly sacrifice your life for theirs if the situation called for it. As it turned out, things weren't quite so simple in real life. There was a murky definition over who exactly were the heroes and villains of this situation. I wasn't sure what we were doing here.

"All good, Sarge," I said blankly to Stanton.

I looked out of the windows of the dark, hot tank and saw the rest of the platoon tanks lining up in formation right outside of this small neighborhood of homes. The rest of the company had joined us. We were staged on the small complex of houses and apartments, ready to move in. Lights were coming on in the different buildings around the complex, and people were tittering around. I wondered if we had stumbled upon some sort of rogue insurgent headquarters. Perhaps it was a meeting and training area for anti-American forces that belied the peaceful feeling of the neighborhood. I hoped that we would find illegal weapons or a plan for an attack on our local bases. I hoped that we would find something that would make the upcoming onslaught of one hundred company soldiers into all of their homes and bedrooms in the middle of the night worthwhile and valid.

I stood guard with the rest of the squad at the very place where bullets had just been flying at us. The tanks in the company roared ahead. It was nearly 4 a.m. The light of the approaching tanks' headlights mixed with the early glow of dawn to create a strange color in the sky. There were times when I would catch the sun rising or setting, or just look off into the distance and wonder how a place so brutal and ugly could be so strangely beautiful.

Howard, Lantos, and I were still a little stunned. Thompson looked indifferent, but Stanton gazed longingly at the soldiers of the company descending upon the various houses and apartments of the complex that housed the suspected insurgents. Doors were kicked in, beds and couches were flipped and searched. A flurry of brightly colored hijabs started to flow out of the buildings as women and children were forced to the sidelines. The soldiers took a more hands-on approach with the men, any of which could've been our shooter. The sounds of the idle engines, some faraway soldiers giving orders, and the cries of the women and children combined to create a bizarre symphony of chaos.

We stood guard like this for about thirty minutes as the rest of the soldiers rounded up the people who were just a few hours ago sound asleep in their homes. Our first sergeant approached Sergeant Stanton to update him. First Sergeant Williams was a big, brawny good old boy from the Deep South. His cheerful demeanor camouflaged any sense of threat that would come from his bulk, at least with us. He spit out some chewing tobacco on the ground near him and shuffled over. His sizable stomach was spilling over his utility belt. Stanton perked up to meet him. He leaned in to speak to him in a near-whisper. I stood up, hyperalert to be guarding the surroundings as I covertly angled myself to try to hear every word.

"We've got nothing. A few AK-47s, but nothing indicating any more than household weapons they're allowed to have. It's martial law here, y'know. You said you were walking, and they just started shooting?" he asked.

Stanton shifted uncomfortably. "Yeah, that's what happened."

First Sergeant Williams looked him up and down cautiously.

"Uh huh. The interpreter says that *hajji* thought you boys were robbers and not soldiers.... Seems one of you was trying to hop over the wall."

Stanton stayed silent. Williams leaned in and lowered his voice even more.

"Look, I'm not sayin' you boys can't have a little fun every so often. Do your patrols, walk around, whatever, but I've got the higher-ups leanin' on me about community relations and shit, wonderin' why these motherfuckers hate us so much. Shit like this doesn't help, especially when I've got shit for contraband to prove these fuckers were up to anything."

Stanton glanced at Williams defiantly. "Oh, so now we're in a popularity contest? I thought it was a fuckin' war."

Williams leaned in even closer and brought his voice down even lower, almost to a whisper. "Watch it, soldier, or I'll have those fuckin' stripes taken off you so fast, it'll make your head spin."

"All clear!"

The yells came from an anonymous soldier inside the complex, effectively breaking up the battle of wits between Stanton and Williams. The first sergeant turned away and headed into the complex, breaking eye contact only when his back was completely to the group. I snapped back to hyper-soldier mode, guarding the area from the imaginary enemy. I was trying desperately not to give off any clues that I had heard any of the conversation that had just happened. Stanton moved to the front of us and eyed me suspiciously. He turned to me. He was close enough for me to smell the odor that came from a mixture of week-old clothes and flop sweat from the night's activities. He looked at me with a mixture of disapproval and anger. He leaned in so that nobody else in the squad could hear him.

"You get all that, Smith?"

He leaned back out, and our eyes met, mine filled with fear and his with anger and defiance. He turned away and motioned for the squad to follow him into the complex.

We walked into a sea of scared, fearful faces. The soldiers of the company stood guard around the men and women who lived in the complex. A table filled with the seized contraband separated them. It wasn't much, perhaps five or six AK-47s and a few rounds of magazine ammo. We had been briefed upon arrival in Iraq that the country and its people had been living under a state of martial law since the ending of Saddam Hussein's regime. The amount of weapons and ammo confiscated from such a large number of homes was perfectly normal, or as normal as could be expected from people trying to live in the middle of a war zone. I walked into the courtyard area behind the squad and stood silent as Stanton talked to yet another higher-up about the situation. This time, I didn't listen. I didn't care. I was too focused on the faces of the people in the complex.

The women clung protectively to their children, most of whom were scared and crying. The wailing voices of the children created a disturbing, almost unbearable symphony of pain. They sat in the dirt, leaning up against the buildings. Some were scrambling to fix their hijabs, for fear of violating their religious beliefs and letting us see what lay beneath. In their eyes I could see fear and sadness, and when they spoke Arabic to one another, it was mostly through choked back tears. I glanced over to the Iraqi men. I locked eyes with one, and he flashed me the most hateful look I had ever seen in my life. It was filled with rage, anger, and utter and complete contempt. He was lined up against a wall with the rest of the men. He wore a T-shirt with old jeans and bare feet. If there were ever a propaganda photo to be taken of what the enemy looks like, I'm pretty sure he would be it. His intense gaze made me uncomfortable. It was enough to make me look away. I could still feel his eyes on me.

I wondered what he thought of me. I wondered if he thought the color of my skin made me some sort of traitor. Perhaps he thought he could hate me with more passion than the white soldiers from whom this sort of behavior was to be expected. I thought about this intently as the soldiers started to leave.

Stanton had been eerily quiet since the double whammy of the fiasco surrounding the attack and the phantom hunt for WMDs that had gone on a few weeks before. Word had gotten out about the circumstances surrounding the so-called attack on the third platoon. Sergeant Stanton was being met with whispers and stares, both from lower-level soldiers and other sergeants who didn't understand his behavior. I got the sense that at least some of the people in the town liked our presence. I sensed that they felt we were doing some good for the country. If we continued invading their space unwarranted, it would obviously push the boundaries of their fledgling acceptance of us. It was very important for us not to wear out our welcome. Even I knew that the events of the past few days had not made us any new allies in a small city like Riyadh, where word could travel easily and quickly.

It was only 9 a.m., but it was already a scorcher. I pulled rear security on the tank as it sped down the road toward the grain factory for our next rotation. My head and upper body were completely exposed to the dangers of being an American soldier on a main road in broad daylight in Iraq. Even though I knew this, I didn't care. The air was hot, but it felt good against my skin. I hungrily devoured it, breathing it in and letting it envelop me. We were notified that we were to stay at the grain factory for the foreseeable future. The rotations between the three staging areas would end. We would still have access to the train station for meals and showers.

After feeling skittish for a few days after the attack in town, I was feeling back to normal again. We approached the gates to the factory. The gates creaked loudly as the soldiers of second platoon opened them for our tanks to come in. Now that we were here to stay, we made ourselves more at home. We placed our sleeping bags on the floors in different rooms of the buildings to provide a buffer from the hard granite floors. Everyone set up their rucksacks, weapons, and gear at the foot of the sleeping areas for quick access. We also converted one into a pantry/rec room where we would pool snacks and leftover food. We watched the lower-quality copies of recent movie releases that we bought for three dollars from the Iraqi kids selling them on the side of the street. We watched them on a portable DVD player the platoon had ordered from a store on the larger base in Kirkuk. They had

227

internet access, a gym, and a general store in Kirkuk. We could load up on snacks and magazines when we visited once a month.

When the thirty members of the platoon were piled into that one room watching a movie, we were like zombies, all transfixed as the bright shadows from the screen flickered on and off of our faces. Everyone looked forward to those movies because they reminded us of the lives we had back home, and that there was even still a home to go back to. It was a place with blue skies, green grass, and people who spoke our same language. It was a place that was very far from where we were.

During the long days in Iraq, it was easy to lose sight of the fact that there was still civilization out there somewhere. We'd been overseas for only five months, but it felt like a lifetime. Even by watching a shitty DVD bootleg of the summer's big event movies, we felt like we were experiencing what they were experiencing back home. We were still in the loop. We were still Americans.


One night, the squad sat on the porch of our building, killing time until we hit the hay. It was one of the darkest nights in recent memory, and the half-moon did very little in the way of illuminating our surroundings. We sat in a half circle around a makeshift bonfire we'd made out of a standard Army-issued citronella candle. They were supposed to keep the vicious and plentiful mosquitoes at bay. The fire burned tall and bright, and our shadows danced against the walls of the many buildings in the complex. Further down, the other squads in the platoon were doing the same thing.

It took a split second before I realized the granite that flew at my face was from the impact of a burst of bullets that had hit the wall adjacent to me. Stanton sat just beyond it. He almost instinctively flew back into sort of a reverse combat roll into the porch area of the building, giving him clearance.

"Fire coming from the east! Direct fire coming from the east!"

I heard the abstract yell coming from above me, most likely from the soldiers who were on guard duty on that side of the complex. Some of the dust from the wall had flown into my eyes. I frantically blinked and rubbed my eyes, tearing up and trying to remove it. Gray granite-streaked tears streamed down my face, and I could feel the pieces in my eyes like tiny shards of glass. Rubbing at them only seemed to be making the problem worse. Stanton was up and ready for action, and he fixed his gaze on Reynolds.

"Take that fire out! Take that fucking fire out!" he screamed at nobody in particular, and some unknown figure in the squad quickly kicked the brightly burning candle over. The flames roared up and then quickly fizzled as Stanton feverishly threw sand on it.

I rubbed my eyes agitatedly to try to regain full vision. All I felt was an intense scratching, as I seemed to be rubbing the debris in further. When I looked back up, I didn't see anyone but Stanton. He looked at me impatiently as I clumsily fumbled for my weapon, doing a quick check to clear it, then loading my M249 machine gun with ammo. "Hurry the fuck up, Smith!" he said. He struggled to keep his head low. His eyes had that same look of feverish and unfocused intensity I'd seen before. I loaded my ammo and heard the satisfying click letting me know the ammo was in and ready to be fired. Stanton glared at me.

"Let's fucking go!"

I could hear the fire being returned from above me as I ran through the complex with my head low and my weapon at the ready. Stanton and I ducked behind a building, and then climbed up the ladder to the roof in order to get a better vantage point. I extended the legs of my weapon and propped it up on the ledge to get a better view of what was happening.

The complex was as dark as the sky. To the front of me I could see the rapid orange glow of the tracers that labeled every eighth bullet so that soldiers could gauge the direction of their fire in the dark. They looked like fireflies moving in the night. I tried desperately to move to a place where I could fire without putting my platoon members in harm's way, but I had a team of soldiers directly in front of me and wasn't able to fire. Without my night vision goggles, I could see nothing but shadowy figures, and I was deathly afraid of hitting my fellow soldiers on the rooftop a few buildings down. They were the ones with the best vantage point, as their building on the east side of the complex was the closest to where the threat was coming from. From what I could tell, our attacker had scaled the large wall and fired blankly into the complex. I backed down below the cover of the wall, looking for an avenue to change my position. The lack of a cleared path to the target didn't stop Sergeant Stanton. He pushed himself into a corner and fired multiple bursts to his northwest direction. He fired directly in between the soldiers posted up in the building in front of us as well as the ones to our right. I looked up at him, and before I realized it, I had yelled, "What the fuck are you doing? We don't have a fucking shot! We don't have a fucking shot!"

"Oh yeah, we have a fucking shot all right," he said between bursts. "You're just too much of a fucking pussy to take it."

I looked at him, and it seemed like for the first time I saw him clearly. He loved every minute of this engagement. I felt my stomach drop. There were people who enjoyed this, people who actually sought this out. He repulsed me. I knew in that moment that I'd never be like him and that if I ever turned into him, no college education in the world would be worth what would be taken from me.

"Fuck you, you crazy goddamned son of a bitch," I growled.

I had never before experienced such revulsion to a human being. "Fuck you," I said and huddled behind the cover of the wall as I listened to the sounds of gunfire rip through the crisp night air.

After a short while, the gunfire stopped, and the threat retreated. I looked over the wall and saw only darkness in the background. In the foreground I could see the silhouettes of my platoon's soldiers, clearing their weapons and checking each other for injury. I heard various abstract soldiers yell, "All clear!"

The threat was gone. I cleared my weapon and stood up. I felt a forceful hand shove me backwards in the chest. Hard. Stanton came toward me and shoved me into the wall as forcefully as he could. He was furious.

I stumbled back, surprised and nervous, but angry. "Yo, Stanton, what's your problem?" He glared at me.

"You know what my problem is, Smith? Pussy-ass motherfuckers like you. What, you just gonna let everyone else get killed so you can get back home and go to fucking college, right?"

"Is that what this is about?" I asked. "I didn't have a shot, Stanton. I didn't have a fucking shot. You want me to just fucking shoot around wherever? I'm supposed to just blindly shoot like you?" I screamed and advanced toward him.

"That's fucking bullshit, Smith, and you know it. I saw you ducking down. You were fucking scared as hell!"

"And what was I supposed to be? What was I fucking supposed to be? Was I supposed to love it, like you? You could've killed one of us on that rooftop!"

This seemed to infuriate Stanton more, and he advanced upon me. He grabbed me by the collar of my shirt. He leaned his face in close to mine. The dark pools of his eyes filled my primary vision. There was nowhere else to go.

"If you think this is as bad as it gets, you have no idea," he said, and the hardness in his eyes dropped slightly. He loosened his grip.

He looked at me and looked around, as if he were talking to some other invisible person in the area.

"I need a fucking soldier, but not this guy. Not this fucking guy," he said, shaking his head. He made his way down the ladder and toward the rest of the soldiers, who had gathered up below just outside of the cafeteria/rec room building.

*Not this fucking guy.* The words rang in my head. I felt a deep disappointment in myself, irrational still due to my feelings toward Stanton. Waves of self-pity, self-hate, and revulsion swept over me. My knees got weak, and my legs buckled. I slumped down right then and there on that dirty rooftop in the middle of the night, my weapon and gear, a forgotten jumble of camouflage-colored equipment, spread sloppily around me.

Everything I was feeling seemed to get caught in my chest. I started heaving and gasping for air. It occurred to me that I was probably having a panic attack. I wanted to sleep, but the adrenaline that flowed through my veins wouldn't allow it. I was up and alert with nothing to do but keep going over and over what had happened. Stanton was unbalanced. I wanted nothing more than to leave the hellish country of Iraq and to never have to see Stanton's face again. I hated him because he'd continually made bad decisions and put me in harm's way on more than one occasion. I was powerless to stop it. I wasn't an officer or a sergeant. I was just another grunt, a bullet-stopper as the old saying went. I wanted nothing more than to leave Iraq and get as far away from this man as I could. I was convinced that he was dangerous.

Eventually my body gave way to a thin and troubled sleep on the rooftop as the rest of the platoon settled down in their various areas of the complex. That night I was plagued by the worst dreams I'd had since arriving in Iraq. In my dreams, the outcome of the evening's events was different. In them, I'd taken the shot from the rooftop and accidentally killed the soldiers in the squad in front of me.

# Chapter 13

# COMING HOME

For the next few weeks, the tension between Stanton and me was as thick as the muggy summer air, but things calmed down in the platoon immensely. The attack on the grain factory had made things more real for all of us. The realization that we could be attacked at any moment made everyone a little squeamish about leaving the security of our surroundings unless it was for a real mission or absolutely necessary. Gone were the nights of laughing and joking with the squad members under the moonlight with our makeshift bonfire burning in the middle of us. The firefight had made it very clear that we were in a life-or-death situation. The mood of the soldiers reflected the gravity of the situation.

When I thought about the blowup with Stanton, I knew deep within myself that his attacks were unwarranted and that I was a good soldier. It bothered me that he remained in charge while so clearly unaware of the difference between bravery and stupidity. He continued to scare me. I spent most of my nights in a deep trance while I listened to Janet Jackson and visualized myself in a place far away from the hellish reality of Iraq. Listening to her soft voice and the lush melodies of her music calmed me. When I closed my eyes, I imagined that I was in a place where all of my dreams had come true.

In my imagination, Iraq and the military were in my rearview mirror. I was Robert L. Smith, famous and powerful television anchor. I had already received my college degree and was in the process of building a career in journalism and exposing the truth in whatever way I could. My body would be dirty, tired, and riddled with sweat, but in my mind I was immaculately dressed and well groomed. I would be living the life I'd dreamed of, the life that I'd risked everything for in the past six months. I didn't know if I would ever get there or if the life I wanted would ever be a possibility for me. I had to believe it, because that belief was the only thing getting me from one day to the next.

In those days, I thought a great deal about Alex. The blind and unconditional love I had for him had given way to a bitter hardness that was new to me. I'd stopped waiting for his first letter after the first four months when I realized it would never come. I had nothing but time. I would spend blisteringly hot days on guard duty on the rooftops thinking about him and our relationship. I would stare out into the vast brown fields of Iraq, but my mind would be in a place further away. I realized that Alex had used me like all the rest. He had used me to get the attention and affection that he couldn't get from his real boyfriend. He needed it to survive and in me had found someone needy, damaged, and lonely enough to give it to him unconditionally.

At first I hated him for not writing me, then I realized that he'd been honest with me all along. He'd never loved me, never pretended to, and had only given me what I thought I wanted. In those waning days of summer as I pulled my guard shifts or ate the same bland food or listened to the same music on my Walkman, I wondered if I would ever find true love in real life. I did get a letter from

Scott, and I hated myself for dropping him so easily when I became so obsessed with Alex. Scott had never deployed to Iraq and continued to do work for the battalion from the unit in Colorado for a while. Earlier that summer, he'd requested and gotten another duty assignment in the South, near his family.

I didn't know when I would be returning home, much less separating from the Army. We knew that summer, despite all the rumors, that American troops would not be quickly rotating out of Iraq. There were reports of escalating violence in other regions. We felt lucky to be stationed in a relatively quiet city, but we knew that the violence and insurgent attacks could very easily spread to other cities, even a quiet one like Riyadh.

Waking up one morning, I turned over to my left and looked bitterly at the makeshift calendar I'd created on the wall. It was September 1, a day notable only because my original separation date would've been a little over a month from that day. I was five short weeks away from hitting my four-year mark in the US Army. I imagined how unrecognizable I was from the seventeen-year-old kid I was four years ago. Above all else, I'd learned how survive, no matter what.

To my surprise, I received my orders to return to the United States. The platoon sergeant informed me that ETS—expiration term of service—dates had been extended ninety days. I would return to the US in just a few weeks so that I could have the full three months to separate from the military. I spent the days packing my things in a state of euphoria, blissfully unaware of the hostility it caused in some of the people in the squad, particularly Stanton. All I knew is that I would be returning home to separate from the Army and begin my new life. I was filled with the excitement, nervousness, and fear that came with making such a huge move.

The company arranged a ceremony to award all of us with the highly coveted Combat Infantryman Badge. It was given only to infantry soldiers who'd served in a wartime combat situation. On a day that seemed somehow so much brighter than all the rest, we lined up as a company as the badges were placed on our uniforms. I winced in pain as our company commander punched the steel prongs of the badge into the flesh beneath the uniform. It was a common form of hazing that came with most promotions and awards. I didn't mind the pain, however, though I was conflicted by the meaning of the award.

I was being given an award and honor that few people ever receive in a place that even fewer ever truly see in their lifetime. The hard part was over. I'd gotten through it in one piece, without ever having to kill anyone. Looking into the relieved and happy faces of all the soldiers, it dawned on me that the Combat Infantryman Badge was an award given for self-preservation more than anything else. The threat of taking life and losing mine had lived with me ever since I'd crossed the border into Iraq. I had only come close to a dead body once.

L ate one afternoon, I felt a rumbling in the train station, almost as if there had been a hurricane. We'd been hit by a mortar attack less than a mile away. The soldiers stationed on guard on the roof had zeroed in on the target. I could hear the sounds of the firefight rage on outside. The gunshots stopped after ten minutes. I noticed several soldiers in the platoon running excitedly outside. I asked one soldier what the commotion was about.

"Going to see a dead *hajji*!" he said excitedly as he ran.

I decided against going to see the dead body. I knew it would be something I would never be able to remove from my mind. I instinctively knew that for the rest of my life I would see the lifeless body and the dead eyes looking up at me when I closed my eyes. I would blame myself for gawking at the shell of the enemy that had been left behind. I stood frozen in place as the soldiers ran back and forth around me, clamoring to see the body before it was removed by the local Iraqi police. I felt disconnected from their excitement. I'd looked death in the eye figuratively, but when the time to do it literally came, I blinked.

No matter what had happened during the previous six months, I couldn't turn this person into a *hajji*. I couldn't dehumanize him to the point where someone who was once a living, breathing human being was a freak sideshow meant to satisfy the curiosity of bored soldiers. I knew that he'd tried to kill us. I hated him and everyone else in the country who had attacked the soldiers, but I knew I couldn't find the detachment it would take to look at his lifeless body and feel nothing. I wondered about the soldiers who weren't as lucky as I was. I thought that if I were to stay for another six months to a year, it would be possible for whatever light I still had within me, that kept me from looking at the body, to be extinguished permanently. I wanted to go home.

After the ceremony, I shared a moment with the squad members, the men with whom I'd shared something I would never share with anyone else. Though things remained chilly between Stanton and me until the end, I knew that, like with all the others, we shared a bond. I thought back to the fear and panic in his eyes as he checked me for gunshot wounds after we'd been attacked out on patrol. I realized that whatever differences we had were dwarfed in the pursuit of the overall goal of survival. I felt guilty that I got to return to the States and embark on a new journey while these men were stuck on the old one that had no end in sight.

Before the squad loaded up into the tank and out of my life, I caught a glimpse of Howard and immediately engulfed him in a bear hug. I wanted to thank him for so much, for being my friend and for listening to me. I replayed all the conversations that we had in the previous years. For once in my life, I didn't have to say anything because he already knew.

I was shuttled up to the base at Kirkuk to stay before flying out in the morning. My last night in Iraq was spent like so many before, in a quiet place to myself as I looked at the broad expanse of the country. I never wanted to see it again. I knew that what had happened over the past four years had changed the course of my life in some way that was too close to be yet defined. As I closed my eyes to sleep on the rooftop of a slightly better building in the middle of the large base at Kirkuk, I heard faint gunshots in the distance. I smiled because I knew that I'd never fall asleep to the sounds of gunfire again, though it would be many years before I was able to again sleep through the night.

# EPILOGUE

When I get the call, I'm surprised that anyone from the unit still has my phone number but saddened by the news that I hear. Specialist Jose Mora has been killed in Iraq. His funeral will be at the base chapel in just a few days. I hang up the phone and sit silently in the living room of my apartment.

It is my first apartment, a small one-bedroom right near Colorado Springs. There is a beautiful view of the mountains right outside. I arrange the cheap furniture that I've managed to scrounge together; I ensure that the head of the bed faces the window. When I fall asleep, I do so lying on my back looking at the mountains as I drift away. I don't remember my dreams.

I decided to stay in Colorado Springs because I knew there was nothing for me back in Ohio. I immediately enrolled in classes at the local community college in hopes of transferring to a four-year university later on.

The classes are hard, but they're interesting. I remain completely devoted to doing the work and following my dream. I maintain a 4.0 GPA, and my professors seem to take a special interest in me once I mention in casual conversation that I used to be a soldier.

I've taken small steps out of the closet, awkwardly coming out to the waitstaff at the restaurant that I work at a few nights a week for extra money. Nobody much seems to care. It makes me happy. I know I made the decision to come out as a result of being forced to lie for so long.

At Specialist Mora's funeral, I am consumed with grief. Though we were never in the same squad, I remember him to be a soft-spoken, gentle man. He spoke frequently of his wife and two children. I remember briefly meeting them once at a company function.

He is the only soldier in my company to be lost in Iraq, so his death hits those of us still around extra hard. I talk with a few other soldiers and hear about how it happened. Soon after I left Iraq, the company was moved to the larger base in Kirkuk. Specialist Mora died during a mortar attack. He was killed instantly.

My tears flow for him. I wonder why I'm still alive, and this man with a family has been killed. I try and try to think of a reason, and I cannot. The only thing I can come up with is that God didn't take me because he has a plan for me. I leave the funeral and drive off the base and back to my new life, searching....

In some way, I think I'll always be searching.

**PART FOUR**

# AMERICA'S FAVORITE FAVORITE BLACK, GAY REPUBLICAN

## Chapter 14

# BECOMING "AMERICA'S FAVORITE BLACK, GAY REPUBLICAN"

In the years between leaving the military and "coming out" as a Republican, I lived a lot of life. I went to Syracuse University, became a raging woke liberal leftist, and moved to New York City where every left-leaning whim was indulged. There's nothing particularly interesting to me about sharing the more hedonistic tales of my early days in NYC. I make no bones about the fact that there was a lot of partying (but no drugs) and meaningless sex. One of the reasons I'm such a strong advocate for more conservative values among gay men is that I've lived the life that the gay mafia is trying to sell as aspirational, and I know as well as anyone that it is anything but. I've never believed there's anything inherently wrong with being gay, and I've never hated myself for it, but I do believe that what is sold as "empowering" to young gays today is really just another form of slavery. They're slaves to their libidos, to hookup apps, to drugs, to booze. I've been there, and perhaps there is another story to be told about those years. But for now, we'll just suffice it to say I did a *lot* of things, came through the other side with my health, life, and sanity intact, and have moved on. Thank God for that.

The most interesting things to happen in my decade in New York City were my indoctrination into woke culture via reality television and becoming an activist in the move to repeal the "Don't Ask, Don't Tell" law that barred gays and lesbians from serving openly in the military. But I'll get to that later, when I take you deeper than you ever thought you wanted to go into what I call the "Cult of LGBT." But for now, let's jump a bit closer to the present—two years ago, precisely. After having become convinced that a $125,000 master's degree from Columbia University was exactly what I needed to break into media (spoiler alert: it wasn't), I became stuck in a rut of shitty media jobs.

What nobody wants to tell the young, scrappy journalists who desperately want to break into the industry is that it's filled with backroom deals and plum jobs saved for the children of the elite. If your parent is/was a famous politician or actor, or if your mother or father is/was a top-tier executive or a legendary news anchor or journalist, you're in. For the rest of us, it's a bit harder. For me, it was damn near impossible. What I didn't realize in those days was that, in the leftist-dominated news media that drips with disdain for people like me (not black people.... They LOVE blacks that can be used to push leftist agendas, but generally loathe people of *any* color from working-class backgrounds), there was just no space for a military veteran who leaned conservative. These people despise military service, and their smug condescension towards anyone who served took me by surprise. They see it as exclusively the domain of the poor, and when it is on your résumé, *you* are coded as poor, and NOBODY hates the poors more than the leftist media elite.

Be it opinion writing, producing, or multimedia journalism, I had done some form of work for all of the big names, and my media career had become a depressing cycle that went something like this: I'd get a job writing or producing somewhere (awful), get laid off, lather, rinse, and repeat. I wasn't learning any new skills, I wasn't using my authentic voice, and I certainly wasn't building anything for myself that would last beyond whenever the bosses at whatever media company I was with tired of me. I mean, take a look at all the blue check mark-verified journalists on Twitter with small followings (I call them Verified Nobodies) practically begging for work when insert-failing-digital-media-company-here folds. I say this with no disdain for these people. They've been sold a lie about the journalism industry and about the value of "higher education," and now they're paying the price. And, a word about "higher education":

You, dear reader, are LUCKY enough to be reading the words of the owner of a master's degree in journalism from none other than Columbia University! Can't you just *smell* the class and Ivy League perfection coming off of the page? If you didn't before, I'm *sure* you now get the sense that I'm typing this wearing an ascot and smoking a cigar with a nicely aged whisky within arm's reach. Well, I'm going to let you in on a little secret: my degree means absolutely nothing. It's not worth the paper it's printed on, and I'm honestly not even sure where it is. Higher education in 2020 is a business and nothing more. And this working-class Army vet from Ohio was so brainwashed into thinking that a degree from Columbia University was a ticket into the upper echelon of society that I was ready and willing to take out (more) student loans to pay the $125,000 price tag. This is why I'm always wary of those "feel-good" news stories about THE NIGERIAN IMMIGRANT WHO GREW UP IN THE PROJECTS AND HAS NOW BEEN ACCEPTED BY EVERY IVY LEAGUE SCHOOL IN AMERICA. Do you notice how nobody ever really explores what happens next? My guess is that they get a crash course in what it is like to be a broke person around the truly wealthy (it takes a strong sense of self to navigate that one—trust me) and to enter into rigorous coursework their likely shitty public school education hasn't really prepared them for. That's a big part of why I think the idea of affirmative action is outdated...but that's another book.

Luckily for me, a group of veteran students pointed me to a VA program that covered the cost of Columbia for me. I'm not the welfare type, but as far as I'm concerned, I wasn't dodging bullets in Iraq for nothing. I gave Uncle Sam five years of my life, and I'm unashamed of reaping whatever benefits are available for me. My philosophy is that if there's a benefit out there for veterans that I *really* need, I'll go for it. And the LAST thing I needed was another $100,000 in student loan debt to add to the $40,000 I took on for my *first* useless degree. And here's another thing they don't tell working-class kids like me about Ivy League institutions like Columbia: not only are they businesses, but, like most businesses, they like customers that can afford it. Columbia is notorious for giving very little in the way of scholarships, so it generally attracts three categories of people: the children of the wealthy/famous/well-connected who can easily write a check for the entire program's tuition, working-class kids like me who bought into the idea of the Ivy League as a way to "level up" in life, and wealthy international students who want to use a school like Columbia to bolster their bona fides back home.

The third cohort is why I found myself in class with an endless stream of international students who could barely speak English, let alone write about the intricacies of American politics—which is oddly what all of them wanted to do. They may not have been able to speak fluent English, were terrible writers, and interrupted class more often than not to ask how local elections in America worked...

but hey, they could pay! *CHA-CHING!* I feel genuinely bad for some of these kids who were promised some kind of job after graduation only to have their hearts broken when they find out that insert-large-media-company-here doesn't feel like sponsoring the visa of some twenty-two-year-old who speaks English as a third language to pay them to write about American politics. SHOCKING! But you know who I feel really bad for? My gorgeous working-class classmate who took out $150,000 in loans for Columbia University and got her first reporting gig out of school for the exorbitant salary of $27,000 per year.

If you look closely, the few in conservative *or* liberal media that have managed to break through have done so because they figured out how to personally brand themselves and harness the power of social media. You're reading this book because I did. This is how it happened.

About two and a half years into my shitty media job cycle, I found myself producing for Trish Regan's then-2 p.m. show on the Fox Business channel. Let me make it *very* clear: Fox News is not a shitty media job. Far from it. I was well paid, treated with respect, and learned a LOT in the few months I was there. In fact, my experience at Fox Business was so good, I could've easily spent the next decade or so of my life producing if I didn't have a burning desire to do more on the other side of the camera. I'd been "red-pilled" (i.e., becoming more conservative in my beliefs) for quite some time, starting with becoming much more educated about the scourge of illegal immigration, leading to my absolute hatred of Hillary Clinton during the 2016 election cycle, and finally reaching a crescendo with the Pulse Orlando terrorist attack.

On June 12, 2016, radical Islamic terrorist Omar Mateen walked into gay club Pulse in Orlando and killed forty-nine gays and lesbians. As you've already read in *intimate* detail, I know what it's like to be a young gay person seeking the sanctuary of a gay nightclub to explore myself, meet people, and feel "safe" to be gay in a way that you honestly can't really be in mainstream bars and lounges. When I woke up that morning to read the news of the attack, I was overwhelmed with grief—grief for those lost, for their families, for the community that was forever changed by such an awful event. One searing memory I have of that morning that I share often was going into the bedroom I shared with my then-fiancé, crawling back into bed, and crying deep, heaving sobs into his chest. I couldn't understand how someone could be filled with such hatred and commit such an atrocity. Even having looked terror in the eye during my deployment to Iraq, this seemed different. This seemed like pure evil. At the time, I was firmly on the left, though I had been flirting with conservative ideas for quite some time. As a black, gay man, I thought the Left was the only place for me. I thought its politicians and media figures were the only ones that would protect me from those "evil" conservative Republicans. As it turns out, those evil conservative Republicans were the only ones who truly had this gay's back.

In the wake of the Pulse Orlando terrorist attack, the response from the Left was curiously neutered. As has become sadly commonplace when Americans are the victims of radical Islamic terrorist attacks, the Left's response is to condemn terrorism in the most ginger terms possible, then to warn against "Islamophobic" attacks and/or retaliation against Muslims. You see this kind of behavior in many different ways. When Muslim political figures on the left are pretty much forced to condemn these kinds of attacks, the condemnation is generally couched in language about attacks of ALL people. This idiocy is twofold. First, it assumes that Americans are morons who think *all* Muslims are terrorists. Remember, the cultural elites of this country have deep disdain for the "deplorables" they feel it's their duty to save America from. In their minds, these hillbilly, buck-toothed rubes see a scary terrorist attack from a "Mooslim" and have to be assuaged from unleashing a reactionary attack on the first brown person they see. You and I know that isn't true because we've probably both actually had a real conversation with a Republican voter at some point in time. These people never have, never will, and are very content to live with the stereotypes they've created in their minds. So, no, literally NOBODY believes that all Muslims are terrorists or sympathetic to terrorists.

This stuff also gives some Muslim public figures on the left the cover of "intersectionality" when they engage in seriously questionable behavior (see: Linda Sarsour's entire existence). In the intersectionality cult of the Left, NO VICTIM GROUP CAN BE LEFT BEHIND. Thus, *anyone* who speaks out strongly against terrorism runs the risk of being smeared as "Islamophobic" and subjected to a round of hate from Woke Twitter. It also sadly encourages the eunuch gays of the Left to open their arms and warmly embrace an idea of Islam's tolerant attitude toward gays that's aspirational at best, fictional leftist propaganda at worst. This is why you'll see rainbow flag-laden banners with such wonderful, inclusive, and not-at-all-batshit-crazy phrases like "Queer LGBTQIA Muslim Alliance" and "Gays for Islam." Seems like an odd alliance to me, especially when you consider that 52 percent of Muslims in the UK polled think being gay should be illegal.[1] That's roughly in line with the 48 percent of Muslims surveyed in America who think homosexuality shouldn't be accepted in society.[2] But GAYS FOR ISLAM, AM I RIGHT?!

---

1   Tim Hume and Richard Allen Greene, "52% of British Muslims in Poll Think Homosexuality Should Be Illegal," CNN, April 12, 2016, https://www.cnn.com/2016/04/11/europe/britain-muslims-survey/index.html.

2   Pew Research Center, "U.S. Muslims Concerned about Their Place in Society, but Continue to Believe in the American Dream," July 26, 2017, http://assets.pewresearch.org/wp-content/uploads/sites/11/2017/07/25171611/U.S.-MUSLIMS-FULL-REPORT.pdf.

I was disgusted with illegal immigration, disgusted with Hillary Clinton and the Democratic Party, and disgusted with the leftist tactics that seemed eager to call the radical Islamic terrorist attack in Orlando by anything other than what it really was. So, when an opportunity came about to work at Fox, it was perfect for where I was in my political evolution.

Working for Trish was amazing. She's intelligent, quick-witted, and a star in every sense of the word. If you're going to do television, *do* it. Don't back down. Have a personality. Have energy. Have a point of view. You need to have *it*. I learned from Trish more than anyone else what it truly takes to have *it* on television and to make it work. During those months I truly learned the ins and outs of the cable news business: how "booking" works, how producers create segments, and how guests are found. While I was sitting at that desk from 8:30 a.m. to 3:30 p.m. every single day, the voice in my head started to get louder: *You can do this.* I would look at some of the people doing "hits"—guest appearances during segments—and would see lots of swamp creatures in suits, emotionless robots, and "millennial conservatives" who acted like a 70-year-old's version of what a young person should be. I thought that I could bring more fire, more energy, and a different perspective to everything that was going on. It was in this moment when I truly started to think about "coming out" as a conservative.

From a purely market-based perspective, a black, gay conservative who is out and open about his political views and targeting a conservative audience had never really been present before, at least not in the era of social media. And I knew I was the one to do it. My career didn't really take off when I was on the left advocating for LGBT rights because I was afraid—afraid to say how I really felt, lest I piss someone off at one of the major networks. I was afraid to be my authentic self because although I saw chinks in the Far Left's armor, I knew I'd be attacked, smeared, and "canceled" if I called them out. I wanted so desperately to be liked and accepted that I was afraid of being honest.

I looked at some of the most prominent black and/or gay faces in the news media and found their perspectives dry and outdated. They always seem to be attacking someone (generally straight white or black men) instead of advocating for what *they* believe in. It's easy to tear America down, and God knows they do it well, but these people have no clue about what they want to build when its destruction is complete.

They hate Trump. They advocate for some idea of "LGBTQ rights" that doesn't speak to me as a gay man. They also have a deep-seated, nearly pathological hatred for heterosexual black men. As if in order to get back at the straight black dudes who called them "fags" in high school, their tweets, think pieces, and lectures always seem to point to the evil straight black man as the source of the never-ending struggle of gay black men and straight women. This lunacy reached its peak in the digital media era when *The Root* published an article titled, and I'm serious, "Straight Black Men Are the White People of Black People."[3]

The "Woke Queens," as I call them, all seemed to be saying the *exact* same things. And why wouldn't they? They're on a path that is well traveled and easy to glide into. If you are a black person selling blacks the idea of themselves as perpetual victims who are constantly kept down by the ever-pervasive spectre of white racism, you will make a LOT of money. You will be celebrated and applauded for "speaking truth to power." You will take photos with celebrities. You will be invited to red-carpet events. You will be well funded by leftist billionaires with a vested interest in keeping the numbers of blacks voting for the Left at upwards of 90 percent. This

---

3    Damon Young, "Straight Black Men Are the White People of Black People," *Root*, September 19, 2017, https://verysmartbrothas.theroot.com/ straight-black-men-are-the-white-people-of-black-people-1814157214.

is why there are so many of them...and why it is so hard for new voices in that lane to break through. It has been done to exhaustion. I mean, honestly. Break up with your talking points; we're bored. I thought I had an interesting voice and perspective to add to the conversation, and it turns out I was right.

On Memorial Day of 2018, the *Daily Mail* published a profile on me titled "Rob Smith 'Comes Out' As Conservative and Breaks Stereotypes That All Black and Gay Men Are Liberal,"[4] which exploded on social media. About a month and a half later, I was "coming out" as a conservative on national TV[5] to none other than Jesse Watters on *Watters' World* on Fox News. It was official: I'd made my transition in front of the camera. Now, the only question was "What the hell did I *truly* have to say?" I'd now become a regular on cable news networks and on the lecture circuit talking about the politics of the moment, but if I had to truly break down the political reasons behind why I decided to take the unrelenting heat and criticism that comes from both sides of the political aisle since I came out as "America's favorite black, gay veteran Republican," they're in the chapters that follow. Come along, because I assure you that you're not getting this perspective anywhere else.

# Chapter 15

# THE CULT OF LGBTQ

Nearly five years after the landmark ruling that made marriage equality the law of the land in America, what was once a relatively stable movement of gays and lesbians trying to live their lives openly and honestly in America has become a feral contingent of far-Left lunatics who have made it their mission to subvert every norm of America and force it on an unwilling populace in the name of "LGBTQ rights." The Evangelical Christian conservatives who resisted marriage equality for decades did so for many reasons, but mostly because they feared the Pandora's box of degeneracy that could possibly open once it happened. When I danced in the street of NYC's famed Christopher Street with a fag hag after the marriage equality ruling came down, I never believed for a second I would ever say what I'm saying right now: they were right.

Not that I think that marriage equality is a *bad* thing; far from it. But even as a gay man and former leftist, the mainstream LGBTQ "community's" transition from normalizing two grooms on a wedding cake topper to normalizing a child drag queen dancing for tips in a Brooklyn gay bar at 3 a.m.[6] is a LOT to take in. That's the thing about cults. You're subject to the will of the cult leaders, forced to jettison your own critical-thinking skills in service of what the cult wants, and risk excommunication from the cult if you step out of line. That's what happened to me. I was barely tolerable to the cult for the time that my military service could be used to push an agenda (at that point, "Don't Ask, Don't Tell" repeal, an agenda I was 100 percent on board with), but once I stepped out of line (i.e., became a public Trump supporter) I was discarded like an old box of condoms after a slutty gay's PrEP prescription has been filled.

## ENTERING THE LGBT CULT

About a decade ago, I was living in New York City as a gay man, two years after a disastrous stint on reality television. You see, I appeared on the first season of a VH1 reality show called *I Want to Work for Diddy* with none other than future transgender icon Laverne Cox. The show was shoddily produced, and I didn't have a great experience on it. I don't remember too much about Laverne except for the fact that she seemed very aggressive about getting me to "out" myself as gay on camera while other cast members were still very confused about her own gender identity. I'd see her around New York City in the years after we filmed, and we'd be fairly cordial. She was as subtle as a very tall transgender woman could be while walking the streets of New York City. One time, when running into her in the Flatiron District and exchanging pleasantries, I remember distinctly hearing someone say "That's a man" loud enough for us both to hear it. I know what she went through, which is why I

---

6    Amanda Prestigiacomo, "11-Year-Old Boy Dressed in Drag Dances at Gay Bar, Gets Dollar Bills Thrown at Him," Daily Wire, December 17, 2018, https://www.dailywire.com/news/11-year-old-boy-dressed-drag-dances-gay-men-bar-amanda-prestigiacomo.

genuinely applaud her success and the success of other adult transgender people who are living their lives without trying to impose language restrictions on the other 99.9 percent of the world. That said, there are some who will call me "transphobic" for pointing out the very real problems with radical transgender ideology that I will go into in depth in this chapter. To me, it's beside the point. Acknowledging the existence of biological sex is not transphobic. Protecting the rights of women is not transphobic. Strongly encouraging society to press the pause button when it comes to projecting transgender identity onto children is not transphobic.

What the experience and exposure on the reality television show gave me was an entry into a world I hadn't been exposed to. There was an emerging world of social media celebrities and activists who were LGBT, and I started to share more about my experience as a closeted gay soldier via writing, social media, and the like. My platform eventually attracted the attention of an activist organization by the name of GetEQUAL. The organization intended to fight for LGBT rights, and the major battle at the time was getting the "Don't Ask, Don't Tell" law that barred open service by LGBT people in the military repealed. This, I understood. I found it fundamentally unfair that I had spent years of my service afraid of being "outed" as gay. I was as good as, if not better, than many soldiers in my platoon. The fact that my service was seen as somehow "less than" was just wrong, so I decided to fight. I got involved with GetEQUAL and became close with Lieutenant Dan Choi.

The fact that many of you have never heard of Lieutenant Dan Choi is a tragedy, and his story is why I'm wary of how my story, voice, and presence is used or co-opted by anyone in any movement. Choi came out as gay on national television while serving as an officer in the Army Reserve. He had been deployed overseas. He was tall, strapping, and good-looking. The moment was iconic, and he became thrust into the movement to repeal "Don't Ask, Don't

Tell." At the time, I'd become involved with GetEQUAL and its crew of LGBT bloggers, activists, and former soldiers who were all united for the same mission. We'd have strategy sessions, talk with one another, and eventually I ended up being arrested at the front gates of the White House in protest of what I felt was a discriminatory law. There was not one moment when I didn't believe in what I was doing, and the same was true for the other working-class military veterans who risked their lives and livelihoods to be involved in this protest. But, looking back, there was a difference in how we were treated versus how the "stars" like Dan Choi and even GetEQUAL co-founder Robin McGehee were treated. First of all, both were being paid a salary by the organization, when many other soldiers and I whose lives and stories were being co-opted were not. Choi and McGehee would be carted around in black cars. Choi was a regular on the cable news circuit and the like. While doing all this, I was still struggling to keep jobs waiting tables and writing on the side in New York City. Other soldiers, like Miriam Ben-Shalom, struggled with their finances as well. Though the push for the DADT repeal was successful, the experience made me very wary of how organizations on either side of the aisle use my face, story, and talents to further their own goals. I told myself after the DADT repeal passed that if I ever got involved in the political realm again, I'd be smarter about my goals, watch my bottom line, and ensure that any professional relationships I enter into are mutually beneficial. And I have.

As for Dan Choi, he was used and abused by the movement and tossed to the side once they were finished with him. He didn't take care of himself. He didn't protect himself. He didn't maintain his mental and physical health in the way he should have when so much was demanded of him. Most importantly, he didn't know how to say no. You see, when you become a "star," your life becomes filled with more and more people in your orbit who have little interest in you outside of what you can do for them, be it a selfie for social media, connecting them with someone who is even bigger than you, or just being friends with a celebrity. These people are to be kept at arm's length, and Dan's biggest mistake was throwing open the gates to let them all in. He was a friend of mine, and his story is a cautionary tale in my head as I move to ever-escalating heights in the conservative movement.

The LGBT cult is fun until it isn't. You get to live in a bubble where anyone who isn't up to date on the most recent sexual minority lingo is a "hater" or a "bigot." Never mind that all these "theories" are coined and developed in academia and disseminated to the masses via the social media accounts of poorly educated gay or transgender "celebrities" who exist solely in their sexual or gender identities because it's a marketing tool for them. If you live in New York City, you'll be invited to glamorous parties with LGBT "celebrities" and open bars, movie premieres, gallery openings, all of it. This was my life for years, until I started to see too many things that I had issues with, and I was kicked out. Here are a few things that I think are subverting and perverting what I call the "Alphabet Soup" of the LGBTQIAK+++ far-Left. Oh, and sometimes all those letters come with a "P" for "pedophile" at the end, you know, for the *truly* woke.

## THE LGBTQ CULT'S WAR ON LANGUAGE

When Kamala Harris walked onstage at the CNN "LGBTQ Town Hall" (or, as I like to call it, "The RNC Presidential Ad Campaign Buffet") and notified the audience that her "preferred gender pronouns" are she/hers[7], it was official: the cult's war on language had entered the mainstream. Now, "male" and "female" are just

---

7    Ian Schwartz, "Kamala Harris: 'My Pronouns Are She, Her, and Hers'; CNN's Cuomo: "Mine Too,' " RealClearPolitics, October 10, 2019, https://www.realclearpolitics.com/video/2019/10/10/kamala_harris_my_pronouns_are_she_her_and_hers_cnns_cuomo_mine_too.html.

not enough to cover the unlimited amount of genders that have been "discovered" on college campuses all over the country. GET WOKE, CLOWNS! We're now seeing the increase of "they" culture, which is basically a group of people so desperate for attention that they call themselves "nonbinary." That means they "identify" as "neither male nor female" (hence the "they"), so in order to feel secure in their delusion, they demand that everyone else use their "preferred gender pronoun" upon introduction or first meeting. The "nonbinaries" also prefer to dress in gender-neutral clothing that is somehow supposed to hide the fact that they tend to be immediately identifiable as either male or female—you know, one of the two genders. Now this is something that may work for, say, a Hollywood type like *Billions* actor Asia Kate Dillon, who has managed to generate a TON of free press for her...um, THEMself by making the central part of THEIR career a "nonbinary" identity. This works for woke Hollywood actors who need attention by any means necessary. For those of us in the real world outside of Hollyweird movie sets, things get a bit more complicated.

If you notice one theme with the cult, it is this: the majority of the population that are just perfectly fine with being one of two genders[8] are ALWAYS the ones bullied into changing how they see themselves to fit into this brave new world of wokeness (I should pitch that show to MSNBC). I'm sorry, I'm not a "cisgender" male (i.e., a male that actually likes my penis) because some trans people in a liberal arts school's Gender Studies 101 class decided that should be the term for the 99.99 percent of the human race that DOESN'T identify as trans. It's insanity. And if decent people don't start standing up to the mob and fighting back against their asinine rules, we'll be destined to a future in which nothing EVER

<hr>

8    Daniel Greenberg et al., "America's Growing Support for Transgender Rights," PRRI, June 11, 2019, https://www.prri.org/research/americas-growing-support-for-transgender-rights/.

gets done because we're too busy trying to differentiate between genders and pronouns.

## THE LGBTQ CULT'S WAR ON WOMEN

The LGBT cult wages war on women by making the argument that anyone who "feels" like a woman and makes even the most basic steps to transition is now an actual woman. OK, fine, you say. Women are women! SLAYYYYY, sis! However, the unquestioning acceptance that TRANS WOMEN ARE WOMEN (a statement generally only expressed via the shouting of hysterical trans activists, hence the caps) has made its way off of social media and into the real world with devastating consequences for actual women. Let's take, for example, the transgender assault on women's sports. Anyone with a bit of compassion would agree that transgender women shouldn't be barred from sports in *general*, but anyone with half a brain could see that maybe trans women competing with actual women isn't working out too well for...the women.

Like the female competitors who were TROUNCED by male-to-female transgender woman Mary Gregory, who broke four women's world records during a powerlifting competition,[9] including: Masters world squat record, open world bench record, Masters world deadlift record, and Masters world total record. Stunning and brave! Fortunately, Mary Gregory was eventually stripped of the titles because—WHOOPSIE!—she didn't tell the competition organizers that she was transgender. I guess she didn't think it was that big of a deal! By doing so, she violated their rules that

9    Alex Lasker, "Transgender Weightlifter Smashes Women's World Records, Sparking Backlash from Olympians," AOL, May 1, 2019, https://www.aol.com/article/news/2019/05/01/transgender-weightlifter-mary-gregory-smashes-womens-world-records/23720231/#.

place competitors into categories based on biological sex.[10] A concept that nowadays is so controversial, Gregory whined about it to none other than the *Washington Post*:

> "I felt like they were invalidating my gender and my identity," said Gregory, who began hormone replacement treatment a year ago and feels she should be allowed to compete alongside any other female.

Yes, you read that correctly. Forty-four-year-old Gregory, after forty-three ENTIRE YEARS as a male before "beginning hormone replacement treatment," feels that she should be allowed to compete alongside any other female—preferably one not competing with forty-three years of male bone and muscular development, I'm sure.

Or, as British Olympic medalist Sharron Davies, one of the few women who dare to speak out about such an obviously unlevel playing field, said on Twitter, "This is a trans woman - a male body with male physiology setting a world record & winning a woman's event in America in powerlifting. A woman with female biology cannot compete.. it's a pointless unfair playing field."[11] And, in case you were wondering why I had to go all the way across the pond to find a woman who spoke up, it's because the LGBTQ cult is so

10    Rick Maese, "Stripped of Women's Records, Transgender Powerlifter Asks, 'Where Do We Draw the Line?' " *Washington Post*, May 19, 2019, https://www.washingtonpost.com/sports/2019/05/16/stripped-womens-records-transgender-powerlifter-asks-where-do-we-draw-line/.

11    Sharron Davies (@sharrond62), "This Is a Trans Woman a Male Body with Male Physiology Setting a World Record & Winning a Woman's Event in America in Powerlifting," Twitter, April 28, 2019, https://twitter.com/sharrond62/status/1122421385232551941?ref_src=twsrc%5Etfw%7Ctwcamp%5Etweetembed%7Ctwterm%5E1122421385232551941&ref_url=https%3A%2F%2Fwww.aol.com%2Farticle%2Fnews%2F2019%2F05%2F01%2Ftransgender-weightlifter-mary-gregory-smashes-womens-world-records%2F23720231%2F.

invested in the idea that TRANS WOMEN ARE WOMEN that they will smear and excommunicate even legendary community icons. That's what happened to Martina Navratilova when *she* spoke out.

Yes, *that* Martina Navratilova. You know the one. Women's sports hero. Lesbian Icon. One of the baddest *human beings* to ever set foot on a tennis court who has been fighting for women (and gay) rights since before the LGBT cult Twitterati had any idea what *gender they were assigned at birth.* Navratilova entered the cult's radar after some rather eye-opening comments about Rachel McKinnon[12], yet *another* male-to-female transgender woman who made another transition from a middling male competitor in cycling to a world-class record-breaker as a female competitor. Navratilova tweeted,

"You can't just proclaim yourself a female and be able to compete against women. There must be some standards, and having a penis and competing as a woman would not fit that standard." Seems like pretty reasonable stuff to me, but not to the cult, who, as they say, pounced. (Turns out it's not just Republicans who do that!)

After these comments, the LGBTQ group Athlete Ally said, "We believe that growth is possible, and we extend once again to Martina the invitation to learn from this experience."[13] Let me put that in cult terms for you: "Apologize and come to us to bend the knee to the cult or you will be excommunicated. This is a warning." Navratilova responded by writing a *Sunday Times* article called "The Rules on Trans Athletes Reward Cheats and

12    Frances Perraudin, "Martina Navratilova Criticised over 'Cheating' Trans Women Comments," *Guardian*, February 17, 2019, https://www.theguardian.com/sport/2019/feb/17/martina-navratilova-criticised-over-cheating-trans-women-comments.

13    Rob Picheta and James Masters, "Martina Navratilova Dropped by LGBT Group over Trans Athletes Row," CNN, February 20, 2019, https://www.cnn.com/2019/02/20/tennis/martina-navratilova-dropped-lgbt-group-scli-spt-intl/index.html.

Punish the Innocent."[14] Hey, you don't become an icon by bowing down to Twitter mobs! And, by the way, don't you think it's a bit...curious that none of these women can find an American outlet to share these kinds of sentiments? That's because the cult has cowed the mainstream media into submission for even *daring* to ask the question. Remember, our mainstream media isn't filled with journalists but with pseudo-activists desperate to be on the "right" side of history and carry water for fringe elements of the Left. They think that being cheerleaders for any and everything trans will put them on the right side of history, but I truly believe it will be the exact opposite. In about five years when the lawsuits and tears start, my guess is they'll finally grow some balls and start doing some actual reporting on the topic. It will confirm what most of us who've been reading the research and doing the reporting they won't do already know to be true: social media-fueled transgender activism has gone too far, too fast, and it is women who are hurt the most. But go off with that pussy hat calling yourself a feminist, sis!

And, it's not just in women's sports where the TRANS WOMEN ARE WOMEN crowd openly wages war on the right of women to their own spaces. This crowd would also like for people who "feel" like they're women to gain access to sex-segregated spaces that are meant to keep vulnerable women safe, like homeless shelters,[15] and spaces where they are even more susceptible to being victims

---

14    Martina Navratilova, "The Rules on Trans Athletes Reward Cheats and Punish the Innocent," *Times*, February 17, 2019, https://www.thetimes. co.uk/article/the-rules-on-trans-athletes-reward-cheats-and-punish-the-innocent-klsrq6h3x.

15    "GLAD Files Complaint on Behalf of MA Transgender Woman Denied Access at Homeless Shelter," GLBTQ Legal Advocates & Defenders, April 4, 2013, https://www.glad.org/post/glad-files-complaint-behalf-ma-transgender-woman-denied-access-homeless-shelter/.

of sexual violence, like prisons.[16] In this agenda they're aided by the woke crowd who vastly misinforms prominent Democratic politicians to the point where we see the front-runner for the Democratic presidential nomination, Joe Biden, openly advocating for women who "feel" like women to be housed in women's prisons. No, I'm not making this up.

At yet *another* LGBTQ town hall in Iowa (these things are the Left's biggest gift to the conservative movement), Joe Biden's response to a question about transgender women in women's prisons went viral on conservative Twitter. Sleepy Joe said, "In prison the determination should be that your sexual identity is defined by what you say it is, not what in fact the prison says it is."[17] Uh-huh. And despite what the TRANS WOMEN ARE WOMEN crowd says about the scarcity of attacks of women by trans women in these spaces, it turns out that sometimes it really *does* happen.

Take the case of Karen White, a fifty-two-year-old transgender woman who raped two women before being sent to jail[18] and admitted to raping a few more once she was in prison. Oh, and according to the *Guardian*, "White has previous convictions for indecent assault, indecent exposure and gross indecency involving children,

16  Madeleine Kearns, "California's Transgender Prison Policy Is a Disaster for Women," *National Review*, June 26, 2019, https://www.nationalreview.com/2019/06/californias-transgender-prison-policy-is-a-disaster-for-women/.

17  Tim Fitzsimons, "Democratic 2020 Hopefuls Tout Their Pride at Iowa LGBTQ Forum," NBC News, September 21, 2019, https://www.nbcnews.com/feature/nbc-out/democratic-2020-hopefuls-tout-their-pride-iowa-lgbtq-forum-n1057236.

18  Nazia Parveen, "Transgender Prisoner Who Sexually Assaulted Inmates Jailed for Life," *Guardian*, October 11, 2018, https://www.theguardian.com/uk-news/2018/oct/11/transgender-prisoner-who-sexually-assaulted-inmates-jailed-for-life.

animal cruelty and dishonesty."[19] Stunning and brave! But wait, there's more from the *Guardian*:

> In 1989, when she was known by her birth name, Stephen Terence Wood, she was convicted of indecent exposure when she deliberately exposed herself near a children's playground.
>
> Twelve years later White would go on to indecently assault and commit gross indecency with two boys aged nine and 12. She was jailed for 18 months.
>
> And in 2003, not long after coming out of prison and while still on licence, she went on to rape a pregnant woman – the wife of a friend.
>
> The defendant, who was then known as Stephen Wood and living in Manchester, had offered to help decorate a flat of the woman, who was two months pregnant.

So, about the awful crimes this transgender woman committed back when she was a male: the TRANS WOMEN ARE WOMEN crowd is so opposed to the practice of "deadnaming"—using the previous name of a trans person pre-transition—that they will tell you it is LITERAL VIOLENCE, and part of their agenda is actively pursuing laws and regulations against this around the globe.[20][21] If what you just read makes you a bit wary about, I don't know, making it legal to COMPLETELY ERASE THE CRIMINAL HISTORY OF ANYONE

19   Ibid.
20   New York City Commission on Human Rights, "Gender Identity/Gender Expression: Legal Enforcement Guidance," February 15, 2019, https://www1.nyc.gov/site/cchr/law/legal-guidances-gender-identity-expression.page.
21   Megan White, "New Law in Australia Could Ban Using Wrong Pronouns for Transgender People," *Evening Standard*, December 10, 2018, https://www.standard.co.uk/news/world/new-law-in-australia-could-ban-using-wrong-pronouns-for-transgender-people-a4013401.html.

WHO MEDICALLY CHANGES THEIR GENDER, that doesn't make you transphobic; that makes you a human being with a brain.

These are the two biggest fronts of the trans war right now, and they are always, ALWAYS, fought on the behalf of male-to-female transgender people who seek access to these spaces. If you don't think that the radical transgender movement isn't a war on women, ask yourself a question: when was the last time you heard anyone make the argument for transgender men to be housed in *men's* prisons? Exactly.

## THE LGBTQ CULT'S WAR ON RELIGION

The assault on religion from the LGBTQ cult and its media allies works on two main fronts. First of all, Christianity itself must be attacked and presented as the enemy of gays and lesbians at all costs. This is why every instance of alleged homophobia from Evangelical Christians is amplified and disseminated within the cult for maximum outrage. This is why Christian-based fast food chain Chick-fil-A has become the cult's obsession, even though the chain broke its own rule of closing on Sundays[22] to feed first responders after the Pulse Orlando terrorist killed forty-nine gays and lesbians. Such hateful homophobes!

However, I'd be lying if I said there wasn't a far-Right radical element in the conservative movement that even in 2020 truly believes gays and lesbians are going to hell. In late 2019, during a stop at the Turning Point USA "Culture War" event with founder and President Charlie Kirk, I found myself face to face with the radically homophobic (and racist) element of the far-Right. At the tail end of one of the most exhausting months of traveling of my career, I

---

22  Hadley Malcolm, "Orlando Chick fil A Workers Reverse Sunday Hours Policy to Feed Volunteers," *USA Today*, June 14, 2016, https://www.usatoday.com/story/money/2016/06/14/chick-fil-a-opens-on-sunday-to-feed-orlando-blood-donors/85868494/.

arrived at Ohio State University tired, jet-lagged, and *totally* un-prepared for the onslaught of hate I was about to receive from a fringe element of the Right. So, when I received a question from the Q and A that asked "How does anal sex help win the culture war?" from a young man I would later realize was clutching rosary beads for maximum effect (I assume he couldn't find any pearls), I was honestly blindsided. Perhaps up until that point I was a bit naive about the conservative movement because I'd been so welcomed by mainstream conservative types that I thought that this kind of homophobia was truly a thing of the past. Well, it wasn't, and it was staring me right in the face.

My answer to the "question" wasn't amazing, though I did manage to get in a good dig about the kid's obsession with anal sex ("maybe you should find someone to explore your curiosity with"). Over the next few weeks, however, I'd be on the receiving end of an onslaught of hate from far-Right internet trolls who seemed to really, *really* hate that I was gay. I decided to face the thing head on and, in a YouTube video, said what would become the five most controversial words I have ever said: "I am a gay Christian."

Look, I have said MANY things in my new life as a famous Republican. I have said things that precious snowflakes would con-sider "racist," "homophobic" (even though I'm gay; that's how crazy they are), "islamophobic," and so forth. But I have NEVER seen the kind of vitriol and hate that was thrown at me when I ut-tered those five words. Luckily, I'm a grown-ass man who stopped giving a single solitary shit what anyone thinks of me long before I became famous, but even some of this stuff was off-the-rails nutty. I'd share some of the comments, but they're right on my YouTube page @robsmithonline under the "I'm a Gay Christian: Get Over It" video. See for yourself!

But here's the silver lining: the response wasn't *all* bad. In fact, some of it was even positive. I'm no preacher or Bible historian, and it's not in my lane to criticize how people interpret God's word, but for the life of me I cannot understand why—out of ALL the "sins" in the bible—homosexuality continues to drive people crazy. People literally compare me being gay to serial killers, rapists, and drug dealers. To these fringe types, it's really *that* deep. As you know by now, I was nearly killed in Iraq more than once. That kind of stuff changes you. I was ALWAYS a believer but moved away from God the more I got caught up in the cult, which is exactly what they wanted.

The cult would have you believe that the nastiest, most hateful messages thrown at me from Christians represented ALL Christians, but we all know that isn't true. I knew it before I uttered those words publicly, and I know it now. The reason the cult wants those people to represent all Christians is because they want to move gays and lesbians away from God and organized religion in the service of their agenda and the state. That is why stories about the small minority of truly hateful Evangelical Christians (think the "God hates fags" Westboro Baptist Church crowd) always get more attention than, say, Chick-fil-A opening its doors on a Sunday to feed people after the Pulse Orlando terrorist attack.

I believe that the tenuous relationship between America's increasing acceptance of gays and lesbians (not the LGBTQ cult) and the right of people to believe what they choose will be one of the biggest cultural battles of the coming decades. The fundamental problem with the cult is that its sense of self is so weak and easily broken that its endgame is using the full control of the government to legislate "acceptance." This can too easily slide into something pretty close to tyranny, like how failed presidential candidate Beto O'Rourke floated the idea of revoking the tax-exempt status of churches that wouldn't perform gay marriages.[23] As I said on *Tucker Carlson Tonight* in 2019 after Beto made those bonkers remarks, if a church didn't want to perform my marriage because it goes against its religious beliefs, I'd just FIND ANOTHER CHURCH. Mind-blowing! Such a simple concept seems unthinkable for the cult, which seeks to shove its views on the world down everyone's throats with the full force of the Democratic Party behind it.

I try my hardest to be a good man, and I am nowhere near perfect. Yet I'm secure in the fact that God loves me, and my relationship with Him is one of the biggest gifts I've received over the past few years. Bigger than Instagram followings, Fox News segments, and even meeting the president! The cult never talks about how many gay-affirming churches there are out there, but I know they exist. I personally don't attend any of them because they too often turn into left-wing political rallies, and I get enough politics in my daily life. In fact, my church—one of those welcoming, inclusive hipster types—firmly believes that marriage is between a man and a woman. It's right there in their bylaws on the internet for the world to see. However, that's not going to stop me from going there, and it won't stop me from receiving the word and knowing that I'm loved by Him. The cult puts so much energy into "warning" young gays and lesbians against Christianity because what the cult really wants them to worship is itself. I've talked extensively about the traps that the 2020 LGBTQ cult sets for young gays and lesbians who don't know God and are looking for something to believe in. I've got news for them: it isn't in identity; it's in something bigger than ALL of that. Don't worship the cult. Worship Him.

---

23   Jeffrey Cook, "Beto O'Rourke Said He Would Revoke Tax-Exempt Status from Religious Organizations That Oppose Same-Sex Marriage," ABC News, October 11, 2019, https://abcnews.go.com/Politics/beto-orourke-revoke-tax-exempt-status-religious-organizations/story?id=66213718.

# THE LGBTQ CULT'S WAR ON CHILDHOOD

## *The Curious Case of Drag Kid "Desmond Is Amazing"*

The saddest and most disturbing thing about the LGBTQ cult in 2020 is its embrace of "drag kid" culture. If for some reason you are lucky enough to not know what that is, I'll inform you, but I hope you're reading this on an empty stomach. In "drag kid" culture, preteen children mimic adult drag queens, complete with exaggerated femininity, makeup, heels, dresses, and, in one case, dancing in a midriff-baring shirt for tips in a gay bar in Brooklyn at 3 a.m.[24] Yes, really. That child is known as "Desmond Is Amazing" (I hate to even use the kid's name because God knows the therapy bills will probably be into the five figures for this one), and I fear he—much like America's first "trans child" Jazz Jennings—will soon become a cautionary tale for the Left's child-perverting agenda.

Desmond started watching *RuPaul's Drag Race* at the age of four, started dressing in drag at seven, and now at TEN YEARS OLD is a social media celebrity among the Alphabet Soup with a following of more than two hundred thousand people across multiple platforms.[25][26] I have personally seen this child escorted around New York City events by his mother, always in exaggerated drag, always with the kind of jaded "seen it all" attitude most of us don't get until our forties or even beyond. I'm sure when the far-Left gets a hold of my writing, I will be slammed as a "self-hating homophobic bigot" by saying all this, but the truth is that I feel for the boy,

---

24  Doug Mainwaring, "11-Year-Old 'Drag Kid' Dances in Popular NYC Gay Club as Patrons Toss Money at Him," LifeSite, December 17, 2018, https://www.lifesitenews.com/news/11-year-old-drag-kid-dances-in-popular-nyc-gay-club-as-patrons-toss-money-a.

25  Desmond Is Amazing (@desmondisamazing), Instagram, https://www.instagram.com/desmondisamazing/?hl=en.

26  Desmond Is Amazing (@DesmondisAmazing), Facebook, https://www.facebook.com/DesmondisAmazing/.

and I question the motives of ANY adults who would let their child become a part of something as adult and subversive as drag culture.

If you think that just maybe there's something a bit "off" with all this, you're a bigot who is "bullying" children. Never mind the fact that Desmond appeared in a YouTube video miming snorting the party drug ketamine[27] with an adult male drag queen.[28] C'mon, folks, be TOLERANT AND INCLUSIVE! If you're a survivor of childhood sexual abuse (which, if you've read this far, you know that I am) or you're just a normal adult who thinks there's a problem with a child being exploited and sexualized in this manner, then you need to just GET OVER IT, BOOMER!

What the Alphabet Soup doesn't realize is that this entire subculture crosses a line that most non-pedophile adults of *any* political affiliation and sexual orientation do NOT want crossed. The same Pandora's box that Evangelical Christians warned us about has been opened, and child drag queens are *sashaying* out of it with the encouragement of leftist adults who either think it is funny or subversive, or, more disturbingly, seek to exploit these kids monetarily and/or sexually. It's sick. However, Desmond is just the tip of a very disturbing iceberg.

"Drag kid" culture is exploding, helped along by left-leaning outlets like Mashable, who produced an internet mini-documentary

---

27   No One (@tweettruth2me), "11-Year Old Drag Kid Demonstrates Snorting Ketamine. Why Would Anyone Think This [Is] Healthy?" Twitter, January 13, 2019, https://twitter.com/tweettruth2me/status/1084332546 895368192?ref_src=twsrc%5Etfw%7Ctwcamp%5Etweetembed%7Ctwter-m%5E1128822708228239360&ref_url=https%3A%2F%2Fwww.redstate. com%2Fbonchie%2F2019%2F05%2F16%2F11-year-old-drag-queen-de-monstrates-snorting-drugs%2F.

28   Bonchie, "11 Year Old 'Drag Queen' Demonstrates Snorting Ketamine, Authorities Stand Idly By," RedState (blog), May 16, 2019, https://www.red-state.com/bonchie/2019/05/16/11-year-old-drag-queen-demonstrates-snorting-drugs/.

on him called "Desmond Is Amazing Is the Future and We're Here for It" that got nearly three million views on Twitter.[29] Thankfully, it seems like most of those views were from people that were outraged and disgusted, taking into account the tweet's unforgiving "ratio"—the number of comments relative to retweets. This tweet got WAY more comments then retweets which means that most people do NOT, in fact, think Desmond Is Amazing is the future. At least not a future any sane person would want to be a part of. Not to be outdone, "filmmaker" Megan Weinberg is unleashing the nauseating documentary *Drag Kids*, which means there are even *more* of these kids out there. I've not seen this film, nor do I have any desire to, but a reviewer for *Point of View (POV)* magazine put it best:

> Although Weinberg's energetic doc makes the point that the supportive parents must deal with community disapproval, monitor the kids' social media accounts, and worry about dangers lurking out there, it doesn't focus much on the disconcerting aspects of little boys voguing in girls' clothes.
>
> Lactacia [a famous "drag kid"] has been photographed with a naked adult drag queen. And for sure, the wigs, false eyelashes, tight dresses, high-heel boots, and lip-synching to Lady Gaga's "Bad Romance" are not entirely neutral.
>
> The parents deny they are sexualizing their children or that drag has anything to do with their sexual identity. As one of the kids puts it, a drag queen is merely a male "who wants to put on a feminine persona.[30]

The existence of Weinberg's film proves a disturbing point about this entire subculture: whenever there is a child being sexualized,

---

29    Mashable (@mashable), "Desmond Is Amazing Is the Future and We're Here for It," Twitter, November 3, 2019, https://twitter.com/mashable/status/1191023982516019201.

30    Maurie Alioff, "Review: 'Drag Kids,' " *Point of View,* April 29 2019, http://povmagazine.com/articles/view/review-drag-kids.

groomed, or exploited in this way, there's an adult around to make money from it.

One of the more insidious parts of the LGBTQ cult's war on childhood is how it has completely taken over organizations that were founded to focus on gaining equal rights for gays and lesbians—and is using them to promote a radical transgender agenda. These organizations, like the Human Rights Campaign (HRC) and GLAAD, have transitioned into far-Left organizations focused on promoting a radical trans agenda, including the aforementioned "drag kid" culture, and now seem laser-focused on using their power in the media to condition society to accept the "transing" of children, the next agenda on their to-do list. If you think I'm going "too far" or stretching the truth *just* a bit, well, dear reader, do I have a story for you.

Do you remember adorable little "transgender" nine-year-old Jacob, who just so happened to ask Elizabeth Warren a very thoughtful and not-at-all-rehearsed question about "children like me" at CNN's aforementioned hot-mess LGBTQ town hall as "his" mother beamed in the background?[31] You could almost *see* the dollar signs from the potential TLC reality TV deal in her eyes. As it turns out, this step into the spotlight wasn't the first time at the rodeo for little "Jacob" and his mother, Mimi Lemay. Little "Jacob" was the subject of an *NBC Nightly News* story way back in 2015, which racked up over one million views on YouTube when he was five years old. Mimi is also on the Human Rights Campaign's "Parents for Transgender Equality National Council," has published a book

31  Nik DeCosta-Klipa, "A Local Transgender Boy Asked Elizabeth Warren a Question during CNN's LGBTQ Town Hall," Boston.com, October 13, 2019, https://www.boston.com/news/politics/2019/10/11/elizabeth-warren-jacob-lemay.

about her "journey,"[32] and has even been the subject of a fawning profile from no less than *Cosmopolitan* magazine![33] A Google search for "Mimi Lemay trans child" turned up one hundred and ninety-four thousand results in less than one second.

I'd personally wager that Jacob's mom is a big fan of that particular money train and doesn't really want to see it end, even if little "Jacob" decides that one day "he" is done playing dress and wants to be a girl again. This is, to me, the fundamental danger of the transitioning of children that the leftist LGBTQ cult has made a centerpiece of their agenda. If you think that this doesn't have very real effects on our society and our rule of law, consider the case of James Younger.

Seven-year-old James Younger found himself at the center of a legal battle and national firestorm when news broke that his mother, Anne Georgulas, insisted that the child was "transgender," that he referred to himself as "Luna," and that she was seeking to place him on hormone replacement therapy. However, Younger's father, Jeffery, insisted that James had no signs of gender dysphoria, insisted on wearing traditional boy's clothes when they were together, and that James's "transgender" identity was primarily the influence of the mother. Georgulas was given full custody of the child by a Dallas jury, but thankfully a judge decided that both mother and father should have joint custody of the child and equal say in any medical procedures that the child should ever undergo.

---

32 Mimi Lemay, "*What We Will Become: A Mother, a Son, and a Journey of Transformation*," Amazon, November 12, 2019, https://www.amazon.com/What-We-Will-Become-Transformation/dp/0544965833/ref=sr_1_1?keywords=Mimi+Lemay&qid=1575339999&sr=8-1.

33 Tess Koman, "The Way This Family Supports Their 5-Year-Old Transgender Son Will Make You Weep," *Cosmopolitan*, April 21, 2015, https://www.cosmopolitan.com/sex-love/news/a39378/jacob-lemay-transgender-video/.

[34] Woke, attention-seeking parents like Georgulas are vulnerable to the messages being pushed by the cult, and it's not outside of the realm of possibility to wonder if Georgulas was seeking a little bit of national attention and a book deal of her own.

We shouldn't be sexualizing children, PERIOD. Nine-year-old Jacob should not be showered with this kind of attention for toying with gender like a child, and legal authorities should not have to step in to prevent seven-year-old James Younger from getting "transed" by an overbearing mother. And, if you think that there aren't transgender people that eventually transition *back* to the sex they were born as, I'd like you to meet a few.

### Meet the Detransitioners

There will be many that will call me "transphobic" for even daring to question the accepted transgender orthodoxy that has become gospel over the past seven to ten years. Criticize a trans person? TRANSPHOBIC! Point out that maybe two-year-old children can't correctly identify themselves as born in the wrong gender? TRANSPHOBIC! Though the cult won't believe it, I truly don't think I'm transphobic, just highly critical of something that seems to have so drastically altered the lives of so many young gays and lesbians only a decade into the social media era. I have more empathy for these kids than the average conservative, partly because I've lived through a lot of the insecurities, self-doubt, and mental health issues they have—which is precisely why I'm so critical of the "one-size-fits-all" approach to happiness the trans peddlers seem to be selling. The "transphobic" line of attack from the cult has gotten so bad over the past decade that many careers have been ruined

---

34    Jackie Salo and Aaron Feis, "Parents of Texas Boy at Heart of Gender Transition Case Retain Equal Custody," *New York Post*, October 24, 2019, https://nypost.com/2019/10/24/parents-of-texas-boy-at-heart-of-gender-transition-case-retain-equal-custody/.

and good people smeared for daring to question *any* of this, but that seems to be changing, starting with a legendary and bold gay conservative voice. In November of 2019, *New York Magazine* writer (and conservative gay icon) Andrew Sullivan took this conversation mainstream with an article called "The Hard Questions about Young People and Gender Transitions." In a *far* more sensitive way than I do, Sullivan lays out the questions about the gender orthodoxy that have overtaken a generation of young people, primarily lesbians. Of the young women he met who had decided to "detransition" back to their birth sex from transgender men, he writes:

> These women are not anti-trans, or religious nuts, or members of the far right. They expressed not a smidgen of transphobia, just a pressing concern that many teen-age women, particularly lesbians, struggling with gender dysphoria, have been convinced too quickly that the only solution is to change their sex. They worry that any kind of therapy apart from affirmation of transgender identity is now seen as transphobic, and that teens are able to get hormones far too easily.[35]

The all-too-easy availability of hormone therapy to gender-questioning young people has been a chief criticism of the current transgender movement. Some of these "gender" clinics have been the source of lawsuits.[36] As Sullivan puts it, "The widespread consensus today is that detransitioning is so rare even mentioning

---

35  Andrew Sullivan, "The Hard Questions about Young People and Gender Transitions," Intelligencer, November 1, 2019, https://nymag.com/intelligencer/2019/11/andrew-sullivan-hard-questions-gender-transitions-for-young.html.

36  Jonathon Van Maren, "Mom Sues Transgender Clinic for Giving 'Inaccurate' Information on Risks of Hormone Blockers," LifeSite (blog), October 16, 2019, https://www.lifesitenews.com/blogs/mom-sues-transgender-clinic-for-giving-inaccurate-information-on-risks-of-hormone-blockers.

it borders on transphobic." He's correct. The small but growing amount of "detransitioners" share their stories via Twitter and social media. The trans lobby and powerful allies like former gay rights (now transgender) organizations GLAAD and HRC make it very clear to the mainstream outlets that give glowing profiles to glamorous transgender actresses and "trans" children like Jacob that any coverage of detransitioners is off-limits. Even the *New York Times* found itself the target of the cult after publishing the story "Chest Binding Helps Smooth the Way for Transgender Teens, but There May Be Risks,"[37] which showcased the negative health effects of "binding," a process where females "transitioning" into men painfully constrict their breasts to their chest in order to minimize their appearance in public. After the story was criticized as "transphobic," the *Times* published the follow-up " 'It's Binding or Suicide': Transgender and Non-Binary Readers Share Their Experiences with Chest Binders."[38] The cult is so sensitive to any exploration of the negative health effects of their methods that none other than the *New York Times* has to backpedal for their absolution. SAD!

And as for those negative effects, well, hear it from their lips to Sullivan's ears:

> "I have back issues, lower lung capacity, and permanent dents around my shoulders," one told me. "Every now and again, I have to push a rib back in to breathe," another recounts. "I have permanent bruising," another explains. "Serious back issues," says another, who cannot carry a backpack for long without pain.

---

37  Amy Sohn, "Chest Binding Helps Smooth the Way for Transgender Teens, but There May Be Risks," *New York Times*, May 31, 2019, "https://www.nytimes.com/2019/05/31/well/transgender-teens-binders.html.

38  Lara Takenaga, " 'It's Binding or Suicide': Transgender and Non-Binary Readers Share Their Experiences with Chest Binders," June 17, 2019, https://www.nytimes.com/2019/06/17/reader-center/chest-binding.html.

The detransitioners are a growing group, and mark my words: when the MSM starts doing their jobs and stops seeing themselves as the public PR arm of the LGBTQ cult lobby, the detransitioners' stories will end radical transgender ideology as we know it. And that day can't come soon enough.

Jamie Shupe is the most famous detransitioner in America—and you've probably never heard of him. Shupe is an Army veteran with severe mental and emotional issues dating back to the sexual abuse he endured as a child. Shupe first transitioned to female and then to nonbinary (neither male nor female), in fact becoming the first person in America to have the sex on his birth certificate legally changed to "X" for nonbinary. He eventually detransitioned back to male. Quite a story, right? Well, as far as what Shupe himself thinks about his story, the title of his first-person piece for The Daily Signal says it all: "I Was America's First 'Nonbinary' Person. It Was All a Sham."[39] He writes:

> Four years ago, I wrote about my decision to live as a woman in The New York Times,[40] writing that I had wanted to live "authentically as the woman that I have always been," and had "effectively traded my white male privilege to become one of America's most hated minorities."
>
> Three years ago, I decided that I was neither male nor female, but nonbinary—and made headlines[41] after an

---

39    James Shupe, "I Was America's First 'Nonbinary' Person. It Was All a Sham," Daily Signal, March 10, 2019, https://www.dailysignal.com/2019/03/10/i-was-americas-first-non-binary-person-it-was-all-a-sham/.

40    Jamie Shupe, "Jamie Shupe," Transgender Lives: Your Stories, *New York Times*, https://www.nytimes.com/interactive/2015/opinion/transgender-today/stories/jamie-shupe.

41    Mary Emily O'Hara, "Oregon Becomes First State to Add Third Gender to Driver's Licenses," NBC News, June 15, 2017, https://www.nbcnews.com/feature/nbc-out/oregon-becomes-first-state-add-third-gender-driver-s-licenses-n772891.

Oregon judge agreed to let me identify as a third sex, not male or female.

Now, I want to live again as the man that I am.

I'm one of the lucky ones. Despite participating in medical transgenderism for six years, my body is still intact. Most people who desist from transgender identities after gender changes can't say the same.

Jamie's story isn't unique. Social media is filled with stories of detransitioners just like him—people like Walt Heyer, who lived for eight years as a woman, detransitioned, and now runs the website sexchangeregret.com[42] for people who seek a path back to their birth sex after transitioning. The stories on the site are harrowing. One mother of a "trans" child authored an article titled "What It's like to Lose Your Child to the 'Transgender Cult.'" One transgender woman writes about how she regrets her surgery. And perhaps most horrifyingly of all, Walt shares his own reporting from the *Federalist*[43] about multiple patients who complained of botched sex changes and mutilation from the Oregon Health and Science University in Oregon. Their stories are nearly uniform, with most feeling like they were rushed into sex-change surgery and left with permanent scarring and irreversible damage to their reproductive area. Unsurprisingly, taxpayers were on the hook for most of these surgeries to the tune of more than three times what was estimated:

> In January 2015, Oregon Medicaid (known as Oregon Health
> Plan) started paying for sex reassignment surgery — the
> same year that (sex-change doctor in question) Dugi went

42  "Home," Sex Change Regret, accessed February 18, 2020, https://sexchangeregret.com/.

43  Walt Heyer, "9 Transgender Patients Complain of Mutilation, Botched Sex-Change Surgeries in Oregon," *Federalist*, December 6, 2018, https://thefederalist.com/2018/12/06/9-transgender-patients-complain-mutilation-botched-sex-change-surgeries-oregon/.

abroad for training. State regulators estimated 175 patients would use the benefit that first year at a cost to taxpayers of less than $150,000. The reality was different by orders of magnitude — more than 700 people used it and the budget was three times higher than estimated.

Any Oregon resident whose income falls below a certain threshold is eligible for Medicaid benefits. A quick look on social media shows one solution being touted for free gender change surgery is to move to Oregon, keep one's income below the limit, and allow Medicaid to pay the entire cost.

Make no mistake: when leftist politicians pander to the cult for votes, this is the brave new world they envision. The rest of us are left shaking our heads at how things have moved so quickly in what is so obviously the wrong direction for taxpayers, for Americans, and for the confused teens who rapidly get sucked into the cult as a way to escape other, more pressing issues.

## GUN RIGHTS ARE GAY RIGHTS

LGBTQ cult members spend a lot of time lecturing the rest of the world about how oppressed they are. Stories of gay men who were gay bashed routinely go viral. LGBTQ cult websites and blogs regularly share poorly sourced and low-information articles about black transgender women whose lives were lost to violence. At the same time, the anti-gun agenda has so thoroughly infiltrated and co-opted the LGBT movement that we have groups with names like "Gays Against Guns" (seriously), and a Pulse Orlando survivor has become one of the most prominent anti-gun voices among gays and lesbians. If the big, bad world out there is so dangerous for LGBT people, why on earth are we lining up to give our second amendment rights away?

I know the feeling of being a gay man walking down the street hand in hand with a boyfriend, and feeling powerless when a group of hecklers decides that they're going to crack jokes about the fags, and hoping that the jokes don't escalate into physical violence. Look, I live in the real world, and I had more than one encounter like that before I started thinking much differently about the second amendment. Violence happens against LGBT people all the time. I'm not arguing that it doesn't. So why on earth would LGBT "activists" spend equal amounts of time convincing the rest of the world that we live in a constant state of fear and advocating for gun bans?

The gays and lesbians being used to push a "gun control" agenda don't understand that they're being used by leftist movements that seek to disarm them to exert further government control. You'd think that a community not too far removed from the years of watching the federal government look the other way while the AIDS crisis killed a generation of gay men would be a *bit* more cautious about advocating to give *more* control to that same government! This is one of the more insidious aspects of the leftist agenda, because the LGBTQ cult is feeding an entire generation of young LGBT people the dueling messages that they're perpetual victims *and* that they should be advocating for "gun control" and against their constitutional right to protect themselves.

Gun rights are gay rights. The right to bear arms given by the second amendment was given to *all* citizens—even the gay ones. Because armed gays don't get bashed.

## THE LGBTQ CULT'S WAR ON CONSERVATIVE GAYS

There is nothing a cult hates more than a defector, and conservative gays have defected from the LGBTQ cult. We call out the outrageousness. We question the unquestionable. We say the unthinkable. I've personally been on the end of the LGBTQ cult's ire for quite some time. Conservative gays and lesbians are dangerous to the cult. The cult gains power by convincing people who don't know any better that the lunacy they're pushing represents ALL gays and lesbians, but as more conservative gays with large platforms like me and others speak up, their arguments become angrier, more emotional, and therefore weaker. Even a few years ago, cancel culture would've all but guaranteed that someone like me couldn't exist. I would've been "deplatformed," smeared as "transphobic," and not be allowed to enter "polite" society. And yes, a bit of that has happened, but something else has happened as well: gays and lesbians are starting to wake up to the cult's tactics and move away from their nonsense. Here's the thing about social media: GLAAD, HRC, and all the different arms of Gay, Inc. who decide among themselves who is or isn't an "acceptable gay," are losing power. The people find me on Twitter, Instagram, and Facebook (@robsmithonline, by the way), and my response from gays and lesbians falls into one of three camps. Either they're conservative gays who think I'm an amazing gay icon and the best thing since silicone-based lube, liberal gays who disagree with my politics but 100 percent (privately) agree with my critiques of the cult, or cult members who are so far gone they scream about the Trump administration's "war on LGBTQ people" that they can never seem to find any facts or statistics to back up.

I believe that conservative gays will save the LGBTQ cult from itself. We represent a welcome throwback to the time when gays and lesbians wanted nothing more than to assimilate into society, live our lives, and be left alone. We're a welcome respite from the vulgarities of the attention-seeking cult, mix well with the heterosexuals, and are honestly the last line of defense against the rapidly growing anti-gay backlash to the excesses the cult seems eager to smear in the faces of Middle America. I've been a gay man for a long time now, and I've been watching trends long enough to know that the excesses of the cult are short-lived. Most gays and lesbians want the same things that our straight counterparts do: the American dream, a house, a few vacations every year, perhaps even a family. By modeling this behavior—not cult excesses—to the younger generation of gays and lesbians coming of age, I think conservative gays can stem the tide of the cult before it overwhelms us all.

## ESCAPING THE LGBTQ CULT

Escaping the cult is hard. Not only do you have to be strong enough to go up against countless A-list actors, celebrities, and entertainers who smugly declare themselves to be on the "right" side of history, but you also stand to lose gay and lesbian friends and acquaintances when you become too hot to handle. That's what happened to me. I'm called a "sellout" Auntie Thomasina (the gays' version of "Uncle Tom" because there truly is NO part of the African American civil rights movement that they won't rip off for their own means), disinvited to parties, a PARIAH in West Hollywood, and so on. But don't cry for me, people; I knew full and well what I was doing when I decided to make a very public defection from the cult, and I know that people like me and other prominent conservative gays are taking the hits so that the liberal gays can finally start discussing the issues I've brought up minus the fear of being "canceled." If there's anything that gives me hope in a sea of social media-verified celebrities that are TERRIFIED to even gingerly critique the radical LGBTQ Left's tactics I've just laid out for you, it's the dozens of DMs and emails that I get every single month from gays and lesbians. They usually go a little something like this: "I'm not a conservative, and I'll NEVER be a Republican, but THANK YOU for speaking out about this stuff! I'm afraid to because, if I do,

I'll lose all my friends!" Here's what the cult doesn't want you to realize: THIS IS COMMON SENSE CRITICISM INDEPENDENT OF POLITICS. It is not a "left" or "right" issue to speak up at the weird and gross sexualization of children. It's not a "conservative viewpoint" to stand up for the rights of women to their own spaces, be they clothing store fitting rooms, sex-segregated sports teams, homeless shelters, or, yes, even prisons. Escaping the LGBTQ cult isn't really about becoming a gay Republican like I have. If you've read this far in the book, you know my politics run much deeper than just the cult stuff. Escaping the LGBTQ cult is about normal, hardworking, everyday gays and lesbians standing up and saying "FALL BACK, HOLLYWOOD WEIRDOS! THIS SHIT DOESN'T REPRESENT ME!" And I hope that if this breakdown of leftist LGBTQ cult lunacy does one thing, it inspires MORE gays and lesbians to do just that. Yes, even the liberals.

## Chapter 16

# THE KANYE EFFECT

## WHY BLACK AMERICANS ARE LEAVING DEMOCRATS BEHIND

I'm not interested in providing you with an encyclopedic break-down of the myriad ways in which Democrats and liberal policies have destroyed African American communities over the past forty years. I won't bore you with pages about how the single motherhood rate in the black community has exploded since the '60s or about how modern welfare systems are set up to incentivize it. I won't delve into how once-great black cities like Detroit, Baltimore, and Cleveland have been decimated by liberal policies, or how Planned Parenthood was founded by the eugenicist Margaret Sanger, who *really* didn't want you to know[44] that one of her aims with Planned Parenthood was "to exterminate the Negro population."[45] Oops!

---

44    TFP Student Action, "21 Quotes by Margaret Sanger That Will Probably Make You Sick," November 20, 2017, https://tfpstudentaction.org/blog/margaret-sanger-quotes.

45    Margaret Sanger to Dr. C. J. Gamble, December 10, 1939, Smith College Libraries, https://libex.smith.edu/omeka/files/original/d6358bc3053c9318

Sorry, Margaret! If you've read anything by Thomas Sowell or listened to the great Larry Elder for even five minutes, you already know all of these things—and if you don't, those two intellectual and moral giants are a great place to start.

I'm more interested in the ways in which our very modern social media and entertainment culture has managed to enslave the minds of young black people all over again. How liberal gatekeepers in our entertainment and journalism fields stoke the omnipresence of white racism to keep them from achieving their fullest potential. How ultra-wealthy and successful rappers and actors feed blacks a near-constant buffet of oppression to stay relevant and line their own pockets. How the constant onslaught of the message of black victimhood in the social media era keeps young blacks locked in constant struggle with their ever-present white oppressors. I'm not a big fan of plantation talk from black conservatives. I find it simplistic and overtly incendiary, as if the mental shackles these young people are kept in by the lies of the Left can be compared to what I believe is the greatest horror and biggest embarrassment in American history.

And yet, a kind of mental slavery is the only way I can explain it. How else can we explain the millions of young black minds who see America as nothing more than a place of evil white oppressors while simultaneously elevating those who look like them who have achieved wealth and fame to a near-mythical status? How else can we explain the insidious nature behind multimillionaire rappers and actors who exist in rarefied spaces, yet speak as if white racism is the primary problem in their lives? To break through the decades of conditioning in even the smallest way, the black conservative movement would need someone so iconic that he couldn't be ignored, someone so massively famous and successful he couldn't

3295bf2df1c0c931.pdf.

be controlled, someone who is such a cultural giant that he could never be "canceled" by the far-Left wing of black Twitter. The movement would need someone like Kanye West. Any movement in black conservatism that happened after Kanye donned the MAGA cap and went instantly viral worldwide would have to be at least partially attributed to him. It would have to be the Kanye Effect.

Kanye West is not the reason black Americans are starting to wake up to the lies of the Left. However, the influence of one of the most iconic rappers and cultural figures of all time on the *visibility* of black Republicans in the Trump era is undeniable. In the whirlwind few months after Kanye donned the MAGA cap, Tweeted about black conservative firebrand Candace Owens (making her *the* most important black millennial conservative in America), and participated in *that* Oval Office conference with Trump, America woke up to the presence of black Republicans in a way that they never really had before. So, of course, that meant that the mainstream media had to destroy Kanye.

## HOW "WOKE CULTURE" HURTS BLACK AMERICA

In order to comprehend how and why one of the most iconic rappers in American history became a target of the entire mainstream media and entertainment complex, you have to understand "woke culture." To be "woke" is—according to Dictionary.com—"being conscious of racial discrimination in society and other forms of oppression and injustice." So, racism, sexism, homophobia, and other forms of discrimination exist. Got it! I'm not the kind of black conservative that denies *any* of these things. I'm more of a "get over it and get money" kinda guy, but the "woke culture" people obsess over any and every perceived racial slight, amplify it for clicks and media attention, and make *entire careers* out of making whites feel guilty for…being white. I heard a secondhand story about a man who makes $80,000 PER MONTH on the speaking circuit lecturing whites about "white privilege." So *that* should give you a sense of the financial incentive that is wrapped up in making whites feel guilty about being white and making blacks feel like perpetual victims.

There is an entire online ecosystem of these people, and they make a TON of money. Maybe they're writers at middling black-oriented websites who await every viral tale of racism like vultures picking at a dead animal to throw the red meat out to their perpetually outraged and aggrieved base of millennial and zoomer blacks. Maybe they're C-list television actors who become tireless "activists" for false idols like Colin Kaepernick to remain relevant on social media. Maybe they're cable television personalities whose entire shtick is fighting the good fight against racism from cable TV sets, Hollywood red carpets, and behind the podiums for speaking engagements that they've been paid five figures to do. These types love to call black conservatives grifters to discredit us, when the reality is that they're running the biggest grift of all.

I was a semi-regular on the cable news circuit during the time of Kanye's awakening, and I'd never seen so many elements from entertainment and journalism come together in an absolute *onslaught* meant purely to destroy a black man who thought differently from the way he was "supposed" to think. "What I saw was a Minstrel show today," said newly crowned Woke King Don Lemon on *CNN Tonight*[46] shortly after the meeting, adding, "Kanye needs help …

46   *CNN Tonight* (@CNNtonight), ""What I Saw Was a Minstrel Show Today," Twitter, October 11, 2018. https://twitter.com/CNNTonight/status/1050523698996731904?ref_src=twsrc%5Etfw%7Ctwcamp%5Etweetembed%7Ctwterm%5E1050523698996731904&ref_url=https%3A%2F%2Fwww.forbes.com%2Fsites%2Fprudygourguechon%2F2018%2F10%2F14%2F3-facts-about-mental-illness-to-wrap-up-the-kanye-west-don-lemon-kerfuffle%2F.

this was an embarrassment, Kanye's mother is rolling over in her grave." Classy! Legendary black actress Jenifer Lewis also chimed in to CNN,[47] saying, "I just feel so sorry for him. They are going to try to get me in a room with him when he gets back from Uganda, and all I can tell everyone is that I will do my best."

And if you think the many, *many* articles written about Kanye's "mental illness" weren't meant to delegitimize him—and by extension other black conservatives—you really must not be paying attention. Furthermore, I'd argue that this treatment wasn't intended only to delegitimize him but to ultimately destroy him, lest any other black entertainers get any ideas about stepping outside of left-wing talking points. Even Chance the Rapper had to *issue a public apology*[48] after tweeting "Black people don't have to be Democrats,"[49] lest he somehow be mistaken for advocating for black Americans to use their hard-won voting rights to vote for anyone but Democrats.

The way the "woke left" treated Kanye during this period is shameful. The same people who promote themselves as exalted figures that are "tolerant, inclusive, and respectful" of everything from the rights of black transgender sex workers to late-term abortion attacked Kanye's admitted mental health issues with glee. I'll never understand the absolute joy these people have in "canceling" people. I was personally on the other end of a few cable TV

47  Lisa Respers France, "Jenifer Lewis Wants to Help Kanye West," CNN, October 22, 2018, https://www.cnn.com/2018/10/17/entertainment/jenifer-lewis-mental-health-kanye/index.html.

48  Carl Lamarre, "Chance the Rapper Apologizes for His 'Poorly Timed Comments' on Twitter, Takes Aim at Donald Trump," Billboard, April 27, 2018, https://www.billboard.com/articles/columns/hip-hop/8395346/chance-the-rapper-apologizes-tweets.

49  Deena Zaru, "Chance the Rapper: 'Black People Don't Have to Be Democrats,' " CNN, April 25, 2018, https://www.cnn.com/2018/04/25/politics/chance-the-rapper-kanye-west-donald-trump/index.html.

battles with black liberals who thought it was completely legitimate to openly question Kanye's mental state of mind, as if the fact that he *dared* to support a political figure that wasn't a Democrat somehow made this OK.

I have no doubt that some of these black liberals mean well, and I'm sure they would tell you that it wasn't about Kanye being a conservative or Republican per se but that they just couldn't get behind him supporting *Donald Trump*! Well, history will tell you that that is just a lie. Why then did it take a full year for Republican Supreme Court Justice Clarence Thomas—the *only* black on the court—to get an exhibit in the Smithsonian National Museum of African American History and Culture?[50] The truth is, the Left in America has a long history of calling black Republicans everything from "bootlickers" to "Uncle Toms" to "coons" to "house niggers" in order to keep us safely "in line" on the left, where we supposedly belong. I've been called all of these things and more since my very public conversion. But that history you can find anywhere. I told you I'm going to give you stuff you can only get *here*, and I always keep my promises.

A few months after my social media exploded, I had apparently made enough noise to attract the attention of producers for the digital media network Vice who were looking for some black conservative voices to balance out a political panel they were putting together. The video, "Black Conservatives Debate Black Liberals," became— and I'm completely serious about this—an instantly iconic internet sensation. The two versions[51] of that particular video[52] combined to

---

50  Bradford Richardson, "Smithsonian Gives Clarence Thomas a Spot in Year-Old African American History Museum," *Washington Times*, September 25, 2017, https://www.washingtontimes.com/news/2017/sep/25/clarence-thomas-spot-african-american-museum/.

51  Vice, "Black Conservatives Debate Black Liberals on American Politics (Extended Version)," Vice Office, March 3, 2019, YouTube video, https://www.youtube.com/watch?v=IVIoC5ROaHk.

52  Ibid.

generate over ten million views on social media, and the panel is still the most visible thing I've ever done. When I'm traveling to lecture at an event and get stopped at an airport coffee shop, that video is what black people want to discuss. When I arrived in Baltimore and was stopped by a young black man at the train station, *that video* was how he knew me. The Vice video struck a nerve because—finally—people were being exposed to a nuanced and respectful conversation between blacks with different political views. Imagine *that*! Black Americans are smarter and more complicated than we're given credit for in the vast majority of the media. We're more nuanced than the screeching black leftists who dominate mainstream media outlets would have you believe, and more balanced than some of the more extreme black conservative voices who think the only way to verbalize their beliefs is to disparage less fortunate people in the community. What the success of the Vice video told me is that America is desperate to see black Americans with differing political views talk to one another outside of the limiting confines of cable news, and they're starting to notice a difference between what their eyes are telling them about America and their fellow Americans and what the endless stream of black liberal talking heads on television are telling them to think about both.

## THE OBAMA MYTH

I'll never really know just *why* the Vice video exploded the way it did, but one of the more talked-about exchanges was when the other black conservatives on the panel and I admitted to voting for President Barack Obama solely because he was black. It's true. I've admitted it on camera to millions of people, and I'm admitting it right now to you. I now look back at the tears that streamed down my cheeks when I watched Obama gain the electoral votes needed to win the presidency that night in November of 2008 with embarrassment and a bit of wistfulness at my naïveté. In that moment I felt powerful. I felt represented. And I felt that I really didn't need to make any moves to take control of my *own* life because a black man would now occupy the White House. And *that* is the problem.

To understand the hold that what I call "The Obama Myth" has on African Americans, you need to get a sense of just how powerful the imagery of *that* family in the White House was to us. The Left is very adept at selling black Americans the idea that black politicians will always have our best interests at heart, and there was no better way to do that than to have an attractive black family occupy the most coveted address in the world. While the black unemployment rate topped 16 percent on eleven different occasions[53] during the Obama years, blacks were treated to a nonstop onslaught of the then-first family featured in the most prominent black-oriented media in the United States. Indeed, in March 2010 when the black unemployment rate was at 16.8 percent—its highest level between 2009 and 2019,[54] Barack and Michelle Obama appeared on the cover of Essence,[55] the iconic magazine for black women.

This was par for the course with how the myth of Obama was sold to African American voters. He was our icon. He was our legend. The full force of the liberal-controlled mainstream media was used to sell the myth, and that was one of the many things that protected Obama from any real criticism. As the former chairman of the Congressional Black Caucus, Emanuel Cleaver, told Guardian opinion writer Gary Younge,[56] "With 14% unemployment, if we had

---

53 "Labor Force Statistics from the Current Population Survey," U.S. Bureau of Labor Statistics, accessed February 18, 2020, https://data.bls.gov/timeseries/LNS14000006.

54 Ibid.

55 Kevin Hall, "Barack & Michelle Obama Featured AGAIN in *Essence* Magazine!" Gossip on This, February 12, 2010, https://gossiponthis.com/2010/02/12/obama-essence/.

56 Gary Younge, "Barack Obama and the Paradox behind His African American Support Base," *Guardian*, November 3, 2012, https://www.theguardian.com/

a white president we'd be marching around the White House. The president knows we are going to act in deference to him in a way we wouldn't to someone white."

The image of Obama that was sold was cool, calm, and collected. Because he looked like us, we were to believe that he was actually doing things for black people without actually, you know, making sure of it. It didn't matter if you weren't working. It didn't matter if you saw diminished opportunities around you. It didn't matter if the economy wasn't doing well. It didn't matter if the black unemployment rate was at near-historic highs. He was "our" guy in the White House. And that was supposed to be enough. Anyone who criticized him in public risked being seen as aligning themselves with "racists" on the right who were trying to "take a good black man down." This is how blacks were taught to see Barack Obama, and it was to our detriment. There is a line of criticism from conservatives that says that Obama exacerbated racism and negative racial relations in a way that no other president has, which I think is only half true and misses the point.

It wasn't necessarily that the man *himself* used his race as a wall with which to shield himself from all legitimate critiques of his policies and actions (or lack thereof); it was the kid gloves with which he was treated by the mainstream media. Obama was the "cool black friend" in the heads of prominent white journalists, thought leaders, entertainers, and media executives desperate to lionize him so as not to seem racist. The black ones saw him as their way to access the power that the Oval Office provided. And when you have so many powerful people with vested interests in selling the myth of someone, it's only par for the course for the ones being brainwashed to buy into it. Most prominent blacks in media, entertainment, and politics still are.

commentisfree/2012/nov/03/obama-african-americans-paradox.

Any mention of him in black-oriented spaces continues to refer to him as the "Forever President" and Michelle Obama as the "Forever First Lady." Even to this day, the "Michelle Obama is a man" jokes made on the Far Right still turn my stomach with the ugliness of the racial hatred inherent in them, and my MANY criticisms of Obama himself remain focused on the way of thinking that exploded during his popularity that I find severely detrimental to the success of blacks in this country. The myth of Obama still holds strong. In essence, what we saw during the Obama years was the EXACT opposite of what we're seeing with the media treatment of President Donald Trump. This is why the Left absolutely DESPISES black Obama-to-Trump defectors.

## THE TRUMP TRUTH

I hesitated to include Trump in this book because I believe that far too many people on both sides of the aisle are too emotionally invested in him as a political figure to judge him impartially. However, the truth is that Trump HAS done good things for African Americans! The "lowest ever black unemployment" touted by right-leaning political figures is a great thing, but the truth is that these numbers had been trending downward for a very long time. However, the fact that they've hit record lows during an exploding economy that Trump's policies are very much responsible for says something. But I'd like to point to two very big wins for African Americans that get very little attention from the mainstream media: the passage of the First Step Act and the Trump administration's Senate passing a bipartisan bill to permanently fund HBCUs (historically black colleges and universities).

So about those HBCUs: a lot of my conservative fans like to downplay any mention of "black" this or "gay" that and like to silence any mention of difference by stating that "We are all

Americans." Look, while that is true, the experiences of minorities just aren't the same as those of white Americans. That's not to demonize white people. I love ya'll! I even married one of you! But black Americans have, to put it *gingerly*, a VERY different experience as Americans—which is where the HBCUs come in.

HBCUs were created in response to racist exclusion of African Americans from mainstream colleges and universities back in the days of segregation and open societal racism against African Americans. They remain an integral part of the culture and experience of African Americans in this country, and when the Trump administration-led Senate passed a bill to PERMANENTLY FUND HISTORICALLY BLACK COLLEGES AND UNIVERSITIES, I thought you'd hear the same black celebrities who profess to LOVE HBCUs screaming about this from the rooftops! According to CNN:[57]

> The bipartisan bill known as the FUTURE Act (Fostering Undergraduate Talent by Unlocking Resources for Education) strives to strengthen HBCUs as well as other minority-serving institutions by providing $255 million annually. The measure makes the federal student aid application process -- the Free Application for Federal Student Aid -- easier by eliminating up to 22 questions and the process that had required some students to verify IRS documentation with the Department of Education in order for aid to be released.

As of this writing, the bill is headed to the House to be voted on again, and as Ivanka Trump indicated on Twitter,[58] the White House is ready and willing to sign the legislation. Of course, you

---

57  Shawna Mizelle, "Senate Passes Bill to Permanently Fund Historically Black Colleges and Universities," CNN, December 5, 2019, https://www.cnn.com/2019/12/05/politics/hcbu-senate-bill-permanent-funding/index.html.

58  Ivanka Trump (@Ivanka Trump), "Let's Put an End to Any Debate on Our Responsibility to Strengthen HBCU's + Minority Serving Institutions,"

shouldn't be surprised that the passage of this legislation was met with crickets from the black members of the media "resistance." African Americans actually being helped during what they will have you believe is the most racist administration in American presidential history doesn't fit their narrative, so they exclude it. Their hope is twofold: that voters of ALL colors are too simple, stupid, and silly to find the facts for themselves, and that regular voting blacks in this country are so cowed by the prominent black voices in mainstream entertainment, media, and journalism that shame and silence black Trump supporters that they wouldn't dare think for themselves. But the truth is...black Americans are waking up.

In two separate polls released within a week of one another in November 2019, African American support of Trump reached 34 and 34.5 percent, respectively. As I wrote at the time:[59]

> I believe it is too early to say whether the two recent polls are indicative of a major and decisive decision among African-American voters to swing for Trump in November 2020, but they represent a pattern that is becoming too common to ignore.

What the Left also likes to ignore, but what is visible among blacks that exist in the real world outside of the coasts and cable news sets, is that enforcing laws against illegal immigration HELPS African Americans...and will probably help Trump snag more of the black vote in 2020.

---

Twitter, December 5, 2019, https://twitter.com/IvankaTrump/status/1202656907925901312.

59    Rob Smith, "Rob Smith: Trump's 34% Black Approval Shows 2020 Momentum," Breitbart News, December 1, 2019, https://www.breitbart.com/2020-election/2019/12/01/rob-smith-trumps-34-black-voters-approval-shows-2020-momentum/.

# DEMOCRATS HAVE TRADED BLACKS FOR ILLEGAL IMMIGRANTS

Illegal immigration hurts black Americans. It's not racist to say now, and it certainly wasn't racist when legendary African American Congresswoman Barbara Jordan took it on as the chair of the US Commission on Immigration Reform from 1994 to 1996. In her bipartisan review of America's immigration policy, she wrote:[60]

> For immigration to continue to serve our national interest, it must be lawful. There are people who argue that some illegal aliens contribute to our community because they may work, pay taxes, send their children to our schools, and in all respects except one, obey the law. Let me be clear: that is not enough.

Of course, she was right then and is right now. But what has changed? The Democratic Party needs its beloved "people of color" coalition to lead it to the promised land of free stuff for everybody! There are two big problems with this. First off, the "majority-minority" theory relies too heavily on the theory that "people of color" are aligned with each other (and, by extension, the Democratic Party) purely because of their status as nonwhite people. That simplistic theory denies the complexity of people beyond their skin tones and outright ignores the elephant in the room when it comes to black and Latino relations. The biggest chink in the Democrats' alleged "people of color" armor is surely its stance on illegal immigration. Think about this: over the course of three decades, the Democrat line on illegal immigration has gone from Barbara Jordan's sane and firm

---

60   Brian Lonergan, "Barbara Jordan's Wisdom Is Needed in Today's Immigration Debate," Hill, January 17, 2018, https://thehill.com/opinion/immigration/369153-barbara-jordans-wisdom-is-needed-in-todays-immigration-debate.

stance on curbing it to every single Democrat running for president affirming their support for free health care for illegal immigrants[61] during a 2019 presidential debate.

It's utterly bonkers, but Democrats and the Left have painted themselves into a corner. Any mention of possibly curbing illegal immigration is now coded as "racist," as is *any* policy pursued by the Trump administration to curb it. Why, it's almost as if 63 percent of non-citizen households in America access some form of taxpayer-funded welfare[62] and the current president thinks that this should be reined in in an attempt to save taxpayers of ALL colors a bit of cash! What a monster! What the "any-criticism-of-illegal-immigration-is-racist" crowd doesn't get is that blacks actually BENEFIT when America's immigration laws are enforced!

Take this case in Chicago, as laid out by Center for Immigration Studies fellow[63] David Seminara in an op-ed for the *Los Angeles Times*:[64]

> This dynamic played out recently at a large bakery in Chicago that supplies buns to McDonald's. Some 800 immigrant laborers, most of them from Mexico, lost their jobs last year after an audit by Immigration and Customs Enforcement.

61  Matthew J. Belvedere, "Health Care for Undocumented Immigrants May 'Haunt' Dems against Trump, Says Ex-Sen. Evan Bayh," CNBC, July 1, 2019, https://www.cnbc.com/2019/07/01/health-care-for-undocumented-immigrants-may-haunt-dems-against-trump.html.

62  Steven A. Camarota and Karen Zeigler, "63% of Non-Citizen Households Access Welfare Programs," Center for Immigration Studies, November 20, 2018, https://cis.org/Report/63-NonCitizen-Households-Access-Welfare-Programs.

63  "David Seminara," Center for Immigration Studies, accessed February 18, 2020, https://cis.org/Seminara.

64  Dave Seminara, "Op-Ed: Liberals Say Immigration Enforcement Is Racist, but the Group Most Likely to Benefit from It Is Black Men," *Los Angeles Times*, March 16, 2018, https://www.latimes.com/opinion/op-ed/la-oe-seminara-trump-immigration-reform-african-americans-20180316-story.html.

The Cloverhill Bakery, owned by Aryzta, a big Swiss food conglomerate, had to hire new workers, 80% to 90% of whom are African American. According to the Chicago Sun Times,[65] the new workers are paid $14 per hour, or $4 per hour more than the (illegal) immigrant workers.

Immigration laws are enforced, and more blacks are hired at a living wage. Imagine that!

The focus on results is working, and the outreach to *inform* black voters about the results is having a positive effect. The risks that many visible black Trump supporters like I and many others have taken are paying off. More and more blacks are becoming comfortable with being open supporters of the Trump administration, even if it can sometimes mean being the target of physical violence.

In early 2019 in Maryland, a black immigrant wearing a MAGA cap was attacked by two men who punched him in the head and upper body. In a press release after the attack, the Montgomery County Police Department[66] said:

The victim, who was wearing a red, Make America Great Again hat, was approached by two men who began harassing the victim and asking why he was wearing the MAGA hat. The victim told the suspects that he was entitled to his own views and kept walking away from the suspects. The suspects began striking the victim and telling him to take the hat off. The victim continued to be struck by the suspects until he

---

65  Frank Main and Dan Mihalopoulos, "At Major Northwest Side Bakery, Labor Issues Pit Blacks vs. Hispanics," *Chicago Sun-Times*, February 16, 2018, https://chicago.suntimes.com/2018/2/16/18355997/at-major-northwest-side-bakery-labor-issues-pit-blacks-vs-hispanics.

66  Mcpnews, "Two Arrested for Assault and Robbery in Germantown," Montgomery County Department of Police, April 15, 2019, https://www.mymcpnews.com/2019/04/15/two-arrested-for-assault-and-robbery-in-germantown/.

fell to the ground. The suspects then removed property from the victim and destroyed items of value. The suspects then fled the scene.

In another incident, a twenty-two-year-old black man wearing a MAGA hat was berated by employees of the Cheesecake Factory because apparently black Trump supporters shouldn't be able to enjoy overpriced chain restaurant food like the rest of America! The Daily Wire reported:[67]

> The Sunday incident allegedly began at the Cheesecake Factory located inside Dadeland Mall when 22-year-old Eugenior Joseph was seated while wearing his MAGA hat.
>
> According to multiple witnesses and Joseph's own account, a woman who worked at the restaurant walked up to him and started pointing at his hat, signaling for the other employees to come over.
>
> "Her finger was literally on top of his head, we were all looking at her like 'what is happening?'" one witness told The Daily Wire. "She was pointing at him, calling her other coworkers, telling them to look at this guy wearing a Make America Great Again hat."
>
> At that point, approximately a dozen or so employees approached the table and began making comments about the hat, with some saying they wanted to punch Joseph in the face. Witnesses also allege that some of the employees also referred to him as a "n**ger" in their conversations among each other.

Tolerant and inclusive! Perhaps these isolated incidents aren't indicative of a larger pattern of black Trump supporters being

67   Ryan Saavedra, "EXCLUSIVE: Cheesecake Factory Employees Attack Black Man for Wearing MAGA Hat, Witnesses Say," Daily Wire, May 14, 2018, https://www.dailywire.com/news/exclusive-cheesecake-factory-employees-attack-ryan-saavedra.

targeted for violent attacks, but even a blind man could see the correlation between the MSM's never-ending "Trump is racist" themes, the attacks on Kanye West for donning the MAGA cap, the attacks on black Trump supporters online, and the *physical* attacks against them that I've just described. We're living in a very strange moment in America, but I believe that Donald Trump represents an opportunity. The black conservatives who have coalesced around the forty-fifth president have been attacked and smeared with the full force of mainstream media and all of its digital arms in the twenty-first century. If we can survive this onslaught with our ideas and integrity intact, the next generation of black conservatives who support, say, a President Nikki Haley, Dan Crenshaw, Ron DeSantis, or Marco Rubio won't have to deal with the lies and smears. We will be able to fight back with ideas and ideals. Imagine that.

# AFTERWORD

*An Inclusive Republican Party for a Changing World*

Black people don't have to be Democrats. Or Republicans. Neither do gays and lesbians, Latinos, Asians, Muslims, or anyone else. One of the chief reasons I've become so public about my own political evolution is to dispel the fiction that either of our two major American political parties *owns* anyone. Democrats don't own minorities. Republicans don't own white men and women. The only way forward as Americans is to lead with our values and ideas, not necessarily our identities. I can just about hear you screaming, "Wait! Is the guy who calls himself "America's favorite black, gay Republican" arguing against identity politics?!" Well, yes and no. I'm of the belief that all politics are identity politics, whether that identity be of a working-class small business owner, military veteran, or immigrant both legal or illegal.

My chief argument is that, for Democrats, the full weight of *racial and ethnic* identity is being pushed to a generation of voters as the chief reason to vote for them in the absence of any real ideas for America's future, let alone a plan to engender a sense of American pride into *any* of the groups they want to claim for permanent victim status. My very existence is a rejection of *those* kinds of identity politics, those that seek to slice and dice Americans into thinner and thinner groups in the hopes that they'll create a coalition big enough to keep the left in power. My guess is that they will not, and the results of the 2016 election should be a big wake-up call to anyone who still thinks in this way.

However, don't mistake my political leanings and writings as a wholesale endorsement of the Republican Party as it stands right now. I see a party with some terrific ideas that is *slowly* realizing that America is changing, and if it is to continue as a nationally competitive party, then it'd better start thinking of some ways to sell its ideas to different minority groups. From what I've seen, the Trump administration is starting to crack the code. The party in general, however, needs to become *much* better at recruiting young leaders of ALL colors who embody its vision for America as a land of laws and prosperity for those who play by the rules, regardless of race, ethnicity, religion, or sexual orientation.

That means evolving beyond elements of race-baiting and homophobia that just won't play in a post-2020 America. I didn't jump from blindly following one party to blindly following another. However, I truly believe that the party is ready for the evolution, and I'm glad to be a part of it. Think about how many Republicans will read a memoir from a black gay guy and think not about how my race and sexual orientation make me different from them, but about how many ideas, hopes, dreams, and experiences we have in common! That's the story of America. And that's the story I'll continue to tell.

# ACKNOWLEDGMENTS

There are a lot of people that saw the vision for who I am and what I'm doing, and without their support none of this would be happening on the level that it is. Candace Owens "discovered" me on Instagram shortly after I "came out," and has been an amazing supporter and friend in this movement, as well as an inspiration when I watch her major moments along with the rest of the world.

To the team at Turning Point USA, you've been instrumental in supporting my rise in politics over the past few years. President Charlie Kirk, Chief Operating Officer Tyler Bowyer, and Influencer Marketing Director Sara Schmactenberger, thank you for your patience, hard work, and support of me. I'm not the obvious choice as a public face for a right-leaning message, but you saw the vision and always had my back. Thank you.

To the team at Post Hill Press, thanks for seeing the vision for this book through, and thank you especially to publisher Anthony Ziccardi. The BLEXIT crew: Brandon Tatum, Derrick Gradenigo, Terrence Williams. It's amazing to connect with other black male Republicans in this movement. You all inspire me daily.

To anyone who has ever tweeted in support, come out to support a speaking engagement, or shared encouraging words on social media: I literally could NOT have done this without all of you! *You* are making the difference, and you matter. I'm just the messenger.

To my best friends Derrick Horn and Shawn Foley, even though you're both lefties you stuck behind me when I became a prominent Republican and lost many other friends. You're the real deal. Nathan Smith, becoming closer with you over the past few years has been a joy, and I can't wait for our next travel adventure. Isaiah Washington, I've been a fan ever since my teenage black gay self saw your magnificent performance in *Get on the Bus*. Your friendship and mentorship have been one of the most pleasant surprises of the past year.

Mom and Dad, I'm so much more like both of you than I ever realized. You both live in me, and I hope I continue to make you proud. To my sister Shellida Simmons, I love you so very much, and will never forget the night we spoke. You literally saved my life.

To my husband Mikhail Safronov: you lift me up when I'm down, you supported me when I was "nobody," you listen to me tell the same stories constantly, you listen to my frustrations, hopes, dreams, and my plans for life. I don't know what I can say other than I love you. You are my person. And I'm so blessed and thankful to have you in my life.